Heart to Heart

Heart to Heart

Guiding Your Kids Toward Courage, Character, and Values

William J. O'Malley

Chandler House Press
Worcester, Massachusetts
1999

HEART TO HEART: Guiding Your Kids Toward Courage, Character and Values

ISBN 1-886284-51-2
Library of Congress Catalog Card Number: 99-66270
First Edition
ABCDEFGHIJK

Published by
Chandler House Press
335 Chandler Street
Worcester, MA 01602
USA

President
Lawrence J. Abramoff

Editor
Ann Linblad

Book Design
Bookmakers

Cover Design
Marshall Henrichs

Chandler House Press books are available at special discounts for bulk purchases. For more information about how to arrange such purchases, please contact Chandler House Press, 335 Chandler Street, Worcester, MA 01602, or call (800) 642-6657, or fax (508) 756-9425, or find us on the World Wide Web at www.chandlerhousepress.com.

Chandler House Press books are distributed to the trade by
National Book Network, Inc.
4720 Boston Way
Lanham, MD 20706
(800) 462-6420

**This book is for
Catherine McGillivray**

Contents

Introduction

The Human Invitation

"To teach morality is neither to preach nor to indoctrinate.
It is to explain."
– *Emile Durkeim*

arewell, *Norman Rockwell*. No longer does our society resemble the sentimental small town scenes he painted just a generation or two ago. As our popular culture spins further and further out of control, parents and teachers in America have experienced the most shocking and gruesome "wake up call" imaginable—kids killing kids in a frightening number of school shootings in across the country. Parents, teachers, reporters and politicians are asking "why?" and are pointing the finger at each other. One thing is clear—it's time we got back to the basics of teaching ethics and moral values to our children. This book is an invitation to youngsters to become good people, good spouses, and good parents.

For 36 years, I've taught moral behavior to young people, the majority of whom came from eleven years of supposed religious "brainwashing," and the sea change in their attitudes over those years has been slow but ultimately shocking. Kids are the same as they were, but their attitudes have changed—*drastically*.

In surveys, 60-70% claim they routinely cheat on quizzes and tests; at least a third are sexually active and feel no compunction about it; nearly all admit they don't give their parents an honest day's work for an honest day's pay; all but a few agree that *anyone* in business must routinely compromise his or her ethical beliefs. Consistently in role-playing moral dilemmas, they make "practical" choices that are often not ethical. "Does anybody else know you cheated for the Harvard scholarship?" No. "Then keep your mouth shut." Pretty ineffective religious brainwashing, I'd say.

Most students I've taught in the last ten years believe that accumulating enough money, fame, sex, and power will deliver fulfillment. But if that were true, how do you explain Elvis Presley, Marilyn Monroe, Janis Joplin, Jimi Hendrix, Jim Morrison, John Belushi, River Phoenix, Kurt Cobain and the others who "had it all?" Did they anesthetize themselves with drugs for years and finally kill themselves because they were so *happy*? Yet every kid I've taught believes those people were successes.

In 1988, the Rhode Island Crisis Center surveyed 1,700 children ages 10 to 13 asking, "Is it acceptable for a man to force a woman to have sex if they have dated for more than six months?" Of the boys, 65% said yes, as did 47% of the girls. And Rhode Island isn't south-central Los Angeles.

What can parents do to make sure their children don't adopt these twisted beliefs? This book will teach parents to help their children internalize the human values that most cultures have tried to instill for the past 30,000 years. And sharing this book is a way for parents and children to talk about the most important factors in their future success: their *personal principles*.

"Do unto others as you would have others do unto you" is not the exclusive property of religion. It is a matter of human survival.

The Basics of Teaching Moral Values

During my teaching career, I've read 80 reflection papers from each one of about 5,000 high school seniors, which totals nearly 400,000 pages—surely a Guinness World Record. This has given me a special insight into kids' *real*—as opposed to *claimed*—moral values. More often than God has heard the Lord's Prayer, more than any mother has heard, "Oh, *Mom!*" I've heard, "Come *on*. If she wants it as much as you do, who's getting hurt?" We have a go 'round on that one at least six or eight classes every year. Oddly, the kids who argue most fervently about it don't even realize they're openly declaring they're sexually active. And because they are ardently defending a vested interest, it's clear that they aren't arguing honestly.

I try to make them see that even if a person wants to do something, it doesn't make it right. I usually say, "Even if she really wanted to be your slave ("Hitch me to your plow, and beat me!"), would that make it a legitimate human relationship? Even if she desperately wanted you to help her commit suicide, would that make it right for you to help?" Groans. The students know my argument makes sense, and they don't like it one bit. One year, sometime in March, a very bright young man, "Joey," tried it again.

"Now look," he said, being gentle with me, "it's perfectly *natural*. When you're thirsty, you go to the faucet and get a drink of water. When you're horny, you call your girlfriend."

He had absolutely no sense of how degrading this was to another human being. But I suddenly got a brain-rush: "Okay, there are two words for having sex. What are they?" About four or five kids piped up with the F-word. "Fine, but what's the other?"

The boy whose girlfriend (whom he'd probably claim he loved) was no more than a convenience said, "Making love."

I skewered him with my eyes and said, "They *don't* call it making *like*." His face closed up like a fist. Finally, after six months, he really knew. And it was inescapable. I walked out of that class floating a foot off the floor.

Ordinarily when kids are ambushed by an epiphany—a sudden flash of insight, when their eyes tell you they do really see the truth and their grim mouths tell you they don't like it at all—the bell usually rings. Their realization gets smothered in the rush to the next class and calls of "Anybody do the math?" But a week or so later, when I was comparing drug addiction to an uncommitted sexual relationship, Joey scowled, "Okay! But how do you get *rid* of it?" His insight—his understanding—had lasted.

I asked the class what the first rule of AA is, and they responded that first you have to acknowledge that you have a problem you can't control. I said, "And the next step is to find someone you can trust and talk to when you think you're going to fall back." Maybe Joey found someone else to talk to. He didn't talk to me. But at least for that one shining moment, he held the truth in his hands.

Another year a very similar boy, who had always been the one saying, "C'mon, if she wants it…," came up to the desk at the end of the last period of the year, hooked his arm around my neck and said, "Pops, we both know you're right. But I can't give it up." That was enough to keep me going, too. He'd come as far as he could toward understanding, and that was a long, long way.

Mentoring Works After Monitoring Ceases

A few years before, a boy came up to me on Monday and said, "Boy, did I hate you Friday night." When I asked him why, he said, "Well, her parents were out, and we were upstairs in her room getting undressed, but I remembered what you said, so I stopped, and said, 'I can't. I'd only be using you.' So I got dressed and came downstairs, and she came down and sat very quiet next to me on the couch, and she said, 'I've never been more proud of you.'" To this boy, the truth of human value was no longer some arbitrary rule, or the ignored whisperings of his conscience; it was part of him now. Groping our way toward the truth is far less efficient than following clear rules and having vigilant supervision, but it is far more effective. *Mentoring works when monitoring ceases.*

Precepts, rules, and catechisms work only when there's a cop. Unless we find ways for kids to internalize the truth about moral behavior, we might as well shout in Mandarin at the deaf.

Teens have three deeply rooted beliefs that all parents and teachers must overcome when encouraging moral behavior: (1) My opinion's as good as anyone else's; (2) Society decides what's moral and then tells us; (3) Morality changes from age to age and culture to culture. Until we blast out these roadblocks, we don't stand a chance.

Only a rare adolescent would deny "My opinion's as good as anyone else's." In fact, most young people have opinions that are self-validating—

ideas that are "true" simply because the teens believe them to be true. This is a manifestly foolish, not to mention arrogant, attitude. Your opinion of a problem in physics isn't as good as Einstein's; your opinion of a symphony isn't as good as Beethoven's.

One's opinion—on anything, including morality—is only as good as the evidence and honest reasoning that back it up. Everyone on the street has an opinion on every topic from welfare to homosexuality to abortion, but most haven't thought out the opinion or read even one book about these topics. One of the greatest resentments among students is the fact that the teacher knows more than they do, has read more than they have, has thought things out more than they have. They think this is unfair. Unfortunately, it happens to be the objective fact, no matter how green the teacher.

Teaching Morality Through Reasoning

Therefore we must make our case for morality based solely on evidence and hard-nosed reasoning. I can testify that *the* most difficult concept for youngsters to accept is the radical difference between objective facts and subjective opinions. Kids often deny facts, but facts remain constant. I try to show kids that opinions are valid only if they're grounded in objective facts and honest reasoning.

Even after six months of relentlessly hammering away at the difference between objective fact and subjective opinion, a third of any class still marks "True" for "Objective morality changes from age to age." I don't know where that deep-rooted and idiotic conviction came from, but kids believe it to be so.

According to this wrong-headed argument, society decides what's morally acceptable and what's not, then it tells us. Morality was different in the '50s; now the media tell us actions forbidden then are not only permissible now, but recommended. But if society decides what is moral and immoral, then doing something against popular opinion, like hiding Jews in Nazi Germany or runaway slaves in ante-bellum America would be *immoral*. And the Incas believed that slaughtering virgins to placate the gods was laudable. And in China, exposing unwanted female infants to the elements to die was an accepted practice. Were these practices *moral* just because the Inca and Chinese societies said so?

The humanity of Jews, Blacks, Incas, and female Chinese is no more debatable than the fact that the earth is round and cyanide is toxic. Morality is based on objective *fact*, no matter what *any* society thinks.

Again, it's crucial to establish the difference between objective facts (which don't change from age to age) and subjective opinions (which of course do). Human beings have gone through the same physical changes since the Cro-Magnons: pregnancy, birth, weaning, playing, learning skills, puberty, marriage, pregnancy, and so on. Humans have faced the same problems that having bodies and brains causes: arrogance, covetousness, lust, anger, gluttony, envy and sloth. This is objective fact. If morality changes from age to age, then Plato can tell us nothing about being human or moral. Nor can Jesus, Buddha, Shakespeare, Dickens, or Camus. Discussing morality then becomes little more than verbal Ping-Pong.

Evolving a Validated Personal Conscience

Unlike the free-wheeling pooling of half-baked ideas you'll find in most "Values Clarification" and "Decision Making" classes (which most public schools now offer), this is based on three truths, facts that can be ignored but not disproved.

- 🎝 **Truth No. 1—*Reality, or truth, comes to me.*** Things tell me, by the way they are made, what they are and how I can legitimately use them. Fire burns without my approval; rape degrades the victim.

- 🎝 **Truth No. 2—*Human beings are not merely higher-level animals.*** There is an "element" in us which raises human value above the value of even the most "intelligent" animals, like dogs and dolphins.

- 🎝 **Truth No. 3—*What being human means (morality) does not change from age to age and culture to culture and morality has nothing to do with religion.*** No matter what any age/culture/religion asserts, killing a human is a more significant act than killing a sheep. The evidence is unchallengeable.

Reality Comes to Me

My opinion is only as good as the objective evidence and reasoning that back it up.

A rock tells me what it is (just by the way it's made) and how I can legitimately use it. It has mass, weight, and electrical charge, and it just sits there, inert. I can do whatever I want with it because it has no feelings. The rock tells me that; I don't tell the rock.

An apple tells me what it is (just by the way it's made) and how I can legitimately use it. It has all the properties of the rock—mass, weight, electrical charge—BUT it also has the potential to take in food, grow, and reproduce its own kind. That's a quantum leap up; it has properties no rock has. This is an objective fact. Therefore, it's wrong to lob apples around a cafeteria in a food war as if they had no more inner value than snowballs. The apple tells me that; I don't tell it.

A bunny tells me what it is (just by the way it's made) and how I can legitimately use it. It has all the properties of the rock and the apple, BUT it can feel, sense danger, and move around. That's another quantum leap up; it has properties no rock or apple contains. This is an objective fact. Therefore, it's objectively wrong to kick a bunny the way I can kick a rock, or roast it alive as I can do with apples, as if it has no feelings like them. The bunny tells me that; I don't tell it.

Humans tell me what they are (just by the way they're made) and how I can legitimately use them. They have all the properties of the rock, the apple, and the bunny, BUT a human being *can* (but need not) reflect on experience and learn from it. Yet since Plato, philosophers have wrongly defined humans as "rational animals," as if humans were only a minor step beyond beasts—apes with computers implanted. That is far too simplistic. There are qualities in human beings of which no beast we know is capable. These are human activities which simply cannot be reduced to the body or the brain: understanding, honor, patriotism, awe, and wisdom.

Only humans are capable of *conscience*. No beast can be wicked; each follows its inner programming helplessly. No tiger gobbles a goat and lumbers back to the jungle muttering, "Oh, *no!* I did it *again!* I need *counseling!*" Humans do express regret—at least good humans do. Bad humans don't.

That's what ethics is about. Ethics is not about religion, but only about being *authentically human*.

Humans are More than Animals

What separates us from animals is that we can (a) learn and (b) love, and (c) grow more intensely human by more learning and loving. Or not.

(a) Learning

Any stag can "know" a hunter is chasing him, but he doesn't say, "What the hell did I do to that guy?" Though we need not, we have at least the potential to ask the human question, "why." We have the capacity to *understand*, an ability that no animal possesses. This is an objective fact. Human beings are the only species that suffer from conscience.

(b) Loving

Animals show affection for their own, even to the point of sacrificing their lives for them. But humans can sacrifice their lives—often without dying—for people we don't even *like*. Ask any teacher. Genuine love is *not* a feeling. It's an act of the will—a commitment that takes over when the feelings fail, when the beloved is no longer even *likable*. Ask any parent.

(c) Growing

No lion can become more leonine, but human beings can become more intensely human. It is unarguable that Abraham Lincoln was a better (more moral) human being than Adolph Hitler. How do we know that? By the way they acted, by the choices they made, by the way they treated other human beings, by the order of their priorities.

$$\text{Marble : Acorn } = \text{ Cub : Baby}$$

or

$$\text{(rock) : (apple) = (bunny) : (human)}$$

At a quick glance, those pairs look more or less similar; the marble and acorn are about the same size and shape; the cub and the baby look and act more or less the same. But they're profoundly different. Plant the marble and the acorn, and the marble will just lie there; it hasn't the potential to be anything other than what it is. But the acorn has at least the *potential* to become something enormously larger than what it is: a huge oak tree. Or not. It could fall onto a sidewalk and wither or into a swamp and rot. But it does have the capability of changing into a size and shape unrecognizably different. In the same way, both the cub and the baby will both grow physically, but the cub is never going to be any more bear-like than it was from the start, while the human baby has the *potential* to become Thomas Jefferson or Helen Keller. Or not.

Therefore, humanity is a spectrum, ranging from pimps, pushers, and terrorists at one end (human, but just over the line from beasts) all the way to great-souled human beings like Oprah Winfrey and Mother Theresa. This book hopes to lure its readers (and their children) further along that spectrum of humanity than they originally planned—and certainly further than the media and popular culture are urging them to go.

📇 *Objective Morality Doesn't Change*

Objective facts are "out there," unarguable: human beings have more inner value than bunnies or apples or rocks. That's a given, whether I like it or not, acknowledge it or not, or approve or not. Subjective opinions do, in fact, differ from age to age, from society to society, from individual to individual, BUT subjective opinions are valid *only* when they're backed up by objective evidence. For a long time people believed the earth was flat. They were wrong. How do I dare say they were wrong? Objective facts.

There is a "law" of nature inside human beings—just as in planets, plantains, and platypuses. The human difference is that we're the only beings free to ignore that law, flaunt it, and uproot it in ourselves and others.

The foundation of this book is the objective fact that each of us is a human being and not merely a rational animal, and that we live in a web of moral (human) relationships with every other inhabitant of this fragile planet. That is the human invitation.

Every parent (or teacher or student) accepts that a purpose of getting an education is to develop into an attractive job candidate. The trouble is that so many believe it is the *only* educational purpose they can understand and appreciate. On the contrary, the purpose of education in this country has always been to train good citizens—men and women of character. Education is called "the humanities" because it encourages us to become more fully human. This book, then, is simply that: an invitation to youngsters to become good people, good spouses, and good parents.

Making Moral (Human) Decisions

In the last several decades, there have been two more or less tolerable methods of trying to address moral questions in public schools, where the touchy issue of Church and State makes dealing with such problems sensitive. During the '60s Carl Rogers developed a method called *Values Clarification,* in which students pooled their ideas about moral questions without any direction or interference from the teacher. In the '70s Lawrence Kohlberg evolved a technique called *Decision Making* in which students faced a moral dilemma and were asked not only to "solve" it but to justify their choices with well-argued reasons.

Values Clarification at least has the advantage of making students realize moral decisions are important. But in my experience not many have really made a study of moral questions—or even of what being human truly means. Their understanding is not based on a grasp of the objective facts about how humans differ from other species, but their responses are most often based on hearsay, uncritical beliefs and feelings. Most students take their opinions "off the rack"—they simply adopt other people's unexamined opinions and apply their own labels. When I argue with students about welfare, for instance, I'm not arguing with them, but with their tax-paying fathers. They have simply adopted their fathers' ideas without question.

Sound moral judgments aren't based on feelings but on objective facts and honest reasoning. Having a moral discussion about using drugs and having sex is not just a subjective decision—especially when some of those involved have a vested interest. That is, if they ever admitted the opposite side was right, they'd have to give up something they like very much—like sex. In effect, *Values Clarification* allows students to make up their own morality (beliefs about what being human allows us legitimately to do). Nothing wrong with that, *as long as* they know what they're talking about and accept the basic objective fact that human beings can't legitimately be treated like animals or vegetables or stepping stones. Otherwise, it is as hazardous as allowing them to make up their own chemistry or their own diet. Personal choices are not *self*-justifying; "This is my opinion, therefore it is the truth." Any opinion is only as valid as the objective evidence that backs it up. You're surely free to hold any opinion you wish on any topic, but that doesn't protect you from being scorned for it by people who have studied the question in greater detail.

Decision Making asked for rational solutions to moral dilemmas such as which of twelve survivors in a lifeboat made only for six should be denied limited food and water. It had advantages over *Values Clarification* in that the participants were required to *justify* their decisions rather than merely express their "feelings" about them. But it had the disadvantage of having to work within the parameters of a made-up story—for instance, accepting the premise that half the people in the lifeboat *must* be denied food and water and, further, that a retarded girl is "less important" than an atomic physicist, or that all but one of the males in a survival shelter should be excluded because one would suffice to impregnate all the females and assure the continuance of the human race. No matter their state, all those people are human beings.

Carol Gilligan, one of Kohlberg's protégés, took exception to his method and to the dominance of male respondents in his studies. Most of the conclusions depended almost solely on left-brain, "masculine," rational values to the exclusion of right-brain, "feminine," inclusive values—which encompass the human as opposed to the merely rational-animal aspects of questions. One little boy's response to the exercises embodied the problem perfectly: "These moral dilemmas are just like math problems, only with people."

Executives with such a mind-set, for instance, when faced with a factory in a small town which was in no way comparable to the corporation's other facilities across the country, would not have the slightest hesitation in merely closing the plant and pulling out. It's the only clear, rational choice. But what about the lives of the workers and their families? What about the auxiliary businesses like dry cleaners, mechanics, groceries which depend on those workers' business? What about the effect on schools when the town's tax base is eliminated? Tough on them. This is perhaps a rational response, but not a human response.

Guiding your children toward character is not making them good debaters but making them good people. Character is one's own set of personally reasoned and accepted principles about how a decent human being should and should not act. Developing character is not like learning how to factor or spell correctly. Nor is it just a matter of knowing *that* such an act is approved or disapproved in this particular society or that some acts are degrading to other human beings and to oneself. Developing character means internalizing that truth, feeling it, caring about it. It is not just a realization but a *conviction*. Most of the time, even in moral debates, we know what is the right thing to do. The tough part is having the conviction that we ought to do it, even if it costs dearly.

Developing a personal conscience (character) depends on *both* powers of the human mind: reason (critical thinking) and intuition (it "makes sense").

A good way of asking the basic question is: Where does the "ought" come from in "I ought to"? For instance, parents *ought* to feed their infants and keep them warm. Why? Because of the objective facts, because of what the infant is and what the parent is in relation to him or her. I *ought* to be grateful to my parents, at the very least for the gift of life. I *ought* to show respect for every human being. I *ought* to be kind, responsible, honest, persevering. Why? The foundation of this book is the objective fact that each of us is a human being and not merely a rational animal and that we live in a web of moral (human) relationships with every other inhabitant of this fragile planet. That is the human invitation.

This book has nothing whatsoever to do with religion. It examines values accepted by all cultures over the last 30,000 years as essential for being fulfilled human beings. No reasonable atheist would—or could—object to his or her children cultivating any of the virtues we will study here. This book does not ask: "What does God want?" It asks only: "What does the nature of being human demand of us?"

Moral questions are inevitable. We live in a world where all the other porcupines have quills, too, and different agendas. You can't become a good person, a good spouse, a good parent until you've wrestled with what makes someone a good (moral) human being. You can't study literature without evaluating moral (human) choices. Studying morality is a matter of survival as human beings.

What will make us humanly fulfilled, happy, more alive than merely "getting by?"

Come and see.

A Conversation About the Introduction

What's your reaction to the following statements?

A = Agree; ? = Uncertain; D = Disagree.

1. Things tell me, by the way they're made, how I can legitimately use them. A ? D

2. Human beings are not just higher-level animals. A ? D

3. What being human means (morality) does not change from age to age. A ? D

4. My opinion's as good as anyone else's. A ? D

5. A society has every right to decide who is fully human and who is less than human. A ? D

6. There's no such thing as an immoral shark or shrub or shooting star. A ? D

7. A person's humanity is no more debatable than the toxicity of cyanide. A ? D

8. Majority opinion is a very unreliable way of discovering the truth. A ? D

9. Morality isn't a matter of religion. Even decent atheists want to be moral. A ? D

10. We don't "make up" morality. We discover it by the way humans are made. A ? D

Help me understand what you understand by any of these statements.

1. It's immoral (less-than-human) to lob food around as if it had no more value than snowballs.

2. It's immoral (less-than-human) to torture an animal for fun.

3. It's immoral (less-than-human) to treat cafeteria workers like unfeeling robots or slaves.

4. Marble : Acorn =   Cub : Baby

5. If society decides morality, then it was immoral to rescue Jews in Nazi Germany.

6. The Golden Rule isn't religion but a matter of human survival.

7. Sound moral judgments aren't based on feelings but on objective facts and clear reasoning.

8. Opinions on moral questions (or anything else) are not self-justifying.

9. "These moral dilemmas are just like math problems, only with people."

10. The goal of a moral education ought to be to prepare good spouses and parents.

For Adolescents (who can probably comprehend the pages for themselves.)

⚜ Start with the title of the introduction. Why do you think it is called *"The Human Invitation?"* It's obvious we're all born human because we had human parents. But an invitation means a request asking you to go someplace, like to a party or on a trip. The book at least seems to say that—unlike any other species—humans are… well, *incomplete*. Can you think of someone you know or someone you've read about who is incompletely human, someone who is even crueler than most animals? That person was born of human parents, therefore…? What do you think might have gone wrong? Can you think of someone you know or someone you've read about who just, well, "vegetates"—puts up with boredom and mediocrity— "gets by"? That person was born of human parents, therefore…? What do you think might have gone wrong?

⚜ Why does the book have such a problem with defining human beings as "rational animals"? Try to tell me some things good humans do that bad humans refuse to do? What kinds of values do good humans appreciate that animals are incapable of? Values that very incomplete humans sneer at, values that simply can't be rooted in a physical body and in the electro-chemical activities of the brain? People call that "the soul." Any trouble accepting that?

You've seen or read *A Christmas Carol* by Charles Dickens. What makes it obvious Bob Cratchitt is a better human being than Ebenezer Scrooge? Think of as many choices as you can that separate them.

Tell me what you understand by this division between the left-brain, "masculine," rational part of us and the right-brain, "feminine," inclusive part of us. What do you think you'd do if you were the CEO faced with the problem of the plant closing mentioned earlier? Why? Which would be more important: the company or the workers? Or something else?

For Young Children

Remember the time you (put your hand on the stove, fell out of the tree, almost drowned)? Why do you think that happened? It certainly wasn't because the (stove/tree/water) got mad at you. It wasn't because you disobeyed me, and I was secretly punishing you for it, right? Why do you think your (Mom/Dad) and I get all steamed up when you do dangerous things? It's because we've been around awhile, and we know pretty much what things are dangerous and will hurt you. It's not that things are mean and nasty; that's just the way they're made. When you pull the dog's tail, he snarls, right? When you slap another child, she cries. It's automatic. That's the way *they're* made.

Okay, so here on the table I've got a rock and an apple, and there's the (dog/cat) and you. The rock and the apple are pretty much the same size, right? But how are they different? I mean, you could take a bite out of the apple but not out of the rock. How do you know that? They tell you they're different, right? And the apple has seeds in it. What does that mean? No rock's going to make little rocks, but just one apple seed can make a tree. That's a big difference, no? Now, we can eat the apple but we can't eat the (dog/cat); that'd be awful, wouldn't it? How come? How do we know that? Okay, now if we lost the (dog/cat), we'd all be pretty miserable. But how do you think we'd feel if we ever lost you? Far, far worse, right? Why? Because the (dog/cat)'s important to us, but you're far, far more important. Why do you think that's true? So, people are more important than pets, and pets are more important than snacks, and snacks are more important than stones. They tell us that, just by the way they're made. So before you use anything, in order to use it the right way, you have to look at how it's made. Does that make sense?

Ways to Use This Book

One on One

Ideally (therefore hardly likely) I had hoped *Heart to Heart* might be an ethics text for public schools. However, in most schools the examination of ethical principles becomes foolishly confused with teaching religious precepts. Therefore, I have written this book to be used primarily one-on-one, by a parent with an emergent adult. This is when conforming to "the rules" is no longer a child's grudging submission to adult edicts, but becomes a prickly encounter with limits on freedom. Young people are beginning to think for themselves, and they want to get out of the constricting corset of parental control. This is perfectly natural; it's what adolescence is for—to prepare oneself to go out on the road alone.

Therefore, adolescence is not only an invitation to a new role for the youngster but also to a new role for the parent. It is no longer enough for the parent to lecture, giving as a reason, "Because I said so." The ordinary young person will react negatively and demand that the parents stop "treating me like a little kid." Either the boy or girl will become outright rebellious or quietly seethe with resentment—or adopt any of a thousand passive-aggressive postures between the two. This is perfectly natural. In fact, the youngster *is* no longer a child. Yet on the other hand, he or she is not yet an adult either.

Adolescence is not a "stage," a sort of suspended state into which one falls at puberty, like Snow White in her crystal coffin, to emerge into adulthood at the conferral of a college diploma or a marriage license. Many children think adulthood "clicks on" with puberty and a driver's license; many parents think it "clicks on" only when the young person leaves home. On the contrary, adolescence is a *process*, exactly like the process of moving from infancy into childhood, when the parent had to cajole the baby to toddle just a few more steps each day. In the same way, a parent has to lure a youngster to rise to the challenges of responsibility, honoring commitments, honesty, self-possession—*freely*—more and more each week.

This is a new parental role. It is no longer enough for a parent to be just the guardian of order in the house. Parents have to insure that youngsters will act ethically even when they are outside the parents' direct control—where they spend more and more time each year. Parents must no longer simply state, "These are the rules," but should ask, "What are *your* rules?" In effect, the parent has to become a *salesperson*. You must convince your child to *want* to "buy" moral, human values (when the prevailing culture has convinced many young people to abandon these values). Parents must begin to hand over control to the youngster, like a monarch assuring a successful succession. Precepts are no longer enough; it is time for *persuasion*.

Pick, say, one evening a week when the parent and youngster are going to sit down and hash out the chapter both have read—a home seminar on that particular virtue. The folk tales, biographies, text segments, and dilemmas are ways to stir interest, focus the virtue under study, offer a common ground for discussion. The important part is the parent-youngster interchange.

In writing the text segments, I had difficulty finding a "voice." In some chapters, I found I was talking to parents, as teacher-to-teacher ("Ask them…); in others, I ended up talking directly to the youngster ("When you find yourself in this situation…"). Therefore, I decided to write the text segments for parents—sketches from which they might draw up their own "class notes." I wrote the questions after each chapter for the young people—writing questions about that virtue that I myself would ask young people.

However, parents can also adapt the chapters to younger children, preparing them to confront their eventual moral independence. They can read the story one time and ask the child what the "lesson" is; another time they can read the biography and ask what kind of person this is; another time they can read the dilemma and ask how the child would advise the people involved. It can be more random and leisurely, less "schoolish." In the questions about the introduction, I've tried to give one example of how to do this. But since my experience has been almost exclusively with adolescents, in the rest of the chapters I have written only with teens in mind.

Groups

The book can also be a starting point for school counselors in group guidance with students, for English or social studies teachers, for Scout leaders, for home-schooling networks. In an ordinary school setting, each chapter has enough material for a full week of classes, but I believe they might better be used here and there over the year lest they become tedious—too much of a good thing. In a religious setting, they can provide a basis for confirmation preparation. Too often religious teachers presume a religious conviction when it simply isn't there. The approach of this book presumes nothing, except the nature of being human, whether there is a God or not.

Despite the fact that societies since cave days have used folk tales to teach moral principles to their young, I was hesitant at first to use them with today's "sophisticated" young people. Today's media has made most youngsters skeptical—if not cynical—about values. But don't worry. For over ten years I've used these folk tales with tough Bronx boys for whom street smarts far outweigh book smarts. Almost invariably, if a topic goes over to a second class, they often beg like younger kids, "Aren't we gonna have a story?" I've used folk tales with adults as well, and they have proven just as effective as hooks to grab their attention.

Whether this material is used one-on-one or in groups, the most important goal is to avoid either of two extremes: being too rigid and saying, "No, that's wrong," or not interfering enough and allowing too many assertions to go unchallenged, as if holding any opinion were self-justifying. The most basic *premise* is that human beings are not merely animals, and they should not allow themselves to act as if they were. Nor should they treat other humans as if they were merely animals. The most basic *method* is an honest sharing of ideas, but—and this is essential—with a critical eye to the objective evidence which validates those ideas.

General Questions Parents and Teachers Can Use for Every Chapter

Folk Tales

1. Every story wants to convince readers of some truth. What's the most important word in the title of this story? (e.g., in Chapter 1, "trust").

2. What do you think the writer is trying to say about (trust) *through* the story? Try to put it into a sentence, which is what a theme is, some kind of important statement about what being honestly human means. (The trust you "feel" from your family leads to a trust in yourself as worthy, and then to the confidence that can move out on your own, to stand even alone.)

3. A story is "faked," exaggerated, manipulated. How does this story sometimes tell you *more* than a straight essay? How does getting into a character's skin and walking around in it awhile open up ways of understanding that hard-nosed "studies" can't? What does this story tell you—or suggest, or make you puzzled about—regarding (trust)?

4. The people of the story aren't "real"—not in the physical, historical sense of flesh-and-blood people. But in what way are they truly *real?* Try to tell me what real questions in your own life having to do with (trusting) make you uneasy? How can we wrestle with that uneasiness and get rid of it?

5. What would happen if the heroines and heroes of folk tales refused the invitation to leave behind what was comfortable and go out on the road looking for something better? What, really, *is* that "something better" in this particular story? Why is it worth what it costs?

Biographies

1. The key word in the title is (trust). Why did the author pick this particular person to show what that value means? How does this person really *embody* that virtue and make it desirable?

2. The person in the biography—just like the people in the folk-tale—started out as a "nobody." What were the factors *inside* this person that simply wouldn't allow him or her to settle for being a blotch on the wallpaper? Who were the people who helped the person overcome fear in order to reach for something more than surviving? In what specific, concrete ways did those people make this person's life come more alive?

3. In both the folk tales and in the biographies, the success and fulfillment the people finally achieve comes about only *through* the course of trying to overcome a great many unpleasant obstacles. What were the obstacles for this particular person in this biography? What were the *inner* resources the person had to call on—often resources he or she had no idea existed before facing the challenge? A wise man named Aristotle once said that you learn courage by *acting* courageous, even though you're convinced you're not. How is that true of the way this person learned (the trust that leads to confidence)?

4. Unlike the people in folk tales, these people really did live in the same world we do. Does this person's story touch anything inside you, make you suspect you could make more of a difference than you suspected so far? What kind of difference can you make—not later when you "get out into the real world"—but right now, here in the family, in school, at work?

5. Think for a minute or two: If you could meet this person right now, what's the one question you'd like to ask him or her?

Texts

Each of the texts, of course, is specific to the value onstage at the moment. One help for parents not used to making "lesson plans" is first to skim the pages of the text quickly to get a general idea of the main thesis (the theme assertion) and the major arguments the author uses to support the thesis. Certainly do *not* just plow in at the first sentence, slashing away with a highlighter. You'd most likely highlight (indelibly) ideas that, however important they seem in the first run-through, are not really as important as others. A better idea on the first go-round is to make small brackets in pencil around segments that seem important and small question marks where you're puzzled or where you think the author is loony.

After that first quick overview, go back and read it slowly, pausing over the bracketed sections, distilling only an essential sentence or two at most to underline. And try to disentangle the segments where you've put question marks.

After those two readings, the section is pretty much "yours." Get a piece of paper and write a statement of what you think is the principal assertion; then under it write in outline form the major arguments the author uses to justify that principal assertion.

Now the harder, more important part. The story and biography try to focus the virtue in question by describing individuals who exemplify it. You've digested the text segment—and perhaps added insights of your own. But your biggest problem will be engaging the interest of *your* unique child(ren). Real learning begins in honest puzzlement—or not at all. What does your child fear about the value in question? Some children fear they have no virtues at all; others are overly cocksure that "I'm OK!", even when they habitually cheat or lie in a tight spot or shred their friends' reputations without a second thought. What will set the question mark hook in *this* child's mind? Only you can answer that question, but it's essential. Spend at *least* as much time finding that "hook" as you spend on all your other preparation time.

Dilemmas

I have tried to pose the dilemmas so that there is no easy answer and so that each of the people in them has at least some shaky ground on which to base the conviction that they are in the right. In some cases, it helps (and is kinda fun) if the parent role-plays the person at fault, using every self-serving dodge he or she can find. Then, if the child's gut feeling is with the person at fault, he or she gets hooked into finding all kinds of reasons to attack that position. Most kids love to argue and hate to lose. Since you're defending "their" position, the only option they have is to attack it!

Don't expect to "solve" the dilemma. But also, don't be surprised if a day or two later the youngster comes back and says, "You know, I was thinking about that dilemma—"Ah!

Conversations

These pages are just one other way of focusing a discussion of each value. Have the child read the first ten statements (or you read them aloud) and ask whether they agree or disagree with each one. Whatever you do, *don't* say that's a "right" or "wrong" answer. The important thing is to discover where your child really stands on each issue. If they think the hero or heroine was a fool, no problem—but let's be sure to talk about *why*.

Another way to understand your child's grasp of the virtue is to pick from the second set of statements the one which puzzles them most or makes them the most uneasy.

In all these discussions, no matter what tack or form they take, the most important thing to remember is to avoid being too "preachy." You don't want your child to merely conform to *your* convictions, but rather you want your child to come up with—and believe—his own convictions.

Trust

If I Can Trust My Family,
I Can Learn to Trust Myself

As contagion
Of sickness makes sickness,
Contagion of trust makes trust.
—*Marianne Moore*

Tatters

nce upon a time, long, long ago, when people were less clear-headed, there lived a very rich, very glum (not to mention very eccentric) widower duke named Dirk, in a grim castle on the crags above the boiling sea. For a time the duke had found joy in his lovely daughter, Lisette. But the girl married a dashing knight named Gaston, whose biceps and pectorals were far more imposing than the muscle housed in his skull. However, Gaston's purse was even lighter than his brain, so to the duke's delight, Lisette and her husband were forced to live in the castle with him.

Soon Lisette gladdened her father with news she was about to deliver an heir, guaranteed gorgeous, given his parentage, though brain power was not so assured—for the same reason. Then Gaston announced he had accepted an invitation to serve in the army of an impoverished prince who, despite a tender conscience, hoped to solve his insolvency by blasting his kingly father off his throne. Duke Dirk was of mixed mind about that. On the dark side, the airhead might be lucky, make a fortune, and take Lisette away. On the bright side, the impetuous ninny might get himself killed, and the duke would have his treasured child to himself once again.

As it happened, the latter option prevailed, though when the news of Gaston's untimely demise reached the castle, the Lady Lisette went into premature labor and delivered a pretty baby girl. But in her exhaustion, she breathed her last and joined her ghostly Gaston.

Duke Dirk was inconsolable. When Hannah, his daughter's old nurse, brought the infant girl to him, he swore he would never look on her face as long as he lived. So he sat himself in a great chair looking out at a tempestuous sea and refused to budge ever again. Day after day terrified servants forced some food into him, but there he sat, his white hair and beard growing down over his shoulders, twining around his chair, and creeping into the cracks in the stone floor.

Meanwhile, his nameless granddaughter grew into a young girl, her lovely face smudged, coppery hair tangled, living off scraps from the kitchen. No one dared care for her, except old Hannah, who gave her bits from the rag bag. The staff batted her away like a stray dog, "Off with you, Tatters!" And she would run off crying to the woods, not knowing where else to go.

Then one day, a new boy named Owen came to the castle to tend the duke's geese. A sprightly lad, he sat all day playing his pipe so merrily his geese huddled near him, dreaming of soaring on unclipped wings high in pillowy clouds. Young Tatters crept through the bushes and sat listening to his music, feeling somehow "at home" for the first time in her life. But that very first day, Owen spied her and called, "Hey, young miss! Come out where I can see you."

Tatters tried to run away, but Owen caught her arm and swung her around.

"Well, aren't you the pretty little thing. Except for that soot. Here," he said, and dipped his sleeve in the water trough and wiped the smudges from her face, and he began to unsnarl her coppery curls, dabbing at them till they were a red-golden froth. "Now, then. A princess!"

Tatters blushed, unused to any kindness, but pleased. Day after day, she sat with Owen, fearfully at first, but slowly letting down her guard. Owen spun her tales and made magic music with his pipe, and Tatters danced, the geese whirling round her like a honking *corps de ballet.*

But one morning, in her nook behind the kitchen fireplace, Tatters awoke to a burst of bustle and chatter: "I never thought I'd see the day" and "Quick, quick! You know the old man's temper!" Tatters crept out and spied old Hannah collapsing like a soufflé into a chair by the fire.

"Hannah," Tatters whispered. "What is it? What's happening?"

"Ah, child," Hannah huffed, "it's not to be believed. A summons from the king himself! Not to be disobeyed! To a great ball at the castle. So the prince can choose a wife."

"And the duke is... going?"

"How can he not? The fines would ruin him! Ah, it will take hours just to cut the old man loose from his chair! His hair's knotted around everything like morning glory vines gone mad!"

"A ball," Tatters sighed, and leaned her head against Hannah's knee.

But just then the cook burst into the kitchen like a Viking invader. "Get that wretched girl out of my kitchen!" she cried. "And Hannah, be off with you! Fetch the hedge clippers!"

So Hannah huffed to her feet, and Tatters fled to her friend Owen and his geese.

"A ball," Owen smiled. "And would a certain young miss fancy an invitation?"

"Oh, Owen," Tatters mumbled, looking down at her raggedy dress. "Don't tease."

"Now, what have I told you of disrespecting yourself? Those people can thump you round, but never hurt the soul inside. Unless you let them. There's a noble lady inside those rags, and don't you forget." So he began to tootle his pipe, and before any of them knew it, Tatters and the geese began swirling, and Owen led them dancing down the road toward the town.

Before they had gone very far, they heard hoof beats behind them. They stopped and turned, and beheld a handsome young man in fine traveling clothes atop a great gray gelding. "Ah, young lad," the young man called, "could you tell me the way to the—?" But he stopped when he caught sight of Tatters. "Oh, my," he said, "what angel walks by your side?"

Even the geese twisted around in puzzlement, wondering what they must have missed.

"I mean," the young man smiled, doffing his hat, "the enchanted young lady by your side. The dazzling swan among your geese." He slid from his horse, bowing deeply to Tatters.

"Oh, sir," Tatters blushed. "It were a wicked sin to tease this way."

Owen grinned. "I have been telling her as much myself, your… I mean, uh… sir."

"I am… my name is Justin. I'm traveling to the castle to attend the king's great ball."

"And so we are ourselves, sir," said Owen.

"Oh, no, Owen," Tatters tugged at his sleeve. "I was just a lark, sir."

Slyly, Owen began to pipe, and Tatters stopped, as if held in a silken cord of music.

"Come, then, my friends," said Justin. "Let us travel together. The young mistress will charm the hinges off the castle gates." So Owen and his geese and a baffled Tatters began to walk with him, chattering of this and that, singing with Owen's pipe, softening to one another.

The castle loomed high above them, encircled by a broad moat. Justin leaped upon his horse and whispered down to them, "I'll ride ahead and see what I can do with the gatekeeper. I leave the rest to you, my lad." He clattered off and stopped at the gate, leaning down to speak to the keeper, who looked up at him, not sure he understood, then back at the boy and girl and gaggle of geese. Finally, he shrugged, and Justin rode off with a wave into the castle.

"Come, Tatters," said Owen, beginning to cross the drawbridge. But Tatters held back.

"Oh, *no*, Owen. We daren't."

Owen took her hand. "Mister Justin has opened the gate to us, hasn't he? Come."

So the raggedy pair crossed the drawbridge, geese honking haughtily like plump matrons on their way to a grand party.

Maids hustled by with their mistresses' glorious gowns, while Owen filched a few buns from overloaded trays. Then they huddled listening to the music from the great feast within.

Suddenly there appeared a most impressive gentlemen dressed in brocade, his mouth drawn tight like a miser's purse. "Ahem," he huffed. "The... uh, Master Justin requests the... well, honor of your presence at the... uh, festivities. If you will... follow me."

And he turned away, assuming the threadbare two would follow. Which they did, eyes and mouths as big as saucers, as they stumbled through great corridors hung with tapestries, ablaze with light. The geese muttered with what seemed a touch short of awe but well beyond approval.

Finally the doors swung open to a great ballroom, where gentlemen and ladies swirled to the music like a dancing garden. Then in an instant, everyone froze, eyes and mouths agape, staring toward the door. Everyone backed away as a flock of fluting, fluttering geese preceded a ragged goose-boy and a cringing, tattered young girl through their midst toward the dais on which the king had stepped from his throne, gawking like a startled boar, wattles atremble.

And from beside him rose Mister Justin, beaming down at them.

"Father," Justin said, "I have made my choice. Here is my bride, the loveliest girl in all the land, and the sweetest as well."

Grinning, Owen began to play his enchanted flute, and before their very eyes, Tatters was transformed. Her rags shimmered into a satin gown, seeded with glittering jewels, and a silver coronet appeared in her coppery hair. In a whirl of white, Owen's geese changed into a flock of pages and maidens, circling their mistress and singing in far better voices than they had ever had before. And Prince Justin came down to the floor to take the hand of his new princess.

No one noticed dark Duke Dirk slink through the great doorway into the night, hurrying to his lonely chair, bitterly swearing again he would never look upon his granddaughter's face.

No one seemed to miss him either.

Christy Nolan

t might seem odd, at first blush—even brash—to write an autobiography at age 22. But Christy Nolan had ample justification. At only 15, he had won two writing prizes and published a book of poems which respected critics compared to William Butler Yeats, James Joyce, and Dylan Thomas—despite the fact he'd been horribly crippled with cerebral palsy since birth. As he himself describes it, "his drunken, drooling body," his "spoiled manhood, birth-brain damaged" often lashed out uncontrollably and poked an unwary bystander in the face or gut—or worse. He couldn't chew or speak more than a yowl or control his bowels or bladder. "The frenzied limbs could wreak involuntary havoc yet he was unable to brush a fly from his nose.[1]

Christy could nod his head, pound the foot of his wheelchair with his feet, signal his needs with his eyes. And he could weep. And he could laugh. Yet all the while he drank in the world inexhaustibly with his ears and eyes, "fiercely listening, nestled in hassled lucidity," wrapping what he knew in webs of words no one else would even unwrap until he was 11 years old.

He had almost died at birth. His tiny body was in a transverse position across the birth canal, his spine wedged into a V-shape by his mother's contractions, cutting off oxygen from his brain for two hours before he was delivered by Caesarean section. Any new infant completely changes his family's whole schedule and priorities for a year or two, but Christy's homecoming would change their lives forever. Here was a child who would never be toilet-trained, never be able to feed himself, never learn to get up when he fell. Yet his parents refused to

---

1. To achieve some psychological distance, Christy Nolan wrote his autobiographical novel, *Under the Eye of the Clock*, in the third person, calling himself Joseph Meehan. Quotations in this piece are from his book.

buckle. Their twisty boy was going to be as loved and challenged as any other boy. "His mother it was who treated him as normal, tumbled to his intelligence, tumbled to his eye-signaled talk." He drew strength from Bernadette Nolan's courage and humor from her down-to-earth, no-nonsense love: "Come on, Joseph, don't be so damn dramatic." Trusting her faith in him, he slowly found "home"—confidence. "She spoke res-urrecting hope when there was no hope at all."

When Christy was 17 months old, his mother took him to a Dublin doctor who was intrigued by the inquisitive baby, who studied *him*. He played games with the child, blowing in his eyes so Christy shut them; then the doctor stopped, and the boy popped open his eyes to see what was wrong. The doctor knew what Christy's mother knew. He suggested physiotherapy, speech therapy, occupational therapy and, in time, schooling at the Central Remedial Clinic in Dublin.

Christy's father worked on a one day on, one day off schedule as a psychiatric nurse so he could also tend his farm in Corcloon, 55 miles west of Dublin. There the boy grew, nestled like any normal boy between his father's knees as he drove the tractor, wheeled from place to place in a wheelbarrow before he was big enough for a wheelchair, which "allowed him access to birds' nests, anthills, and sheep farts." His father took him to football matches, but most importantly every evening he sat his wobbly boy on his knee and recited poetry to him, told him nursery rhymes and all sorts of bawdy stories. He "meddled in medleys of cheery but breathtakingly beautiful thought. Words seemed his tools of trade as he ferreted for mollification in his bondaged world."

His sister might be, because of her age, the most remarkable member of a truly extraordinary family. "She cradled his head when he was sick, but when he was well she gave him hell." One day when they were older and he involuntarily grabbed her bosom, she merely sniffed, "Let go, you sex maniac." When she was seven and he was five, their parents gave her a speckled Connemara foal as a birthday gift. When Christy signaled with his eyes that he wanted a try, at first she refused, but he sat "determined to look hurt and bruised," and finally she said, "Look here, brat, I'll give you one ride, that's all." With one parent on each side, they heaved him tottering into the saddle and followed beside him, and he demanded to go faster. They even allowed him a jump. As his mother said, "Falling off is less painful than not having a chance."

When he was four, Christy's mother took him to a psychologist, who assured her that his intellect was superior, equivalent to a seven- or eight-year-old's. But still he couldn't speak. Except with his eyes.

When Christy was five, the family uprooted itself from the farm to move to Clontarf, three miles north of Dublin, to be near the Central Remedial Clinic. It was a school filled with all kinds of impaired children, from slightly to seriously wounded. There he encountered superbly sensitive teachers, who earned his trust. "The mute boy became constantly amazed at the almost telepathic degree of certainty with which they read his facial expressions, eye movements, and body language... It glimmered in their kindness to him. It glowed in their keenness, it hinted in their caring, indeed it caressed in their gaze."

At age 11, Christy was set free by a typing teacher named Eva Fitzpatrick and by a new drug, Lioresal, which calmed his spasms— more or less. With Eva soothing his panicky nerves, cupping his chin, and with a stick banded to his forehead "the unicorn stick," Christy began giving wing to his imprisoned soul, one letter at a time. "But for Eva Fitzpatrick, he would never have broken free." And after awhile, "his belief now came from himself." One day, when Eva pretended to be called away, she asked Christy's mother if she could support his head for a moment. And his mother could *feel* the need in his head, pulling her hands to the right letters.

Finally, it became time for Christy to move to a secondary school. Or not. His father told a psychiatrist friend his son's applications kept being refused, and Christy brashly conversed with the two in his own language, "leaving no doubt in the doctor's mind that here was a boy ready and willing to face school life bravely, if only a school would have him." The doctor got on the phone, and within minutes the boy was scheduled for an interview at the Mount Temple School. Despite Christy's terror and sweats, John Medlycott, the headmaster, looked at this glaring, drooling, punching, gibbering apparent-idiot and said, "Well, Joseph, when can you start?"

The principal enlisted two understandably skittish boys to wheel Christy from class to class, wipe his drooling face, and over the months begin to intuit his mute signals. "He was full of hope for he sensed the sincerity and kindness in them." Gradually, three or four more boys and girls joined them until finally he became their taken-for-granted brother:

"Lift up your feckin' head until we see what you're saying." They became his life-line to the world of school.

"My mind is just like a spin dryer at full speed; my thoughts fly around my skull, while millions of beautiful words cascade down into my lap. Try then to imagine how frustrating it is to give expression to that avalanche in efforts of one great nod after another." But tap he did, a single page taking a whole day's work. Then he cajoled his mother to send his boyhood story to the Spastics Society Literary Contest in London. To everyone's astonishment, he won first prize. On Christmas Eve, he heard eminent Britons interviewed on the BBC about the most important moment of their year, and Edna Healey, an author, wife of the Chancellor of the Exchequer, said the high spot of her year had been reading Christy Nolan.

When he had won the prize again the following year, the London *Sunday Times* wrote an article about him, soliciting funds to buy Christy a computer. Thousands of pounds poured in, enough to inaugurate a drive to highlight the communication needs of "tongue-tied but normal-rational man," and to fund research for new mechanisms to open and free their minds and souls.

Then, when he was only in his third year of secondary school, Christy's book of poems, *Dam-Burst of Dreams*, was published, and within ten days it was on the best-seller list. The BBC did a documentary on Christy and his family, and from all over Europe came reporters from radio, magazines, and newspapers. Only one, an American, showed less than profound respect for the boy. He sat unsmiling, wrote nothing, yawned as Christy showed him how he typed. When the magazine finally appeared, the article was a shock. The American had written that the entire Christy Nolan phenomenon was a total fraud; a boy of fifteen—much less a wreck of a child—couldn't possibly have written the boyhood story or the poems; it was obviously his mother's work, using a freak to get notoriety. That night, Christy cried "tears of pristine despair."

In 1987, Christy Nolan's autobiographical novel received the $35,000 Whitbread Award. His mother read his acceptance speech: "Tonight is the happiest night of my life. By choosing my book as the Book of the Year, you have fashioned me as an equal to any other writer, be they creating words by hand or by head."

Christy has his dark moments. Yet he is indomitable, because his parents and sister were. When someone asked if he ever feels despair, he typed his response: "No. I haven't time."

Feeling at Home

he closest any of us has ever been to paradise—or will be—is in the womb: warm, fed, floating, secure, "at home," without a care or desire, because we couldn't think. Then, through no fault of our own, we were ejected into cold and noise with a slap on the butt to make us cry, breathe, and eventually, think. Being born is the first in a lifetime of natural crises which summon us to grow more fully human—or not. But the first thing doctors and nurses did was to clean us up and lay us back against the heartbeat that had been our reassurance for the last nine months.

Just so, when a child awakes from a nightmare, alone in the dark, she's completely lost, so she cries out, and almost instantly her mother comes, flicking on the light, hugging her: "It's ok, honey, it's ok." And everything *is* all right again, because out of the darkness has come someone she knows can be trusted unquestionably. The child feels "at home" again, confident again.

When we learned to swim or ride a bike, Dad was there, bigger and stronger than he truly was, reassuring, dependable, solid. Only because we were sure the people around us were reliable were we able slowly to develop the *self*-reliance to swim, ride, speak and move out on our own. As with Christy Nolan, "after awhile his belief came from himself."

Trust, I suspect, is the *sine qua non*—the most necessary—of virtues. Without it, there is slim likelihood we will ever be confident enough to be curious, empathetic, responsible, persevering, because unless we can trust those around us, it's doubtful we will ever truly trust ourselves.

Without trust (and the ironic union of vulnerability and confidence it can give rise to), no one would ever risk loving.

One need only look at young people, especially young men, who have had no solid figure in childhood against whom to hone their adulthood—like the young man in 1998 who spread HIV—the virus that causes AIDS—to dozens of women in southwestern New York State. His grandmother was a crack addict; his mother had prostituted herself and her ten-year-old daughter to support her own habit; the boy roamed from one crack house to another with no one to pay him much attention, much less respect. In Freudian terms, he was raw Id—primitive urges—without the slightest taint of a governing Superego—respect for society's moral commands.

Striking a Balance of Cherishing and Challenging

Every Tatters needs an Owen. Every Christy needs a Bernadette. Not only someone we trust to catch us when we fall, but someone who sees a goodness, a potential, a genuine value in us few others seem aware of. What a good mentor offers is another ironic union—cherishing and challenging—unconditional acceptance, coupled with a love unafraid to be tough.

Anyone, young or old, who deals with kids can "tell" which ones are "at home" inside themselves, who have had a healthy balance of cherishing and challenging. No need to grab attention, prove themselves, or to seek out caves to hide in—these kids are hard-working, at ease. They take their licks with a resigned smile and are above alibis, scapegoating, and requests for extensions.

We can also tell those who have been overly cherished or overly challenged (and in my experience the former far outnumber the latter). The unfairly cherished are too often smug, small-minded and lazy. They usually have A minds and C averages; their parents fight their battles for them and call the school to report them sick the day of the circus. The unfairly challenged are the nail-biters, the perfectionists, yearning for some, all too momentary, evidence that they have value. These are the athletes who come off the losing field punishing themselves for not giving 110 percent (which no one has), the scholar for whom a B+ is an F, for whom winning the Silver Medal just means being number one among the losers. Such good kids have unconsciously internalized a conviction their own parents are unaware they have inflicted on them: If I don't succeed, I won't be loved.

If one bad apple can spoil the barrel (to coin a phrase), the root of the apple tree can blight even more thoroughly and permanently. Unless both the parents are "at home" within themselves—authentically adult, their child has a great struggle ahead. Psychologists say the purpose of adolescence is to evolve a personally validated self—which few adolescents (future parents) are encouraged or helped to do. That process of emerging from adolescence as an adult is, by nature, necessary preparation for offering oneself to another in the intimacy and partnership of marriage. Then in the natural order of things, the couple has children, whose very spirits depend on the character of the parents and on the solidity of their union. All of which is strong evidence that the primary task of schools and parents is not to train kids to ace the SATs and get children into good colleges, not to prepare attractive job candidates or even good citizens, but to cultivate *good spouses and parents*. If those who motivate the young succeed in that, all those other goals will take care of themselves.

For the first year or so, the ordinary infant is little more than a healthy young animal—eating, sleeping, pooping, crawling—and good parents yield to that. If the child soils the diaper, or spits up, or tosses the cereal, they take care of it, no matter how inconvenient. But somewhere in the second year, the child begins to exert muscle control, along with a curiosity to reach beyond the blanket, climb out of the crib, pull the lamp down on his head. What's more, the parents have grown somewhat disenchanted with the steady stream of diapers and glop. So the infant has to be weaned and potty-trained, which is the next annoying invitation for the child to become less dependent and more self-confident, less "healthy animal" and more fully human.

But up to that point the child has been, in the normal case, unconditionally loved and served. Now, for probably the first time, he or she hears two words they have never heard before: "Good" and "Bad"—or at least "Yes, *yes!*" or "No, *no!*" The child is incapable of connecting cause with effect yet, any more than a dog can comprehend why wetting the rug causes its owner's anger. For some unfathomable reason, it's ok to throw the ball to Daddy but not the spaghetti. Pretty confusing. More importantly, if weaning and potty-training begin too early and brusquely, the child will end up anal-retentive—scrupulous, a perfectionist. If they begin too late and parents are too permissive, the child will grow to be self-absorbed, thick-skinned, demanding—at least until he finds some kindly psychiatrist, spouse, or drill-sergeant to change his (unconsciously) warped personality. One suspects Woody Allen was weaned too soon and Hitler too late.

Understanding the Difference between Personality and Character

There is a real difference between "personality" and "character," which one can see in, "She's got a lot of personality" and "She's got a lot of character." Personality is a set of habits we develop unconsciously before age three in response to the family; character is our set of inner values and convictions. Personality is mostly external, and we have no responsibility for "causing" it (though we do have responsibility for what we make with it); character is internal, and is formed neither unconsciously nor automatically. Character takes real work. In fact, in great part, character *is* responsibility.

Personality

A first-born child of demanding (or overly busy) parents often reacts instinctively from fear of losing their approval, protection, support. So the child tries to do everything perfectly. A second child may see the jangle of nerves the parents made of the first child and, without reflection resolves that the same won't happen to him or her. Introvert perfectionist and extrovert contender. Neither is better nor worse, but parents and teachers—and later the child—must first recognize the differences, then try to make the introvert more assertive and the extrovert more reflective. The key is not to fret over what "mistake" the parents made, without realizing it, or to blame them, but to be aware of a child's personality and ways to balance it.

In this regard, I'd suggest that all students (plus parents and teachers) might do well to read a book on the Enneagram—which refers to nine basic personality types: reformer, helper, climber, artist, thinker, team-player, sampler, boss, peacemaker. Each is a fundamental set of habits in dealing with others we "picked up" in our first three years. Again, none is better or worse than any other, but studying them could help us understand ourselves and others better, empathize with the assets and liabilities of each type, be more aware of what choices (though initially repellent) will make us healthier and what choices (though initially appealing) will make us weaker human beings. Each child is unique, but certain general observations about personality types bring them into better focus.

It is important to realize personalities can be *changed*. Often teenagers say, "I'm a procrastinator"—as if it were some incurable genetic disease. They blame their faults *on* their personalities instead of blaming their personalities for their faults. We are not prisoners of personalities we formed unconsciously as children, any more than Christy Nolan was an irretrievable prisoner of his uncooperative body. A shy child can become confident; a wild child can be tamed. What it takes is Bernadette Nolan's persistence and typing teacher Eva Fitzpatrick's imagination.

Aristotle said we become brave by acting bravely, even if we don't feel brave. You go out on stage and project a confidence not totally genuine—in *order* to achieve a confidence that is genuine.

Character

Unlike personality, character can be purposefully forged only by each individual, and the road to a good character is an obstacle course. We achieve a personally validated self—ethical principals which are *our own* rather than hand-me-downs—by rising to challenges.

If you ask good parents what their major tasks are, they invariably say: to give our children the best we can and to shield them from harm. But like weaning, those laudable goals must be handled sensitively, because giving children *too* much and shielding them *too* carefully prevents them from becoming adults, from achieving character. They must hear "No!" once in awhile, and they have to suffer the legitimate consequences of their choices. Otherwise, parents are equipping them only with the skills to play volleyball before sending them out into the minefield of life.

Adolescence—A Process of Evolving

The word "adolescence" is inchoative, that is, "-escence" means a process begun but not yet finished, as in "convalescence." Too many parents and youngsters believe adolescence is a "stage" kids fall into from puberty to college graduation—a sort of moratorium for a child in an adult body. On the contrary, from the moment a boy or girl becomes capable of producing a child, they no longer have the option to consider themselves children. Rather, adolescence is a *process*, exactly like the process of evolving an infant into a more independent child: "Take just a few more steps; come on, you can catch it; up onto the Connemara pony." Coaches know that: "Today we're going to take two more wind sprints." Just so with adolescence: "You've got to take a bigger role in the family this year; you've got to learn to cook (boys, too); you've got to get your own alarm clock." Irritating words, but necessary.

Most of this book's readers are preparing a parent, and every reader has to deal with his or her own parents. But when most actually do become parents, their preparation has usually been haphazard, a mixed bag of half-perceived, half-remembered recollections of how their own parents "handled things." And in dealing with their parents now, understanding them is an equally confusing operation. Therefore, it might be valuable to have youngsters reflect a moment on parenting, on making children feel confident and "at home," since for most it will be a greater part of their life's work, and since it might ease relationships at home.

The style of parental discipline can run the spectrum from totalitarian at one extreme to laissez-faire (non-interference) at the other. The overly strict style has the advantage of predictability—orderly rooms, and unstained carpets—but the liability is raising dispirited kids deprived of the exuberance that gives joy to young lives—not to mention to the parents' lives. The overly lenient (or indifferent) style frees the exuberance of the child at the expense of the limitations and control which give spontaneity its power. We're back again with the gray areas, as with cherishing/challenging. "Where do I draw the line?" Sorry, no answer to that. It depends on the parents' sensitivity, common sense, openness to criticism, and ability to sort out contrary advice.

One way to enable children to develop a trust in adults which leads to self-confidence is by finding a way to let them know they can be honest about what they've done wrong (just as a married couple must find such a place of peace and forgiveness with one another). Children must know they can say, "Yes, I did that," without fear of a too-strict reprisal—or an equally unsatisfying, "Oh, well, so what?" Too often parents, like judges, have set penalties for each "crime." That's very businesslike, but quite anti-human and teaches nothing.

One of my fictional heroes, a model of authentic fatherhood, is Atticus Finch, in Harper Lee's *To Kill a Mockingbird*. The Whites of a small southern town are incensed at Atticus for defending a Black man accused of rape. A neighbor woman says some pretty nasty things about Atticus, so in retaliation his son, Jem, uproots her garden. Atticus doesn't impose arbitrary sanction on the boy "in reparation." Instead, he says, "Son, I have no doubt you've been annoyed by your contemporaries about me lawing for niggers, as you say, but to do something like this to a sick old lady is inexcusable. I strongly advise you to go over and have a talk with Mrs. Dubose." Not "*order*," but "*strongly advise*." The boy is free to take ownership of his actions—or not. The result? Jem takes it upon himself to repair the garden, and he and Mrs. Dubose become friends.

Trustworthy Parents—Self-confident Kids

The key to a child's developing confidence, I think, is in parents' proving themselves trustworthy. The child can rely on the parent not merely to "be there," like a 911 number, but to be *alert* to the child's every mood and action—exactly like a mother with her infant, rearranging all priorities around the parents' most important task and "product." It means putting aside the ironing or the newspaper, closing the mental file drawer on the contract that's due tomorrow, and really *listening*, not because the news or the questions are intriguing, but because the *speaker* is. Good teachers need to do the same. On the inside cover of my grade book, I have a note in large print: "Make me feel important!" When I'm lucky enough to see that, it reminds me that what I'm trying to do is far more meaningful than covering a lesson plan.

Another way of establishing trust is through honesty. Too many parents believe that, for the child's sake, they have to project an image of solid perfection. But humans, being what they are, are usually found out, and the idol crashes, often with scarring results. Admitting one's mistakes isn't a sign of weakness but a sign of strength. Apologizing to a child when one has been wrong or too extreme forges a bond between two people who are both trying.

The basis for engendering all the other virtues and values is that children feel grounded, confident they live in an environment where they can make mistakes yet still be cherished. I suppose what I've been talking about all along is open-hearted—but level-headed—love.

What does a young person do if he or she has parents who at least *don't* seem to offer the security that leads to confidence? The only answer is to *find* some adult mentor they do trust—a teacher who is both savvy and kind, a member of the clergy, a scout leader. It's *essential* that each of us has someone we trust, someone to whom we can unburden, someone we can talk to when we're scared. Someone who says, "I'm here. I'm willing to listen, if only you can overcome your fear—just a little."

A Dilemma

"Yeah, I can sing. I mean I could always belt out those corny old songs at Boy Scout camp. Till I bagged *that* nonsense. I only did it because the Old Man forced me to, said his scouting days were the best in his life—and the band played on, right? But now this teacher's on my case, see? I mean, she's a really nice lady and all, cute and really sharp, but she directs the school musicals, and she says my speaking voice sounds like I'd be a good singer. They're doing something about a guy named Joseph and some kinda coat, and they need a lot of boys. What's worse, at the PTA meeting she told my *mother*, which is sorta like telling the Gestapo. And now I get all this blah-blah, from the time I get home from school till the time I go to bed. 'Oh, Danny, it'd be so *lovely!*' She uses 'lovely' a lot, which just about kills me.

"Anyway, this Miss Ganley's a lot more cool than my Mom. She just grins and rolls the baby-blues, and says, 'Aw, Dan, give it a try. You might even get the lead.' Like I want to get out there with my face hanging out and everybody staring at the ape in the zoo? And what kinda guys would go out for something where you've gotta sing? Buncha dweebs, and nerds, and cream puffs. And what girls would come all the way over to a guys' school, and get out there and make fools of themselves trying out?

I'll bet they're all the Bride of Frankenstein. They only come to con some geek into inviting them to the junior prom. Which is another thing my Mom wants me to go to, and she wants my sister to teach me how to *dance*! I'll join a monastery first.

"And this musical's *every* afternoon! No hoops, no MTV, no video games, no hangin' out, no nothin'. So, you're my best friend, right? So how do I get out of this thing? Maybe without doing myself some actual bodily harm?"

A Conversation about Trust/Confidence

What's your reaction to the following statements?

A = Agree; ? = Uncertain; D = Disagree.

1. Under every unpromising face/body there is usually a valuable person. A   ?   D

2. To safeguard the rest of the family, Christy should have been institutionalized. A   ?   D

3. Over-cherished and under-challenged children usually out-number their opposites. A   ?   D

4. The primary task of schools and parents should be to prepare spouses and parents. A   ?   D

5. To be practical, personality pays off a lot more than character. A   ?   D

6. A teacher who gives even a D for a top-of-the-head essay is a menace. A   ?   D

7. It isn't enough for family merely to "be there for me" like a 911 number. A   ?   D

8. A parent's apology for over-reacting is a sign of weakness.
   A ? D

9. Better for a parent to err on the side of strictness than to be too lenient. A ? D

10. A shy child can become confident; a wild child can be tamed.
    A ? D

Help me understand what you understand by any of these statements.

1. "Falling off is less painful than not having a chance."

2. What a good mentor offers is another ironic union: cherishing and challenging.

3. Unless parents are authentically adult, their child has a great struggle ahead.

4. We're not responsible for forming our basic personality, but we are responsible for what we make of it.

5. Children must be led to know they can say, "Yes, I did that," without fear of undue reprisal.

6. Too many parents believe that, for the child's sake, they must project an image of perfection.

7. It is as important that children understand their parents as it is that parents understand their children.

8. Making young people respect themselves is more important than covering the lesson plan.

9. It's essential that each of us has someone we trust, someone to whom we can unburden.

10. People blame their faults on their personalities rather than their personalities for their faults.

Questions

Christy Nolan's parents seemed to find a healthy balance between cherishing him (tending to the hundreds of needs he simply couldn't attend to himself—without any fuss) and challenging him to do far more than most parents would "demand" of such an impaired boy, never allowing him to feel too sorry for himself too long. On that balance between cherishing and challenging, where do you think (Mom/Dad) and I stand? Tell me times when we were too tough on you. Too easy? When you have kids, what choices do you think you'd make with them different from those we made with you?

Here's another set of balances—about personality. Make an X where you think you are now.

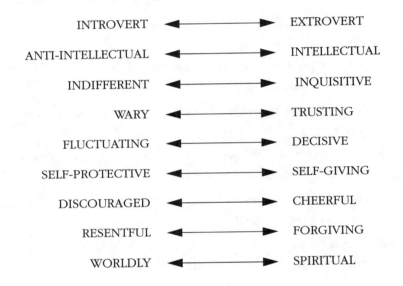

INTROVERT	⟷	EXTROVERT
ANTI-INTELLECTUAL	⟷	INTELLECTUAL
INDIFFERENT	⟷	INQUISITIVE
WARY	⟷	TRUSTING
FLUCTUATING	⟷	DECISIVE
SELF-PROTECTIVE	⟷	SELF-GIVING
DISCOURAGED	⟷	CHEERFUL
RESENTFUL	⟷	FORGIVING
WORLDLY	⟷	SPIRITUAL

Where do you think you need to move some of those X's to the right or left? How?

Good fathers want to be caring, and good mothers want to be decisive, but think for awhile: what qualities, attitudes, "positions" do you expect more from Mom and what qualities, attitudes, "positions" do you expect more from Dad?

Curiosity

It Won't Kill the Cat:
Only the Lack of It Will

Four be the things I'd been better without:
Love, curiosity, freckles, and doubt.
—*Dorothy Parker*

Digger

nce upon a time, long, long ago, when conformity domi-
nated curiosity, there was this boy named Digby. But they called him
Digger, because he was always trying to figure out what things are for.
His favorite word was "why." But he lived in a gray town where people
had very serious faces as if they all had terminal toothaches. So whenever Digger asked, "Why?" they'd snap, "It's compulsory," or "It's
forbidden." So, as you can imagine, they all thought Digger pretty curious. Not just inquisitive. Downright queer.

Well, one day there came to town an old beggar with laser-beam
eyes. His cloak was a tangle, his battered hat like a blackbird's nest, his
smell was so bad it was eye-crossing. Naturally, when they saw him, the
townsfolk turned up their collars and bustled about their business. But
Digger went right up to the old codger, tugged at his raggedy sleeve,

and asked the question of all questions: "Please, sir," he said, "what are people for?"

A rainbow smile spread across the old man's face. "Ah," he sighed, "at *last*! What are people for! Yep, that's the only question all right!" And he reached in his coat and pulled out a map covered with mysterious symbols and runes. "All right, young fella, you've got to find your way to Castle Heder. Meet the three weird sisters." And before Digger could close his gaping jaws for another question, the old man was gone like smoke.

Digger sat on a milestone awhile and puzzled over the curious chart, none too sure he even had it right side up. All the words were in some cryptic code, but fortunately there were pictures as well, some none too welcoming: Griffins with great hawk heads and wide warped wings, dragons with flinty fangs fluming flame, and other beasties he could not put a name to, but from whose acquaintance he would prefer to spare himself.

So off Digger went, clutching his map, and that's when his troubles began. Which, of course, is what a quest is for.

A few hours outside the village, Digger came upon a dense wood crowded with craggy outcrops of rock. And as he pawed his way through the brush, he came upon a griffin perched on a boulder, his cruel eyes lancing from either side of a silver beak. Unaware at first of Digger's presence, the griffin sat idly picking his formidable teeth, and at his taloned feet lay a bloody lion skin, recently emptied. Then Digger caught his savage attention, and the griffin's eyes skewered him.

"Excuse me, Sir," Digger said, doffing his cap. "I'm searching for the Castle Heder."

"Haven't the slightest," the Griffin said, and belched.

"You see, I'm trying to find what people are for."

"Well, then," the Griffin said, with what seemed a smile, "I can spare you the trip. People are for eating." He cast a disdainful glance at the empty lion skin. "Much more tasty than beasts. Fortunately for you, I'm quite full at the moment. Hmm," he said, eyeing Digger. "No more than an hors d'oeuvre. Still, you ought to be on your way. I have quite a marvelous metabolism."

So Digger quickly took his leave and plunged back into the forest. For hours, he pushed onward, one tree looking exactly like the last, which made him wonder if he weren't traveling in circles. And he dearly wished he'd stopped at home before he set out and packed a lunch.

Then suddenly he broke through the trees and found himself face to face with a cliff, and at its feet a long line of hairy men with slave-slack faces trudged toward what seemed to be a cave. Another line of men stumbled out of it, laden with great rocks glinting with gold. Along the line paced a tiny fellow with a scrunched-up face and orange hair spuming from his wrinkled brow. The troll cracked his whip on the prisoners' legs and shouted, "Faster, louts! Only work can set you free! If you don't get moving, I'll double your quota! Move! Move! Move!"

Digger was about to scoot back into the brush, but the little fellow was his only hope. So he buckled his courage and clambered across the fallen rocks and cleared his throat. The troll turned and scowled him up and down.

"Too small," he snarled. "Go away."

"Excuse me, sir. I … I'm looking for the Castle Heder."

"Waste of time," and he turned back to lashing his whip.

"But I'm looking to find what people are for."

"Foolish question. Obvious. Look," and he pointed to the slave lines. "People are to work. All those bags of bones have hired themselves for gold. Hah! Feel sorry for 'em? Knee-jerk silly. If we set 'em free, they'd beg us to shackle 'em up again. They know after twenty years we'll set 'em free with enough gold to retire to the South Seas. If they survive."

"Please, sir. Castle Heder?"

"Oh, it's over there somewhere," the troll said, batting in the general direction of the west.

"Thank you, sir," Digger said and turned to take his leave.

"Start lifting things!" the troll shouted. "Build up those arms. No use for spindleshanks!"

For hours more, Digger plodded on till he broke out of the forest onto a broad green plain. A stream wove through its flowered flanks and silvered in the setting sun. At the center sat a huge castle, its turrets shafting up into the dying light.

Digger made his way across the grassy meadows and over the heavy drawbridge. He reached up his fist and rapped on the big oaken door. Slowly it swung back and framed a stern-faced giantess with iron-gray hair and spectacles the size of barrel hoops. "'Bout time," she snapped. "You must be Digger. Old Solon said you might be by. Name's Dame Verity. Sounds like charity. 'S not. Nowhere near the same thing. Charity's m'sister. You're not ready for her yet. Come." And she led him into a room big as a dragon hangar, piled floor to roof with junk: astrolabes, anvils, chemicals, Bunsen burners, and what looked like all the parts to several atomic reactors, among other oddments. "Well, sort it out. Off you go," Verity said, and off she went.

So Digger dug in, setting the place to rights, separating things that looked alike, putting up shelving, asking everything's name and what it was for, dusting, oiling, washing, polishing, till the place looked like heaven. "Dandy," Verity snorted. "You're ready for my sister, Charity, now." So she gave him a bag of peanut butter sandwiches and sent him off down the road.

When he finally got to the end, Digger found a beautiful park around a lake that glistened like glass, and at the gate was a sweet little old lady like Glinda in "The Wizard of Oz." "Hello, dear," she smiled. "Come in, Digger." So Digger followed into the park, but stopped in his tracks. That beautiful place was filled with limping fawns, and broken-winged birds, and rickety little boys, and misshapen little girls. Digger's heart felt bruised, and he looked up at Dame Charity. "Yes, dear," she said. "Aren't they beautiful?" Digger stammered, "But … why?" Her tiny brows pinched. "Oh," she said, "Why are they like that? So we can love them, dear."

So Digger began shyly to nod at the broken animals and children, and gradually he began to smile at them, and talk to them, and to hold their twisted hooves and shaky hands, and to look deeply in their knowing, grateful eyes. He did tricks and sang songs in his silly breaking voice, and soon they were all laughing and trying to bring their clumsy hands together to clap for him. And Digger had never been happier in his life. But one day Dame Charity came to him and said, "It's time to move on, Digger." He pleaded, but she assured him he could come back. Now he had to make the final stop at Fortress Fearless and meet her sister, Tenacity.

So off Digger whistled till he came to a great bulwark with a moat, crossed the drawbridge and hammered on the big door. It creaked open, and there stood this bolster-bosomed giant lady in a sweat suit with a whistle around her Old Sequoia neck. "Well, Digger!" she bellowed. "Come on in and meet my kids." And she led him into a big yard, where all these impressively fit boys and girls were leaping and cavorting like a herd of kangaroos on cannabis, and she introduced each one: Patience,

Bravura, Moxie, Paladin, Appassionata, Will, and a host more, including the runt of the litter, Spunk, and his Jewish cousin, Chutzpah.

So for a month, Digger joined them in their training games: Stand-Up-and-Be-Counted, Keep-the-Ol'-Chin-Up, Stick-Your-Neck-Out, Beard-the-Lion-in-His-Den, Take-the-Bull-by-the-Horns, Bell-the-Cat, and Put-Your-Self-on-the-Line. Till finally one day, Digger was summoned to the gate where they waited for him: Verity, and Charity, and their big sister, Tenacity. "It's time, Digger. You're ready. Now you know what people are for."

"But," Digger stammered, "what am I s'posed t'do?"

The three sisters smiled. "When it happens, you'll know. From now on, it's all improvisation." So Digger trudged glumly up the path. But the Three Weird Sisters called out, "Don't worry, Digger. You're filled with magic now." So Digger smiled, and stuck out his chin, and climbed on up the road, whistling.

(This story was previously published in the author's book, *Clever Foxes and Lucky Klutzes* (Tabor Publishing, 1993).

Helen Keller

 ifteen years after the Civil War, Helen Keller was born in Tuscumbia, Alabama, the third child of Captain Arthur Keller, a former Confederate officer, wealthy landowner, and newspaper publisher, and his second wife, Kate. The family adored the baby, but at 19 months, Helen fell victim to a mysterious illness doctors now believe was scarlet fever. When the fever finally broke, the family rejoiced, but almost immediately they realized something was terribly wrong. The baby girl slept badly, almost as if she were smothering in frustration, and she constantly hid her face from light. Finally, the doctors realized that Helen's eyes and ears were sealed forever.

As she grew older and stronger, Helen became more difficult. Her moods swung from despondency to fierce anger. Some thought she must be simple-minded and should be institutionalized. What's more, her unpredictable moods and behavior became dangerous. One time, finding her baby sister sleeping in her own doll's cradle and incapable of knowing what it was, she overturned the cradle, but fortunately her mother was there to catch the baby. As her inner intelligence grew, so did her frustrations, like a child in a straitjacket in an airless room.

Without any help from outside, she nonetheless began to use signs to make her feelings and her demands known: a shake of the head meant "No," a nod "Yes," a pull "Come," a shove "Go away." If she was hungry, she mimicked cutting bread; if she wanted her father, she pretended to put on glasses; if she wanted her mother, she pulled her hair into a knot at the back of her head. By age five, she had a "vocabulary" of about 60 gestures. And all of this with no more input than what she'd been able to ingest as a child of a year and a half, before the darkness.

But Helen's mother refused to give up. Reading a book of Charles Dickens's notes on his travels in America, she found an item describing his meeting a girl named Laura Bridgman, blind and deaf from a very young age, who had learned to communicate at the Perkins Institution in Boston. Meanwhile, a Baltimore eye specialist suggested Helen go to Washington, DC, to see Alexander Graham Bell, whose telephone had come about from his efforts to teach deaf children.

Bell invited Captain Keller and Helen to dinner, and he warmed to her immediately. "He understood my signs," she wrote later, "and I knew it and loved him at once. But I did not dream that that interview would be the door through which I would pass from darkness into light, from isolation to friendship, companionship, knowledge, and love." Bell also suggested Perkins.

Imagine what her life was like—without color, without tones. She could contact only surfaces and vibrations with her hands. She knew by the smells and textures when she was in the house—but she didn't know it *was* a house. She'd worked out a safe path through it, a dark little world where she could remember where harmful objects were. Outside was different, too big to plot a safe path through it. When she felt the soft thing under her feet (which was the lawn), every step she took was taken in fear, because the next step could be the edge of everything.

She was the only *person* in her dark, little world. Others were just bodies. She was utterly alone, and everything else was enemy—dark, unseen, always threatening. But inside this girl was a fierce intelligence, agonizing to break free, like a ship trapped in impenetrable fog.

Captain Keller wrote to the Perkins Institution, pleading for a teacher for Helen. And the teacher was Annie Sullivan, 21, abandoned by her immigrant Irish parents at age nine and sent to the Massachusetts poorhouse in Tewksbury. There she had spent five years with the castoffs of society: alcoholics, the helpless elderly, and the insane. Almost blind herself from an eye disease contracted when she was very young, Annie was illiterate until 14, when Perkins accepted her. There, after six years of eye operations and education, she had most of her sight restored and graduated first in her class. Annie spent many hours with the aging Laura Bridgman, still at Perkins, and from her she learned the secret, silent, lonely place Laura had wandered in so long.

When Annie arrived in Tuscumbia on March 3, 1887, she carried in her case a doll for Helen that the Perkins students had pooled their allowances to buy, clad in doll clothes made by Laura Bridgman. She met a near-savage child with wild hair, who punched away Annie's attempt to embrace her. When her mother stopped Helen from grabbing Annie's purse, she rocked and howled on the floor. "There is nothing pale or delicate about Helen," Annie wrote to a friend at Perkins. "She is large, strong, and ruddy, and as unrestrained in her movements as a young colt."

But in the middle of Helen's tantrum, Annie handed her a pocket watch, and the girl calmed, feeling it with her fingers, her empty eyes signaling puzzlement. Somehow, her inaccessible mind intuited that watches had something to do with time, and that there would be candy, later. Helen was excruciatingly curious, which is the only place from which any true learning can begin.

Next morning, Annie began. First she spelled "doll" in Helen's hand, then put the doll from the Perkins children in her hands. Helen went along, mimicking the word, but with no idea she was spelling, or even that words existed. She was simply imitating, with no more comprehension than a monkey. When she grew bored, she batted Annie's hands away, then hurled the new doll, smashing it to pieces. A couple of weeks later, Helen punched out two of Annie's teeth.

No one had made much effort to curb the child. Whatever she wanted, she got. If she refused to be cleaned up, they allowed it; at meals, she pawed anything she wanted from anyone's plate. But one morning when Helen grabbed food from Annie's plate, Annie slapped her hand. Shocked, Helen tried again, and got another slap. The Kellers were furious, but Annie simply ushered them out of the dining room and locked the door. Helen lay on the floor, kicking and screaming, trying to pull Annie's chair out from under her. She pinched her, and Annie slapped her every time. Helen felt her way around the table and knew they were alone. After a few minutes, she returned to her place and began to eat her breakfast with her fingers.

Captain Keller bristled at Annie's discipline but reluctantly began to see that, without control, all Annie's work would be useless. So Annie and Helen moved into a small cottage on the farm, and gradually began to know one another. Slowly, Helen began to associate Annie with "home," with something (not yet "someone") reliable. She found it more pleasant to be clean rather than dirty, and that when she was willing to eat with a spoon, Annie would let her eat. And always there was the strange game in the palm of her hand. Whenever she held her doll, four funny signs; whenever she got a glass of water, five funny signs. That's all it was. Just a game.

Then one day, it happened. Helen was impatient and angry at her lesson, so Annie took her for a walk, out in the yard, near the pump. She hit the pump and shoved Helen's hands into the water, writing the word "water" in her other hand. Something inside the girl was beginning to connect; something choked into her throat. And from her twisted mouth came the only word she could remember from her babyhood, before the darkness: "Wa-wa."

It had happened. The invasion. Helen had discovered things have names. There was a world beyond her darkness, and—even though she couldn't see them—there were other *persons*, like her, people who could communicate to her through the strange game in her hand. Poor frightened girl. She'd made the most liberating of all human discoveries: She wasn't alone.

In an ecstasy of understanding, Helen breathlessly touched the pump, her tugging hand begging its name. Then the trellis, the well house itself. By the end of the day, Helen had learned 30 words, but most importantly, she knew what they *meant*! In their walks after, she was relentless to know everything she contacted: eggs, chickens, piglets, flowers, puppies, a dead squirrel. Within three *months*, Helen accumulated over 300 words, and Annie decided it was time to read Braille. She spelled each letter in Helen's hand, then touched her fingertips to the nubby raised letter embossed on a card. In one day, Helen learned the whole Braille alphabet. "When her finger lights upon words she knows, she fairly screams with pleasure, hugs and kisses me for joy."

By June, Helen had learned to write, using a board marked with deep horizontal lines, guiding her right hand with her left. Annie rejoiced in Helen's joy and her restlessly inquisitive mind. In November, Helen went to her first circus, and the performers let her feel and feed the elephants. She stroked the lion cubs; a leopard licked her hand; a big black bear offered her his paw. When she kissed all the circus performers in grinning gratitude, some of them wept.

At eight, Helen went with her mother and Annie to Boston to visit the Perkins school. "What a joy to talk to other children in my own language!" The library held the country's largest collection of Braille books, and Helen's fingers scampered over the raised dots, hungry for more. And she met Laura Bridgman, the woman who "bridged the chasm between mankind and me."

Helen learned to sculpt, she began to learn French and Greek, and her English fluency was astonishing: 80 words a minute. Then, she spelled in Annie's hands: "I must speak." So Annie took her to Sarah Fuller, principal of Boston's Horace Mann School for the Deaf, and Fuller painstakingly taught Helen—by allowing her to feel her mouth as she formed words, and within an hour she could pronounce six sounds. After ten lessons she was able to gargle to Annie: "I am not dumb now." She never learned to speak clearly, but Sarah Fuller taught her to lip-read by touching the lips and throats of the speaker. She learned to "hear" music the same way.

Because of her father's failing businesses, Helen's chances of further education—or even a continued salary for Annie, looked bleak. But through the begging of Alexander Graham Bell and Mark Twain, money accumulated to send her first to the Cambridge School for Young Ladies, where she interacted easily with ordinary young women, and then to a private tutor so that, at age 19, she was prepared to take the entrance examination for Radcliffe College.

Despite Radcliffe's initial reluctance, Helen excelled, even though she had to rush home after classes to transcribe into Braille what she could remember of Annie's fingered communications of the lectures. In 1902, the *Ladies' Home Journal*, offered her $3,000 for her life story, an amount she was hardly able to turn down. The following year, when Helen was only 23, it appeared as a book, to enthusiastic reviews. Eventually, it was translated into 50 languages.

Helen was restless, tired of writing about only one subject: herself. She became interested in the plight of the poor, women's rights, economics, politics, and pacifism. Many thought her impertinent; who was she to write about complex subjects? Always in search of money to survive, she and Annie toured the country giving "lectures." With Annie now in ill health, Helen finally accepted an annuity from Andrew Carnegie which allowed them to hire an assistant to take care of their housekeeping and finances, a Scotswoman named Polly Thompson, a quick learner, who typed, managed the books, cooked, and dealt with the endless visitors.

In three years, Helen and Annie toured 123 cities, raising more than a million dollars for the blind, a mind-boggling amount in the '20s. She captivated presidents from Grover Cleveland to Lyndon Johnson (even Calvin Coolidge!) and the great figures of her age like Enrico Caruso, Jascha Heifitz, Maria Montessori, Henry Ford, Eleanor Roosevelt, Charlie Chaplin.

In 1936, Annie Sullivan, nearly blind now herself, died. Her last words were, "Thank God I gave up my life that Helen might live." Friends wondered if Helen could survive, but with Polly Thompson, she continued to write and lecture, campaigning for blind workers. During World War II, she toured military hospitals, encouraging soldiers who had been blinded or deafened in battle. After the war, she toured 35 countries promoting programs for the handicapped.

At the age of 88, Helen died quietly on June 1, 1968. She had moved from utter loneliness in the dark to a rich, full life, known and respected by millions, because her restless mind and fingers refused to yield. As Helen said, "Life is either a daring adventure or nothing."

The Cost of Fascination

icture a group of babies on a blanket in a park—sweet, smiling, wide-eyed, tirelessly exploring. Then picture a typical cluster of people in a subway car—gray, slack-faced, guarded, eyes fixed in a ten-yard stare. They were once just like those babies. What got lost?

More often than not, I fear, people sort of "drop out"—they settle for a "realistic" acceptance of what seems inevitably to be "the way things are." They adjust to the humdrum, even to the anti-human, which somehow becomes the norm, a "stunting" they share with everybody else. And after a while they don't even notice how impoverished they've become.

Children are born with ravenous appetites—both mental and sensory. Child-care experts exhort parents to feed that hunger every moment the child is awake—with goo-goo eyes, senseless prattle, singing, patting, brightly colored toys that make tiny noises. Without such constant stimulation, neurons and synapses in the child's brain actually shrivel and die, incapable of rejuvenation. In their first years, well-nurtured children ingest a larger body of new information than they'll assimilate in all their formal schooling. It is difficult to assess how much mental damage occurs in an infant when his or her mother returns to work a few weeks after the child's birth, turned over (however reluctantly) to people who might be caring but who are responsible for many children at once.

The Death of Curiosity

I suspect the death of curiosity begins sometime in the second grade. Up till then, a child's life has been a fascinating odyssey: "All experience is an arch where through gleams that untraveled world, / Whose margin fades for ever and for ever when I move." (Alfred, Lord Tennyson, "Ulysses"). There are the constant stimuli from eager parents, stories experienced in the security of an adult lap, then puzzles and games, *Barney* and *Sesame Street*, inventive play with other children, like turning boxes into turrets and mud into pies. For most children, pre-school, kindergarten, and even first grade are usually stimulating: "Mommy, look! I can write my own name!"

But then around second grade, "the system" takes over. Time to get efficient and serious. The purpose of education is to prepare children for "the real world," and that means developing the verbal and computational skills to make them attractive job candidates. Even the humanities fall victim to those goals. English, for instance, must resolutely focus on the SATs (Scholastic Aptitude Test), memorizing words from lists rather than developing an addiction to books from kindergarten on. Even poetry doesn't serve to move the soul except as analysis fodder: the ability to separate a simile from a metaphor (as if that mattered) and to point out where the poet uses alliteration (without the slightest sense of the effect the poet intended by it). The iron-clad syllabus and lesson plans become more important than judging whether children's minds and hearts are still growing.

Education vs. Schooling

Winston Churchill once said, "My education was interrupted only by my schooling." And truer words were never spoken. Granted, learning need not (and cannot) always be fun, but it ought always to be intriguing, engaging, puzzling—because without curiosity, genuine learning is impossible. It's a totally different—but no less stimulating—kind of fun. The key is the radical distinction between "education" (learning) and "schooling" (endurance). Schooling begins when a bell rings, as it did for Pavlov's dog; education begins with puzzlement, or it never begins at all.

Most students and parents—and, sadly, even most teachers—believe one has to have "a good education" in order to get a well-paying job. Utter nonsense. One doesn't need a good education; all one needs is a diploma. In fact, one doesn't even need that. Henry Ford, Thomas Edison, Mark Twain, and Abraham Lincoln never finished *grade* school, and they managed to secure rather good jobs. Peter Jennings, Edward Bronfman, Jim Carrey, and Julia Roberts dropped out of high school. Walter Cronkite, Harrison Ford, Steven Spielberg, Candice Bergen, Don Hewitt, Ann

Landers, and Clint Eastwood never finished college. *Bill Gates* never finished college! John Steinbeck and Eugene O'Neill both won the Nobel Prize for Literature without finishing college. All you need to be "successful" in life is the four D's: Discipline, Drive, Determination—and a Dream. And I don't know of any graduate school that teaches those.

My hunch is that the Dream is what calls the other three into being. As my friend, Thea Golson, told her sons, "Education is to find the passion of your life." Ah!

The most basic of all puzzlements is Digger's question: "What are people for?" If we find the answer to that, we'll be happy, successful, fulfilled—no matter what our bank balances. Retrievers wag their tails like mad metronomes even when they're exhausted from retrieving. That's what they were born to do. Just so, we will "wag our tails" with joy—even when we're exhausted, stymied, misunderstood—if only we can find the answer to Digger's question.

What separates us from other animals is that we can learn and love and grow more fully human—the more learning and loving we do.

Curiosity Leads to Learning

Ironically, the school "system" can inhibit young people's learning. Harried teachers often presume interest—or at least non-intrusive politeness. The object of these classes is to get this novel "done," rather than to seduce youngsters into loving reading. Too often students take subjects simply because they're "required." When schooling becomes merely a matter of passive endurance, students claim they're lazy. No one is lazy, just incurious, bored and unmotivated. The get-a-good-job motive doesn't turn on seriously until March of senior year in college; even the SAT motive doesn't turn on until a week or two before the actual exam, when it's too late. Despite *Sesame Street's* evident success, too few teachers realize that, like salespeople, they have to find devious ways to outfox the customers' resistance and create a "need to know" where there was none before. Before *anything* else, a mentor's first job is to pique curiosity. If a student has a teacher who doesn't do that, the authorities have to be told. And if nothing changes, they must be told again, and again. Otherwise, the teacher goes *on*. And children's minds die.

Schools can also undermine young people's loving. Most have an initial getting-to-know-you orientation in the first year, but after that the focus is on the SATs, unlittered corridors, and acceptable behavior. Most administrators are untroubled by insulated cliques or by the hapless kids who eat lunch alone, cower in the library carrels, and leave school like sprinters at the final bell. I know only one school (in Australia) which requires every student to be in one athletic activity and one extracurricular activity. In 35 years, I've never had a year where some student didn't ask another senior's name—even after four years. You can't love people unless you know them, and you can't know them unless someone or something has forced you at least to *notice* them. If a student isn't in an after-school activity, he or she is losing at least a third of their education.

But one of the best things many schools now require is the completion of service projects before graduation—a wonderful idea, since schools claim to teach the humanities. Trying to make a person in a nursing home smile, feeling the palpable need for love in an impaired child, reading to someone who is blind can be a more profoundly educational experience than getting through *King Lear*. It opens your horizons, which is what being human is all about.

Very often, for the best of motives, parents also shield their children from learning and loving. Granted that one of their primary functions is to curb their children's curiosity when young children are likely to get hurt ("Don't touch; hurt, hurt," "Never talk to strangers"). But as the child grows older and (one hopes) more reflective, parents have to give them a bit more leeway. Experience (if reflected on) is the best teacher. Once, as a child I put my hand on a hot stove plate; I never did it again. Also remember, your best friend was once a stranger.

Just as with the spectrum between totalitarian and laissez faire parenting, and between cherishing and challenging, the parents' common sense has to be the pivot on which balances the spectrum between protecting and the thrill of a successful risk. As the child's self-confidence begins to build, so must the parents' confidence in the child's prudence grow. As Bernadette Nolan said, "Falling off is less painful than not having a chance."

It's a given that a young child is going to "get into things," and until the child develops some appreciation of cause and effect, the parents simply have to keep harmful objects out of the child's reach—just as they would with a healthy puppy. But as the child matures, parents have to find ways to show him or her which things are OK to be curious about and which are not. And the parents have to maintain perspective. Kids are going to exercise their artistic instincts with their crayons on the wallpaper, but allowing it to cause a mild tantrum in the *parent* is no good lesson for the child. Kids are going to get into rough-and-tumble games and mess up or even ruin their clothes—so be it. They're going to crack open their heads and break their arms, but their learning is more important than the parents' panic or the time lost to rush them to the clinic.

The Human Question—Why?

The same is true of their endless curiosity about reasons and causes: "But *why?*" Parents have to be reminded (even by their own children) that "why" is the human question; we are the only species blessed and cursed with it. It's the question we were born to ask, and keep on asking. We were meant to doubt, to "smell rats," to ask odd questions, to cross-examine what "everybody says." Unless we do, we become no better than sheep—or worse—*robots*. In order to cope with the endless string of "whys," the parents need more than brute patience. They need words, they need the power to reason and the imagination to go looking for better explanations. Psychologist Jerome Bruner showed that you can explain anything to a child, at any stage, *provided* you can adapt it to his or her receptivity—or capacity to understand. The purpose of schooling, formal and at home, should be to prepare an articulately wise spouse and parent, not just an attractive college and job candidate.

To maintain curiosity costs. But to lose it—in the interests of safety or conformity or a more serene life for the parents—is dehumanizing.

Sadly, for the same understandable reasons (safety, conformity, serenity), parents can also stifle a child's curiosity about people. Limiting a child's range of friends by the color of their skin or their ethnic background or their social standing is, of course, bigotry—though most of its victims might call it by less truthful names.

I've known young people whose descriptions of their parents come close to the inflexibility of Nazi drill instructors or the protectiveness of Secret Service agents. In most cases, the descriptions are pretty exaggerated, and I have to remind them they are defending a vested interest; if they ever agreed their parents have a point, they'd have to give up something they really want. Still, some parents are too strict and over-protective. In such cases, the young person must find some adult his parents really respect and ask that person to intercede. They've got to have slack, both control and freedom. Sooner or later, Hansel and Gretel have to control their own freedom.

Like confidence, curiosity requires vulnerability—in both the child and the parent. Vulnerability to the truth, wherever the puzzlement might lead; vulnerability to other people, no matter how initially repellent, and vulnerability to the quest, to leaving behind something comfortable in order to risk something better. As Alistair Reed wrote in his poem, *Curiosity:*

> Dying is what the living do,
> Dying is what the loving do.

A Dilemma

"Mom," Ann Marie Vacca asked her mother who sat at the kitchen table grating parmesan from a smelly, yellow hunk, "OK if I go to the movies with a bunch of the kids tonight?"

"Ann Marie, I've been working all day on this meal. Your aunt and uncle are coming."

"But I'll be here for part of it."

"Part? You mean stuff a couple meatballs between two pieces of bread and it's, 'So long, everybody, I got more important things to do!' No."

"But, Mom, they come over every other week. This is—"

"You heard me, young lady. Now go do some homework."

"But it's Friday afternoon."

"I don't care. Do you see me goofing off because it's Friday afternoon? Besides, you've got to get that scholarship to Nazareth College."

"Mom, I want to go *away* for college. Teachers say it's an experience nobody should miss. Meeting new people, getting away from the family, which I have to do sometime. Becoming indepen—"

"Independent? Just take a look at your room. You'd live in a pigsty if I didn't keep your room clean. You're too young to be off on your own at some school with a lot of boys. Hah, tell me about boys. One thing they're interested in, and they're not getting it from you."

"Mom, there are a lot of decent boys."

"Right. Till after a few beers."

"I've got to make my own decisions *sometime*."

"Yes, the day you get your college diploma. Your father and I worked ourselves ragged so you can go off to some school and come back a couple months later and telling us you're … in the family way? Now go upstairs and study. And if you're not interested in your own future, start making a salad."

A Conversation About Curiosity

What's your reaction to the following statements?

A = Agree; ? = Uncertain; D = Disagree.

1. People like Digger who are always asking questions can be a real pain. A ? D

2. Many sighted and hearing people live almost as isolated as young Helen Keller. A ? D

3. Annie was far too rigid with Helen; she should have shown a little more "give." A ? D

4. Helen's successes are probably out of reach for "ordinary people." A ? D

5. I really seek out other people different from myself and try to get to know them. A ? D

6. In order to get a well-paying job, you must have a college diploma. A ? D

7. If I had a genuinely ineffective teacher, I'd complain—and not once or alone. A ? D

8. Curious people are curious in both senses: inquisitive and weird. A ? D

9. Better safe than sorry. A ? D

10. Limiting a child's friends by race or ethnicity is at least a kind of bigotry. A ? D

Help me understand what you understand by any of these statements.

1. When Digger finished, he didn't understand what people are for, but he knew.

2. Helen Keller was the only *person* in her safe, dark, little world.

3. The death of curiosity begins sometime in the second grade.

4. "My education was interrupted only by my schooling."

5. "Education is to find the passion of your life."

6. If you answer Digger's question, you will be happy, successful, fulfilled.

7. A service project opens your horizons on what being human is all about.

8. Maintaining curiosity has its costs.

9. Like confidence, curiosity requires vulnerability.

10. Dying is what the living do; Dying is what the loving do.

Questions

❦ At school, in the cafeteria, say, or during games, do you usually hang out mostly with people who are "like us," the same color, same kind of economic background, that kind of thing? If so, it's understandable in a way. You feel more "comfortable." You have a lot of things in common you can just take for granted. But what advantages would you find— as a person who's trying to grow as a human being—if you took the chance and sat down with people you're not really used to? You know, "Mind if I sit here?" It'd be a bit embarrassing at first, but do you think it would be worth it to make more friends, with people who would make you "stretch" as a person? When you get into college, and certainly when you get out into the business world, you're going to *have* to deal with all kinds of people who aren't at all "like us." But probably more important, how would that willingness to risk approaching someone different enrich you as a person?

Let's talk about Digger's Question: What are people for? The text says what separates us from other animals is that we can know (understand versus just being aware of) and love (sacrifice versus just feeling affection), and that we fulfill the human invitation by learning and loving more and more and more. Tell me how you feel about that—Not just in your head, but in your heart, in the choices you make. Don't just tell me about the school subjects you like or the ones that have a dynamo teacher, but tell me about the unappealing subjects or the ones with a really dull teacher. How can we make them intriguing, even if it's "from the outside," like you coming home and saying, "Mom, I didn't fall asleep even once in Miss Gulch's class"? Why do you think "people-who-ought-to-know" believe that everybody ought to take (math/history/languages) in order to be better able to cope with the world and people—even those who are going to be salespeople or managers or computer programmers or designers? There's got to be a reason, right?

3

Impartiality

Discovering the Primary Truth

In times like the present, one who desires to be impartial just in the expression of his views, moves as among sword-points presented on every side.
—*Herman Melville*

Colin

nce upon a time, long, long ago, when a man won a maid with his mitts, not his wits, there lived a squire named Colin, a rangy lad with an easy smile and butterscotch hair, who could fence with either hand or both simultaneously. He would surely be knighted within the month.

Except for one small problem.

Colin was deranged with love for the Lady Patrice who lived in the neighboring castle. She was lovely but she cared less about young Colin than about spherical geometry. He convulsed with frustrated desire. He hardly ate or slept, fashioning hymns to her eyes, lips, earlobes, etc. Colin's friend, Aidan, tried to use reason with him—an utterly pointless weapon against a madman.

Each morning, without fail, Colin stood below Patrice's window to pour forth his devotion in airy arabesques of melody, praising her eyes like moonlight, her lips like rose tips, her honeysuckle breath. Just as unfailingly, Patrice sent a squad of squires to drive him off her property and hie him home.

One day, Aidan resolved to cure his friend. As Colin positioned himself under the dawn-streaked casement, out the door like knights from a clock came four grim squires to roust this unwelcome chanticleer. Colin cut off in mid-arpeggio and bowed, smiling, crossing his hands to reach for his swords. The four hemmed him in. Colin whirled round and caught one on the side of his head with the flat of his heavy sword, and the man caved to his knees, eyes crossing, and bit the dust. A second rushed him with a blood-freezing yowl. Colin merely twisted with bullfighter deftness, and the knight hurtled headlong into the wall, his helmet clanging like one o'clock. Wielding their swords with full side-swings, the other two charged with terrible roars. Colin simply squatted to the ground and let them slam one another senseless over his head.

Colin merely sat there amid the four benumbed bodies and waited, humming, trying out rhymes for "honeysuckle breath," finding no better than "death" or words with a lamentable lisp.

Aidan shook his head as two more squires came out the door, grabbed Colin by the heels and dragged him, grinning, into the castle. A few moments later, he reappeared, beaming like a bridegroom. Aidan scuttled down to him. "You were successful this time!" he cried.

Colin grinned. "She cursed me quite inventively. 'Whoreson bore' has a nice ring to it."

Aidan glared at him, open-mouthed. "You're insane."

"No, no, Aidan," Colin said excitedly. "Don't you see? She's *testing* me! She *knew* I could easily dust off four men. She didn't want me hurt. Why not just tie me up and drop me in the moat? She must *see* me! She must see her beloved groveling at her feet!"

"I'll make her love you without all this childishness, or make you hate her and be free."

"I'll wager anything I have you can't."

"Your horse?"

"Done."

"And the saddle?"

"Done. They're as safe as the Crown Jewels."

"Tomorrow, then," Aidan said, his fine jaw set. "I'll go in your stead. I'll lure her out and plead your cause. You wait beyond the garden wall, and within an hour the spell will be broken."

Next day, Aidan bowed low to Patrice and introduced himself. "My lady, might we walk to your arbor," he said. "The sun is so warm here."

"I suppose we might," she said and nodded him to the lawn. "Just what is this about?"

"Colin. I am here to tell you he will not be coming today."

"Really?" And Aidan was hard put to tell whether she was disbelieving or disappointed.

"Yes. I have rid you of him."

"What?" she said, stopping, her mouth agape. "Dead? Seriously hurt?"

"His pride mostly. But he will be in bed for some weeks."

"That long?" she said, wistfully. "He was such a... boy. Yet somehow... endearing. Won't you sit?" So they sat in the shadowy arbor, and she poured glasses of chilly white wine.

"I... I can understand his madness," Aidan said, hanging his head ruefully. "My lady, I too suffer the same disease. I desperately love a lady. But she refuses to acknowledge my existence."

"A fine-looking young man like you. The woman is a fool and not worthy of you."

"Then help me, my lady. Plead my cause with her."

"Of course. I shall do anything I can to persuade her. Who is this woman?"

"The woman is you, my lady."

"What?" She paused from refilling his glass. "Perhaps you need no more wine."

"Not in your intoxicating presence, my lady." So, each unobtrusively refilling the other's glass, the next hour they sat in the shady arbor, whispering and getting more than slightly tipsy.

Meanwhile, squatting behind the wall, Colin fumed, ticking the seconds off on his fingers, marking each minute with a sword-scratch on the oak he crouched under. But when Colin was more or less sure there were 60 scratches, nothing happened. Something was wrong. He climbed the oak and dropped lightly down. There before him, their heads together within the arbor, were his beloved and his best friend! Asleep! Smiling!

Blood thundered in Colin's temples. He reached for a sword and walked slowly toward them. Manipulating hussy! Fiendish friend! At the height of his swing, he paused. No. He could not kill them sleeping, like a coward. He would wait. Serious love craves serious revenge. They would grieve their perfidy—their betrayal—in shame.

He laid the sword lightly across their throats and slunk back to the wall. Back at his quarters, he pushed through his puzzled mates. "I will retire to my room. I will never touch meat or mead again from this moment. I will *die!*"

Meanwhile, in the arbor, Aidan and Patrice wakened from their doze. They turned to look sheepishly at one another and felt a constriction at their throats. They reached up their fingertips.

"It's—" Lady Patrice whispered.

"A sword," Aidan whispered back.

They sat slowly up. Aidan took the sword by the hilt, and they both looked down at it.

"Colin's."

"Yes," she said. "I've seen it enough. But you said you had laid him low. You *lied!*" Then, scrambling to salvage some dignity, she cried. "How *could* you? That poor, sweet boy!" *Out!*" And she drove Aidan to the courtyard gate and turned furiously to enter the castle.

As she did, the guards appeared, and the sergeant said, "If'n you please, my lady, might we take a bit of a break now? That pesky squire ain't comin' back no more. Ever."

"You're probably right," Lady Patrice snapped, muttering to herself, "and it's all my fault."

"Oh, no 'prob'ly' to it, ma'am. He's a goner all right."

"What? Is he slain? For me?"'

"As good as. One o' them squires tole me. Boy's gonna starve hisself t' death."

"Get me a horse!" Lady Patrice shouted, and off she went over the hill.

When she arrived in a flurry of dust, she slammed into the squires' quarters and demanded the way to Colin's room. She followed along the hallway and burst into the only closed room.

Colin lay on his cot, pale as parchment, immobile as a monument.

"My *only* one!" Lady Patrice howled, hurling herself across the room. "I cannot allow you to do this, for *me!*" And she heaved herself on his manly bosom to clutch at his inert form.

"Oooof!" Colin sat up, staring at the mass of satin pinioning his bosom. "What the devil!"

Patrice thudded to the floor. "My *dearest*," she cried, tears dribbling her damask cheeks.

"Out!" Colin roared. "You trull! You minx! Hussy! Drab! Jade! Jezebel! Delilah!"

And in the midst of that stream of insults, Patrice fled in terror.

When he had exhausted his thesaurus regarding abandoned women, Colin stood, his lungs heaving for air. He saw Aidan grinning in the doorway, arms folded, legs crossed at the shins.

"For a moment in the arbor," Aidan said, "I was petrified. I peeked through my eyelashes and really thought you were going to hack off our heads. But only for a moment."

"I would have," Colin said, his fury somewhat diminished by sheer malnourished fatigue.

"Would this be a tasteless time to ask for the horse and saddle?" Aidan grinned impishly.

"Why you insolent—" Colin began, raising his fist.

"I should have doubled the bet," Aidan said. "After all, I didn't do one-or-t'other. I did *both*! Made her love you, and made you hate her. If either of you understands love at all."

"I ought to—" Colin began again lamely.

"But you won't," Adrian grinned, hooking his friend's big neck. "Now, shall we eat?"

"I'm absolutely starving," Colin grinned.

And off they went for eels and ale.

Dag Hammarskjold

ag Hammarskjold's stern father, Hjalmar, became governor of the district of Uppsala, the ancient Viking capital of Sweden, so Dag and his three brothers grew up in a huge red castle—a place of wonder for boys of imagination. His mother was the direct opposite of his rigorous father—effervescent, charming, religious—and Dag took after her. Because of the family heritage of public service, the boys were simply expected to follow in their forebears' footsteps, especially when, in 1914, their father became prime minister of Sweden. In a time when all the countries around them were easing into the horror of World War I, Hjalmar Hammarskjold proclaimed a strict policy of Swedish neutrality, believing political differences should submit to international law rather than to general carnage. Young Dag learned that the only honorable position was above strife, giving fair hearing to all sides, and settling conflicts with honesty and justice.

He excelled in all school subjects, eventually becoming fluent in English, French, and German, but the successes of his father and brothers were enough to keep him doggedly humble. Although Dag achieved his bachelor degree in literature and philosophy at age 19, his father was adamantly unimpressed; he had earned *his* at 18. Dag later took advanced degrees—one in law and another in economics. He was an eager reader and equally avid about debating any subject whatsoever, from Freud to Marx to romanticism.

In 1933, at age 28, Dag began working as an economist for the Swedish government in Stockholm. So impressive were his knowledge and dedication that three years later he was appointed Undersecretary of Finance. But, true to his principle of inner impartiality, he refused to give himself over to any particular party or "-ism." When World War II broke out in 1939, Sweden again declared herself neutral, though the private sympathies of most Swedish officials were with the Allies, especially their neighbor to the west, Norway, which had fallen to the Nazis in 1940. As chairman of the National Bank of Sweden, Dag was able to funnel funds to the Norwegian government in exile in London, often risking flights through skies controlled by the Germans.

At the end of the war, Hammarskjold became a member of the executive committee of the Organization for European Economic Cooperation in Paris (the Marshall Plan), trying to reorganize the financial chaos in Europe and build a whole new world out of rubble. Later, as vice-minister while the foreign minister was on vacation, he calmly took over after the Soviets shot down a Swedish plane over the Baltic, then shot down the plane sent to rescue the survivors. He defused the political bombshell with a tact and fairness that impressed both countries.

Then on March 31, 1953, he was offered the position of secretary-general of the United Nations, a position he later called, "the most impossible job on earth." Born like a phoenix from the ashes of the ill-fated League of Nations, the new assemblage of most of the states of the world was meant to face international differences with reasonable compromise rather than mutual destruction. Essentially, his task was to do for the whole world what he had helped to do for a war-torn Europe. Since the offer came on the last day of March, he was convinced it was someone's April Fool joke. But with his experience in international affairs, his evident workaholic nature, his knowledge of languages, his allegiance to a country with no vested interests—and most especially his resolute impartiality, Dag Hammarskjold proved an inspired choice.

At first, it did not seem so. By nature a quiet man, he seemed no more than a bureaucrat, colorless and uninspiring. What's more, UN prestige around the world was limping along, and as a result, UN staff morale was as listless. It was the time of the Cold War, and the U.S. and Soviet Union were each trying to control the UN. But when the U.S., mad with McCarthyism, insisted several Americans working with the UN were secret communists, Hammarskjold informed them they had no right under the UN charter to interfere. Nor did they have any right to send FBI agents into the UN to investigate American workers. The U.S. government backed off. Quietly, he had exerted his authority. No nation could dominate the UN.

His first international challenge had arisen even before he took the job. In 1950, North Korea, backed by Red China, invaded South Korea.

The UN sent a multinational force to aid the beleaguered South Koreans, but by the time Hammarskjold took office, the war had dragged to an impasse. During the temporary cease-fire and Geneva peace talks, however, the communist Chinese still held American airmen in custody. Hammarskjold saw only one solution: he would go to China.

It was the first time a UN secretary-general had ever officially visited any nation. His reputation for integrity and nonpartisanship was absolutely on the line. Hammarskjold kept discussions with the premier, Zhou En-lai, at a hectic pace, avoiding all intended distractions such as touring this garden or that palace. The core difficulty was that the internationally recognized government was that of Chiang Kai-shek in Taiwan; Red China was not even a member of the UN. But there were two vested interests in the balance: Dag wanted the American airmen released, and Zhou wanted recognition in the UN. Chess time.

Six months later, the American airmen were released, and Dag Hammarskjold had become a world leader. His unassuming, easy, steady way *was* his power. Yet his job was something like being mayor of a village of arsonists. As soon as he had put out a fire in one quarter of the world, some other discontented faction was setting another. But he was convinced that, with the superpowers wielding immense clout in pursuit of their own agendas, the UN was the only hope for the smaller emerging nations. And for all intents and purposes, Dag Hammarskjold *was* the UN.

One of the world's most demanding trouble spots grew from the infusion of a flood of Jews, fleeing persecution in Europe, into predominantly Arab Palestine. When the British, who had overseen Palestine since the end of World War I, relinquished their mandate, the UN voted to recognize two separate states, one Jewish, the other Arab—much to the displeasure of the Arabs. Raids and reprisals became commonplace, but the Israeli army drove the Arabs from much of Palestine, even from territory allotted to Arabs by the UN. Finally, in May 1948, when the British finally withdrew, five nations—Egypt, Jordan, Lebanon, Syria, and Iraq—declared war on the new Israel, confident that such a tiny, scarcely established state could not withstand them.

They were wrong. Israel not only held onto the territory they had established before the war but extended it even further. As a result, when Hammarskjold took over as UN secretary-general in 1953, there were nearly one million Palestinian Arabs herded into camps all over the Arab world, resented by their reluctant hosts for being a drain on their economies and equally unwelcome in Palestine—now Israel— which had been their home for their entire lives. What's more, though the UN had argued the warring parties into an armistice, it was violated again and again by raids and counter raids. The bomb was ticking.

In April, 1956, Hammarskjold arrived in Beirut, Lebanon, to begin "a diplomatic marathon"—winging back and forth among the capitals of all the countries involved—trying to uproot a mutual loathing planted and nurtured for centuries. Gradually, although their reciprocal hatreds didn't diminish a single degree, their respect for the mediator—Dag Hammarskjold—became genuine. It was only his "rigid honesty of purpose" that held the shaky peace together.

Crisis followed crisis in the secretary-general's life. In 1956, Egypt seized control of the Suez Canal from the British and French, controlling not only its enormous revenues but the shipment of Arab oil to Europe and the West. Britain and France threatened war. But Hammarskjold met with all the parties and achieved assurance that the canal would remain open. Nonetheless, Britain, France, and Israel attacked. Hammarskjold took the question to the General Assembly, where a simple majority was sufficient to ratify UN intervention. That came at 4:30 in the morning. He and his assistant, Ralph Bunche, put together an international peacekeeping force, comprised solely of soldiers from small nations, bypassing the "great powers." It was the first time in history that a multinational army was formed not to wage war but to *prevent* it.

In 1958, a civil war in Lebanon threatened to detonate the whole Middle East powder keg. Painstakingly, despite unwelcome and ill-informed intrusions from Americans and Soviets, Hammarskjold defused it. In the summer of 1960, only a few days after Belgium had given independence to the central African country of Sudan, Sudanese soldiers rioted against their Belgian officers, then began harassing, beating, and raping Belgian civilians as well. Within days, with the approval of all other African UN delegates, Hammarskjold sent in 3,500 peace-keeping troops, all from African nations, to replace all Belgians still in the Sudanese Army. Hammarskjold flew to Africa to take charge of the operation himself.

Frustrated that the secretary-general had foiled his attempts to manipulate the newly freed nations of Africa, Soviet leader Nikita Khrushchev decided to join the 23 heads of state and 57 foreign ministers gathered for the opening of the 15th UN session in September 1960. He purposely made a fool of himself—and of the Assembly—heckling speakers, denouncing Hammarskjold for siding with Western colonialists, and proposing that his office be replaced by a three-man committee. One by one each African delegate, even those leaning toward Russian policy, rose to support Hammarskjold. And when Hammarskjold addressed the Assembly, he received a standing ovation.

On September 17, 1961, Dag Hammarskjold boarded a UN plane for a meeting in what is now Zambia, trying to settle a dispute between one Sudanese province and the others. On the flight, he worked on his translation of a book by the German Jewish philosopher, Martin Buber. Ten miles from the airfield, the plane's engines suddenly cut, and it tumbled end over end into the jungle. As Richard Sheldon describes it: "He was found lying on his back, a peaceful look on his face, one hand holding a clump of grass."

He was a man of enormous courage, discipline, and open-mindedness who gave his life to protect the newborn nations from the manipulations of the Goliaths. In his book of poems, *Markings*, he summed up himself, "For all that has been—Thanks! For all that shall be—Yes!"

Impartiality

ne winter when I was teaching in upstate New York, we had eight consecutive snow days in early January. No one could get out of the house, even to the store. It got pretty claustrophobic—family members were close to matricide, patricide, fratricide, sororicide, and suicide— among other diversions. Because we had lost so many school days, the administration decided to cancel the February Presidents' Week vacation. Bad move. The tensions built back up again, this time in the school. Pranks escalated to the point of serious harm. So at a teachers' meeting, a couple of us suggested that we cancel the three days before the Easter break to have a full two weeks vacation to let all the tension ease. But the physics teacher was adamant. "If I lose those three days," he said (pretty intensely), "I won't be able to get to magnetism at the end of the year!" I said that I supposed somebody taught me magnetism in my senior year, but I couldn't remember a single thing about it, and therefore no one would be that impoverished to miss it. We argued on and on, but eventually his opinion prevailed. (And the following year he became principal.)

At the root of all that's wrong with the educational system is simply this—losing the forest for the trees. It becomes of pressing importance that we "cover" magnetism. It doesn't matter if anybody finds it useful, important, or worth remembering. It's "on the syllabus" and therefore as unchallengeable as death. Some people graduate from high school without having read "Hamlet" or *Lord of the Flies*. They've missed some interesting stuff, but as long as they learn how to read increasingly more challenging material and understand it, and as long as they want to keep on reading, they do just fine. Some graduate without calculus, but they don't need calculus to create a budget or balance a checkbook. As long as they have a reasonable knowledge of coping with complicated sets of numbers, they do just fine. But those fundamental skills are only the most basic *tools*, like learning to hammer a nail or fit pipe—essential as a start—but hardly enough to build a house. Once you've mastered the basic skills, you're ready to *begin*.

What differentiates someone who has achieved an education from someone who has endured schooling is the development of higher skills that enable him or her to *reason and come to honest decisions*. This is what legitimizes spending 12-16 years in school. In a nutshell, it is achieving the ability to make honest decisions.

The Reason for Education is Learning to Reason

Reasoning to impartial decisions (rather than just going with "everybody says") requires that we (a) gather all the pertinent evidence, without ignoring *unpleasant* pertinent evidence, (b) sift out the most important facts (most of your research you'll never use), (c) put the best evidence into a logical sequence (if you don't know how to outline, you don't know how to think), (d) draw a conclusion (the report, the essay, the editorial, the recommendation), and (e) submit it for a critique to someone more experienced (the teacher, the boss, the IRS, the judge).

This is *the* reason for education: (a) gather, (b) sift, (c) outline, (d) conclude, (e) critique.

Learning to master the basics is what one does in every school department: English and history essays, lab reports, spinning out math formulas, term papers. It's what we do for the rest of our lives— reasoning to honest conclusions—when the boss asks your best recommendation on the Smith account, when you're deciding on a career or a spouse, buying a stock or buying a home. Reasoning in this manner is also used when resolving moral questions. It's the way the human mind is made.

And each year, students wrestle with ever more complex data. The data—the plot and characters of *The Odyssey*, the factors that led to the rise of Napoleon, the area of this particular circle—are all forgettable, most of it completely unusable in later life. The important thing is not the data but the *process*: gather, sift, outline, conclude, critique.

Every time we arrive at a decision, each of us acts as a judge—even if the matter for decision is trivial (whether to see a movie or go bowling, to eat a balanced diet vs. junk food, to take Spanish rather than French) or whether the matter for decision is very important like choosing a career or committing to a spouse. In cases all along that spectrum—and with increasing importance as the questions become more consequential—we have to ask ourselves to be like any judge should be—*impartial*.

Overcoming Bias

Ah! There's the rub. An honest, impartial judgment has to be free of bias, which can come about in any number of often-undetected ways. I'll consider only four basic ones, plus a related one, reductionism, which is discounting pertinent facts if they don't fit our preconceived notions. The most obvious hindrance to honest judgment is (a) ingrained prejudice, but also there is (b) inadequate study of the alternatives, (c) vested interests (what will benefit *me?*), and (d) unquestioned acceptance of false propaganda.

(A) PREJUDICE

Bigots—of whatever race, creed, social class, ethnic origin—have rock-hard opinions based on no evidence at all other than hearsay, crowd-think, or unexamined "traditions." What's worse, they often *act* on their ill-founded beliefs in groups like lynch mobs, terrorists, street gangs and Hitler's SS Troopers. In *West Side Story*, the Jets hate Bernardo because he's a Puerto Rican, and the Sharks hate Tony because he is not. Racial and ethnic groups detest one another because "they" are taking "our" jobs. For 400 years, the Northern Irish have been killing one another over a religion neither side seems too eager to practice. Many of the wealthy scorn those on welfare, and many of those on welfare despise the wealthy because they're the reason for welfare. What all these closed-minded folk deny is that, beneath our differences, each one of us is equally *human*, with exactly the same hopes and dreams and with exactly the same rights, which our very humanity (not *The Declaration of Independence*) confers on each of us—life, liberty, and the chance to pursue happiness. And if every human has a right to life, he or she also has a right to those goods without which life is impossible: food, clothing, and shelter. These are objective facts.

Unlike bigots, most of us console ourselves with the belief we are open-minded, generally without serious prejudice. But check that belief—with complete honesty and impartiality. Are there not a few "types" for whom we haven't the slightest "fellow-feeling," types who, in fact, make us cringe? What about overweight, acne-faced girls at a dance? What about loud-mouthed, know-it-all jocks? What about painfully shy people? What about the boy who is a klutz at sports? What about homosexuals?

Are they all persons, just as—and just as much as—we are? Do we sense their need for attention, respect, even understanding? Even if we did feel some kind of empathy for those "unacceptables," would our need for our friends' approval keep us from striking up a friendship—or just a conversation—with one of them?

There's no assignment of guilt here, just an honest assessment of one's own impartiality of judgment. Once someone accepts that he is not totally without prejudice he can start to rectify it. That's what learning is for—to prepare youngsters for making honest, impartial decisions—especially about people.

(B) INADEQUATE STUDY

A severely limited point of view—or perhaps more forthrightly, "courageous ignorance"—is poor basis for impartial judgment. The sheer number of inquiring reporters proves that everybody in the country has an opinion on any question under the sun—on the coach of the Knicks, on the effects of secondary smoke, on the morality of abortion, on welfare and on extramarital sex. But precious few have actually reasoned their answers out for themselves (gather, sift, outline, conclude, critique)—or read a book on the topic. Even reading one book is hardly enough to answer any complex question, since books themselves are often biased. But one book is far better than no serious consideration at all, and surely better than "I know this guy—" or "I saw a TV show once—"or "Everybody knows."

(C) VESTED INTERESTS

When a conflict arises over any issue, trivial or grave, legal or moral, you're not going to get a fair trial when the judge has something to lose by being impartial. Discuss the effects of smoking with the CEO of a tobacco company, or welfare with someone who pays heavy taxes, or what legitimizes sexual activity to an already sexually active teenager, you can be sure the other side is going to maximize the evidence that supports them and minimize—or outright ignore—any that threatens them. Every one of us has been in an argument, especially with parents and teachers, when we suddenly realized, "Uh-oh, they're right," but we kept *on* arguing. Why? The question is: Do you honestly want the truth or do you just want to win (or at least not appear to lose)?

(D) UNQUESTIONED ACCEPTANCE OF FALSE PROPAGANDA

No inquisitor, no cult master, no Gulag brainwasher could hope for more than the sponge-like audiences which now absorb everything the media spews out on TV, in rock lyrics, and in the glossy magazines. Most people are no longer genuinely "free" after dinner to play Monopoly, sew, do carpentry, go for a walk or read a book. Like automatons, we head for the couch and the TV remote control, as if saying, "I hear and obey!" The TV programs and commercials "tell" us, without a direct word being said, that "The more things you have, the happier you'll be." (The best brainwashing is the brainwashing you swear you've never gotten.) Rock lyrics convince us, without a direct word being said, that "If you're a virgin by age 18, you're either queer or a fool." Face it. It's really true, isn't it? People in the '50s, before TV and CDs, thought completely otherwise. We *felt* the same urges; we just didn't *act* on them as readily as many do today. Why?

By far the majority of today's voices trying to sway our opinions are saying (without a direct word being said), "You'll achieve success as a human being if you can just accumulate enough money-fame-sex-power." I challenge anyone to deny that such propaganda has been overwhelmingly successful. But is that eminently effective propaganda *true*? Again, recall Elvis Presley, Marilyn Monroe, Kurt Cobain, River Phoenix, and the rest who had all that—in spades—but killed themselves anyway. It's an undeniable, objective fact those things *didn't* make them happy.

As Bertrand Russell said, "Many would rather die than think. Most of them do."

REDUCTIONISM

All fair judgments about questions of morality (or any decision) are jeopardized by resolutely resisting genuinely pertinent data. Prejudice blinds us to the objective fact that skin color or ethnicity or homeliness doesn't diminish a person's humanity. An unflinching ignorance of the evidence severely obstructs honest judgment, and most often makes the judge look like a fool. Self-serving interests put objective evidence into a perspective skewed out of kilter to the advantage of the arguer. Unquestioned acceptance of what "everybody knows" sentenced Socrates to death, silenced Galileo, and nearly kept Columbus from sailing west.

We all want to be free. But, ironically, to be free *has costs*. Genuine freedom requires the effort to gather, sift, outline, conclude, and critique. But our animal inertia resists. Genuine freedom requires that we accept all pertinent data, even facts that threaten the clarity (and consoling security) of our conclusions. Otherwise, all the actions we base on skewed conclusions will be at the very least inappropriate, at the very worst deadly to other people—and ultimately deadening to oneself.

In the end there is only one choice: be an authentically free human being or be a slave to your Id's (primitive urges) snarling selfishness and your unexamined Superego's (respect for moral values) contradictory voices.

It's as simple as that.

A Dilemma

The following statements ought to test the impartiality of any group or individual.

- The Silver Medalist is merely the first of the losers.
- The majority of people on welfare cheat.
- My opinion's as good as anyone else's.
- Objective morality (legitimate human behavior) changes from age to age.
- Children of parents who worked hard deserve to live more comfortably than others.
- Authentic conscience comes from socialization, from parents, peers, media, society.
- If my brother dealt drugs, I would protect him rather than his victims.
- Commercials are morally neutral.
- Better a live slave than a dead hero.
- Cheating the phone company is not stealing.
- A wife's career should always yield to her husband's.
- Homosexuals make a free choice of their sexual orientation.
- Anyone in business routinely has to compromise his or her principles.
- Rock lyrics and MTV have no effect on a person's values.
- People dumb enough to leave lockers open can't complain about thefts.
- If a friend stole a copy of the final exam, I wouldn't look at it.
- Human sex is just a healthy animal activity.
- Jealousy is evidence of distrust.
- Strangers have a claim on your money when they have a life-threatening need.

A Conversation About Curiosity

What's your reaction to the following statements?

A = Agree; ? = Uncertain; D = Disagree.

1. Colin and Lady Patrice really loved one another. A ? D

2. A true friend tells you when you're making an idiot of yourself. And doesn't stop. A ? D

3. Willingness to look at all sides is going to make you look indecisive. A ? D

4. If a teacher doesn't cover the complete syllabus, he or she has failed in some way. A ? D

5. When I set out to write an important paper, I spend a lot of time on heavy research. A ? D

6. I never write a serious paper without a carefully reasoned outline. A ? D

7. If a person loves to read, his or her education will never stop. A ? D

8. There are no people, no matter what their "type," that I find unacceptable. A ? D

9. When I discover I've been bested by objective evidence, I admit it. A ? D

10. Money-fame-sex-power guarantee happiness. A ? D

Help me understand what you understand by any of these statements.

1. The root reason for education is to train people to make honest decisions.

2. Education is basically only about one process: gather, sift, outline, conclude, critique.

3. The best brainwashing is the brainwashing you'd swear you've never gotten.

4. Only two alternatives: Think and be free, or be a slave to both your Id and Superego.

5. My opinions are legitimate only as far as objective evidence validates them.

6. Once you've mastered the basic educational skills, you're ready to *begin* learning.

7. After the basic skills all you need is the four D's: discipline, drive, determination, and a dream.

8. In any question—especially about human behavior—we have to be like a good judge: impartial.

9. The media have become the "conscience" of our unthinking society.

10. "Many would rather die than think; most of them do."

Questions

Try to tell me what values your school really puts most emphasis on—not from what they say at assemblies and in brochures—but from the real time and emphasis they put on them and by budgets. Are the SATs more important to them than anything else? Sports? How do they feel about music and art? Do you really believe every teacher—or most teachers—care more about helping you to become a good thinker, an honest decision maker, than they care about "covering the syllabus?" If there's something important that is genuinely lacking, what do you think you and I could do about that?

Propaganda has a lot of negative vibes about it, like "Oh, that's just a lot of propaganda." But it's really a neutral word; it just means "to spread the word in the hope of changing people's minds and behavior." The *process* is neutral; what makes it good or bad is what the propagandists are trying to convince you to believe. A campaign to cut down drug use is good propaganda; a campaign to get you angry at Blacks or Jews is bad propaganda. *Commercials* are propaganda. Underneath all the specific products, what's the basic message the advertising industry is trying to make you buy? The *programming* has some kind of common message about people, too. What kinds of models does it project in "twenty-something" sitcoms? Are any of the people having sex on those shows actually married? *Rock lyrics*, even though you may not have been aware of it until now, also have a "point-of-view" about human relationships. What kind of ideas about people (especially about sex) can you distill out of them? You know them better than I do.

Imagination

An Essential Ingredient
In Building a Moral Character

Poets do not go mad, but chess players do.
—*G. K. Chesterton*

Hansel and Gretel

nce upon a time, long, long ago, when children were supposed to be seen and not heard, there lived at the edge of a huge forest a woodcutter, his second wife, and his two children, Hansel and Gretel. Times were difficult—in fact, disastrous. Drought stalked the sun-parched land; crops peeped up, looked around awhile, then drooped over and shriveled to straw. One night, unable to sleep for the bellowing in his belly, the woodcutter moaned, "Ah, wife! What shall we do? How will we save our poor children, not to mention ourselves?"

His portly and far more practical wife snorted, "Simple, simpleton. Tomorrow we take them out and pretend we're going to cut wood. Then we walk away, and we're shed of them."

"Oooh," the woodcutter said.

"You're such a mealy-mouthed, shilly-shally, lily-livered, chicken-hearted jellyfish," she harrumphed and folded her beefy arms across her ponderous bosom.

"Oooh," the woodcutter said.

"It's for their own good," she snapped. "Best way to teach 'em how to swim is toss 'em off the back of the boat. Maybe they'll get some spunk. Use their wits."

"I—I just couldn't. Wild beasts will come and gobble them up."

"Them or me," she growled. "And you can't cook." She gave him a cobra eye and no peace till he consented.

Meanwhile, because of the hunger cramping their own bellies, Hansel and Gretel were on the other side of the wall, listening to the whole thing. Gretel began to weep, but Hansel hushed her and said, "I'll take care of us, sister." So he crept out of the house, filled his pockets with pebbles glinting silver in the moonlight, hustled back to his bed and waited for the dawn.

Next morning the family set off into the forest, and as they went, Hansel slipped the silver pebbles from his pocket onto the path. When they reached the darkest part of the woods, their stepmother sat them down and gave them a small sack of food. "We'll be back," she whinnied. But they knew she wouldn't. At noon the children ate their dry bread and fell asleep. When they awoke, it was dark and the wind whipped the trees like balky prisoners. Gretel began to weep again, but Hansel hushed her. "Just wait for the moon," he said. And as it rose, the two children followed the pebbles shining in the moonlight back home.

Imagine their stepmother's surprise when she found them on her doorstep next morning. "You naughty children!" she huffed. "We searched for you everywhere. We've been worried sick." She shot a look at her husband, and Hansel knew the story wasn't over yet.

A few weeks later, without any warning, their stepmother appeared in their little room. "Up, you lazy scamps! We're going to cut wood again. Here's your bread. Now *move!*" What could Hansel do? There was no way to pick up pebbles again without their stepmother seeing. So the two children followed their parents glumly into the forest. But clever Hansel had an idea. He broke chunks from his bread so that he could follow them as he had the stones. Again, the parents left them and went off, they said, to cut wood.

Gretel shared her bread with her brother and, again, the two fell asleep. They woke in the dark and waited for the moon; then they began to search for the bread crumbs. They were gone; birds had come and eaten them. But artful Hansel, with more confidence than he honestly felt, said, "Don't worry, Gretel. I'll get us home." But he couldn't. For hours they walked, until their legs were stiff as andirons and their bellies gurgled like a chorus of frogs. Then suddenly, out of the trees emerged a most wondrous house. Its walls were bricked with wedges of chocolate cake, the roof was nubby peanut brittle, and the moss on the eaves was pink cotton candy! So, without the slightest urge to ask permission, the two children began to gobble at the house.

Abruptly in the doorway there appeared a crone with long snarled gray hair and ostrich eyes, her skin crinkled like dead leaves. "We-e-l-ll!" the old hag giggled, "*children*! How simply *lovely*! My name is Miasma, my pretties. Oh, do come in. You must be hungry. We must *fatten* you up, mustn't we! Oh, yes!" So she patted them and ushered them into her mystical house, fed them blueberry pancakes with butter and syrup, and led them to two crispy white beds where they fell asleep and dreamed they were in heaven.

No sooner had they fallen into a heavy sleep but Miasma swooped on Hansel and hauled him, still groggy from fatigue, out into a dark shed where she clanged him into an iron cage. Then she scuttled back to her house, which had returned eerily to what it really was: green slime oozed from the rotting walls and rats scampered about in the decomposing straw roof. She shook Gretel awake. "Up, you lazy young hussy!" she snapped. "Stir up the fire! You must cook your sweet little brother a lovely meal to fatten him up! And when he's all pink and plump, I'm going to *eat* him!" And she brayed like a camel who smoked too much.

Day after day poor Gretel labored, broiling steaks, baking potatoes, chocolate cakes and lemon meringue pies for Hansel, all the while scouring her mind for some way to save her brother and herself from their hideous fate. Better if they'd been eaten by bears. And three times each day Miasma crept into the dark shed with Hansel's meal to check on his progress. But before he could eat, she hissed: "Put out your arm, boy! I want to see how you're plumping up!" But after the first time, shrewd Hansel poked through the bars a ham bone he'd gnawed clean.

"Fiddlesticks!" rasped the witch. "More starch and fat! More sugar! More cholesterol!" And off she went to beat poor Gretel for skimping on the sugar and cream. Then she went down into the cellar to paw over her gold and jewels to see if the mangy brat had gotten into her things.

After a month of that, Miasma came back one dark evening with the remains of Hansel's duck à l'orange and chocolate eclairs, muttering under her breath. "I've had *enough* of that stringy little shrimp! Fire up the oven, you worthless rapscallion! Plump or skinny, I'm going to eat your mangy brother *today*!"

Poor Gretel was at her wits end. Whimpering against her tears, she tried to fumble the wood and lose the flint until she could find some way to outwit the witch. "Bag the tears," Miasma shrieked. "Get that oven going, or I'll do it myself and have you for dessert!" Her brow crinkled at the idea. She liked having a scullery slave, but the little tart looked toothsome.

But a light popped on in Gretel's mind as well. "The oven is ready," she called to the witch. "But there's a terrible smell coming from it. I think something's inside."

Miasma elbowed her out of the way. "I don't smell anything," she snarled. "But then I've got a bit of a cold."

Gretel swung open the big iron door. "There," she sniffed and made a face. "Something rotten. It could be a poisonous snake."

Again, Miasma pulled a face and sneered. "Imagination!" But she didn't relish being poisoned. So she leaned into the cavernous oven and sniffed again. As she did, Gretel shoved her with all her might, clanged the oven door, and wedged it with an ax. The witch caterwauled inside, and within a few moments there was indeed a most unhealthy smoke leaking out around the oven door.

Gretel ran to the dark shed, banged open Hansel's cage with a rock, and the two ran into the starlight, capering for joy. Then they scampered down into Miasma's cellar, scooped up burlap bags full of gold and jewels, and blissfully dragged them away in a little cart just as a great white moon broke from the clouds. There in the path they found the shiny pebbles Hansel had dropped that first day, and they found their way home.

Their parents were genuinely overjoyed to see them—not to mention the gold and jewels—until they discovered that Hansel and Gretel had no intention of staying.

(With acknowledgment to the original tellers of Hansel and Gretel, Jacob and Wilhelm Grimm.)

Jim Henson

 e was the boy they always stuck out in right field—like Holden Caulfield's brother, Allie, in J.D. Salinger's *The Catcher in the Rye,* who wrote poems on his mitt so he'd have something to do while he was idling out there. Jim Henson spent his first few years in Leland, Mississippi where Deer Creek meanders through town toward the Mississippi River. It was a happy, "Huck Finn" time, swimming, fishing, day-dreaming. He was, in his words, "a quiet kid, introspective, articulate, always involved with art, a fairly good student, but a terrible athlete." He was enthralled by the movies, especially *The Wizard of Oz.*

Before 1950, there were very few television sets, but the radio provided the same smorgasbord of choices—news, soaps, dramas, comedies, variety shows—but with a difference: the listeners had to use their imaginations to supply the faces, the chases, the places. So Jim hunkered by his radio fleshing out super heroes, detectives, cowboys. One of his favorites was ventriloquist Edgar Bergen and his dummies, wisecracking Charlie McCarthy and goofy Mortimer Snerd. "I don't ever remember thinking of them as one man and his puppets. To me they were all human."

By the time he was in fifth grade, his father's work took the family to Washington, DC, where Jim slowly adjusted to being transplanted. But when television began to sprout and spread all over the country, Jim badgered his parents until they bought a set when he was in seventh grade. He fell in love with TV, especially "Kukla, Fran, and Ollie," a puppet show featuring Fran Allison as the human hostess and two puppets—Kukla, a circus clown, and Ollie, a rather cuddly dragon—both worked by puppeteer Burr Tillstrom. In high school, Henson worked at his art, making posters, drawing cartoons, designing stage sets—and joining a group of kids interested in puppets. When he was 17, local TV station WTOP advertised for a puppeteer for a morning children's show. So he and a friend whipped together three puppets: a French rat named Pierre and two cowboys named Longhorn and Shorthorn. They got the job, but they were dropped after three weeks. Fortunately, they were picked up by another station, WRC-TV for the rest of the summer.

When Henson entered the University of Maryland to study acting, stagecraft and scene design, he continued working at the station, and at the end of his freshman year, they offered him his own show. It was called *Sam and Friends*, and was a late-night filler between a live show (which sometimes ran short of an hour) and *The Tonight Show* with Steve Allen. As a partner, he chose a classmate, Jane Nebel, because she had his same weird sense of humor as well as deft hands, and the ability to ad-lib situations. Their puppets didn't speak but would lip-sync to recordings while the characters cavorted and ended either by blowing up or gobbling up one another. One of his hand puppets was a green "thing" cut from Jim's mother's old coat with two halves of a Ping-Pong ball for eyes. Jim called him Kermit. He was supposed to be a lizard, but he evolved into a frog.

Jim used the frame of the TV set as the stage, and he and Jane stood under the "floor" of the tube with the puppets upraised over their heads, watching themselves on monitors so they could edit themselves as they went along. Steve Allen happened to see them a few times and invited them onto *The Tonight Show*, where Kermit, in a blond wig, sang *I've Grown Accustomed to Your Face* to a purple monster in a happy-face mask, which he proceeded to gobble up—before he gobbled up Kermit. In 1957, when Jim was 19, he signed to make eight-second commercials for Wilkins Coffee. In one, a happy puppet asks a grouchy puppet how he likes Wilkins Coffee. The crabby guy snarls that he's never tried it, so the happy puppet rolls out a cannon and blasts him. Then he turns the cannon at the screen and asks the audience, "And have *you* tried Wilkins Coffee?"

Two years later, *Sam and Friends* won a Peabody Award for Best Local Entertainment Program, and Jim and Jane were married.

In 1960, when Jim went to his first puppeteers' convention in Detroit, he met Burr Tillstrom from the *Kukla, Fran, and Ollie* show, and they became lifelong friends. Tillstrom directed him to an agent named Bernie Brillstein—who took one look at this rangy, bearded guy in a loose shirt, jeans, and a headband and saw "this young Abe Lincoln wearing some kind of hippie arts-and-crafts clothes"—and decided he had better things to do with his time. But then he got word that they wanted to book Henson into Radio City Music Hall, and Brillstein's priorities quickly rearranged themselves. They never signed a contract, but both were satisfied with a handshake that lasted 30 years. Jim was honest, and he expected the same of everybody else.

When Jane retired to take care of what would become a family of five children, Jim went to California looking for new "Muppeteers." There he met Jerry Juhl, who would become chief writer for all Jim's projects; Don Sahlin, a talented craftsman who made all his Muppets; and Frank Oz, just a kid of 16 who, when he finished school, joined Henson and went on to create Bert, Cookie Monster, Fozzie Bear and—on the spur of the moment—the divine Miss Piggy.

Jim and Frank were an inspired pair, one quiet, the other exuberant, often ad-libbing and picking up on one another's lines, which is how Miss Piggy (literally) came from the chorus to become an instant star. While they were taping one day, Jim was operating Kermit while Frank worked a nameless female pig in a chorus of barnyard players. Suddenly on a whim, Frank pushed his lady pig forward and burst into a solo, then turned and began to woo Kermit. A superstar was born. Oz kept probing Miss Piggy's subtext to find her past filled with hardship, unyielding ambition to become a star, and a devouring lust for Kermit.

But their first star was Rowlf the Dog who was invited by country singer Jimmy Dean to play the piano, fool around and sing duets with him on his variety show. Rowlf's body was actually a hood covering two puppeteers, one to work the head and one arm, the second to work the other arm. Puppets with tiny arms were worked with wires on very thin rods, painted the same color as the background.

"The only way the magic works," Jim said, "is by hard work, but hard work can be fun." Muppets' jaws don't mimic every syllable, which would make big-mouthed figures look too agitated. It would also take long practice to pick up the knack of mouthing the important syllables— usually a full year just to become "reasonably" good enough to work background puppets.

Operating a Muppet is like rubbing your head in one direction, your tummy in another, while tap dancing and singing, and the entire operation was, as Henson said, "a triumph of art over chaos."

The key to the Muppets is innocence. As Jim said, "the simple-minded young person meeting life. Even the most worldly of our characters is innocent. Our villains are innocent, really. And it's that innocence that I think is the connection to the audience. The most sophisticated people I know—inside, they're all children. We never really lose a certain sense we had when we were kids."

Children's Television Workshop asked Henson to come up with ideas to help inner-city children prepare for school. They needed puppets (who could hold the children's attention), who were able to convey the way real kids feel facing real-life problems. Using real actors and cartoons, jingles and stories, they wanted to teach children how to count and say their ABCs, and to teach concepts like up, down, in, out. They wanted the fast pace and sound bites of commercials. Thus, at Jim Henson's hands, on November 10, 1969, *Sesame Street*, an hour-long, daily program, was born, airing on 179 public television stations across the country. The characters were destined to become immortal: Bert and Ernie, Cookie Monster, and Oscar the Grouch. Probably the most important character was Big Bird, a naive and childlike Muppet that Henson created to "stand in" for the average child in the audience, who tries to figure out what is going on. *Sesame Street* opened a whole new understanding about learning—as long as it was *intriguing*, learning could be fun and easy. The show expanded beyond teaching basic reading and math skills to teaching about life—childbirth, death, prejudice. In its first year, *Sesame Street* won a Peabody Award for Meritorious Service in Broadcasting, and every year after that it won more and more Emmys.

Each Muppet ceased to be a piece of cloth and foam and a little wood and became a character that guest stars interacted with as if they were real. Kermit, Henson said, is "an Everyman trying to get through life whole. He has a sense of sanity, and there he is, surrounded by crazies. He's the solid thing in the middle—flip, snarky, a bit smart-alecky, but a nice guy." Bert and Ernie quarrel, Oscar the Grouch is contrary, Miss Piggy is vain, the Great Gonzo is a hook-nosed creature unsure of what he is. Through these characters, children can better understand themselves and their friends, which are what folk tales have been doing for centuries.

For years, Henson tried to convince network executives to back a regular Muppet evening series, but they kept insisting it was a children's show that adults wouldn't watch. But after a few one-hour specials like *Hey, Cinderella* and *The Frog Prince*, the British entrepreneur Lord Lew Grade decided to back them. Thus was born *The Muppet Show*, a half-hour at the threshold of prime time, shot in England, with a celebrity guest each week. New characters began to appear, like the Swedish chef who says, "odie-odie" and Statler and Waldorf, two old fuss-budgets who heckle the cast from a theater box. It was a wearying—and chaotic—schedule: taping 12 episodes of *The Muppet Show* in the summer, a season's worth of *Sesame Street* in New York, then back to London, with scores of puppeteers and crew. But by the end of the third season, 235 million people followed the show in over 100 countries.

After *The Muppet Show* came *Fraggle Rock*, an underground world where feathery Fraggles coped with big shaggy Gorgs and tiny round-headed Doozers, teaching children the lesson that, somehow, we have to get along with one another, no matter our differences. It was the first American TV series allowed in what was then the Soviet Union.

Then it was on to Hollywood for *The Muppet Movie*, which shows the regulars on their way to make it big in the movies in an old Studebaker. It took a lot of genius. In the opening scene, Kermit strums a banjo while sitting on a log in a real swamp—which had Jim Henson in a tank sunk behind the log, moving Kermit's mouth and plucking with one arm while another puppeteer moved his other arm with an invisible wire fingering the frets. All the regulars were in the car—with two puppeteers apiece crammed beneath—while a dwarf drove the car from inside the trunk, with only a TV monitor to tell him what was ahead!

In the spring of 1990, Jim Henson began to have trouble with a sore throat and persistent fatigue. He thought he had the flu. Then he began coughing blood. In the hospital he was diagnosed with a rare kind of pneumonia, and even with huge doses of antibiotics, the struggle was ultimately futile. He died on May 16 at age 53.

Despite his young age, he had written letters to his five children to be opened only after his death. He insisted that no one was to wear black at his funeral and that it should be open to the public. More than five thousand people in bright colors filled the Cathedral of St. John the Divine in New York City. At the door, Muppeteers handed out two thousand foam butterflies suspended on rods to mourners, and when Harry Belafonte sang *Turn the World Around*, the air inside the cathedral was aswarm with whirling butterflies. Finally, Carroll Spinny, dressed as Big Bird, came forward to sing the theme song Jim Henson had sung as Kermit, *It's Not Easy Being Green*. Several times his voice broke, but at the end, looking up toward heaven, Big Bird said, "Thank you, Kermit." Then he bowed and slowed walked away.

Imagining What If...?

f you took the story of Hansel and Gretel literally, it would be monstrous—parents strand their own children out in the woods in order to save themselves! But the story does tell a truth. Sooner or later, kids have to cut the apron strings and set out on their own to fend for themselves using their wits. That's why so many epics and folk tales take the form of a journey, because that's what life is—a journey. We form character—achieve unique selves—by setting forth to face the unexpected. We hope that our family and teachers have given us a few sound guidelines, but there's no telling what uninvited ogres or dragons are lurking around the next bend. We have to use our wits, and not just our calculating intelligence but our *imaginations*.

Brain scientists tell us our brains have two lobes. The left brain processes data analytically and puts them in some kind of logical relationship (an outline), so that we can draw a tentative conclusion and ask someone wise to critique it. This is called reasoning. The right brain processes data intuitively, getting the "heft" of it, feeling an imaginative hunch about it. Facts are essential, but often they don't go far enough. For instance, my dictionary has 43 tightly packed lines to define "love," but when I come to the last line, I wonder, "Is that all love is?" On the other hand, a little kid with a bunch of droopy dandelions saying, "For you, Mommy," says love, too—and far more satisfyingly. A symbol makes the untouchable (like love) "touchable," sort of like the clothes the Invisible Man had to don in order to be seen.

Left Brain. Right Brain

The left brain works for clear-cut definitions, theories, rational philosophies; the right brain works with much more slippery symbols—fiction, poetry. The third section, the text part of each chapter in this book, is left brain stuff; the first section—the folk tale—is a story which is right brain stuff. Each tries to probe the same value, in quite different ways—the essay analytically, the story symbolically. Both methods are essential for coming to a well-balanced, probable conclusion, whether in picking a career or a spouse, deciding to have children, or forming personally validated moral principles.

In the first place, there are few conclusions we can arrive at with enough evidence for undeniable certitude. There can always be variables we haven't anticipated, as with the atomic bomb. The best we can hope for, even in science, is a high degree of probability from left brain, rational assessment. Then we turn the conclusion over to the right brain to see if it "feels" right. We use our imaginations.

In the second place, reality is a lot more complex than our cookie-cutter definitions and theories. We always have to be wary of reductionism, that is, leaving out important evidence because it fails to fit our preconceived notions. For instance, some pro-choice people say a fetus is nothing more than part of a mother's body—like an appendix—despite the fact that half the fetus's DNA is the father's, and if left alone, won't yield a panther or a peach. Conversely, pro-life people say a fetus is a human being from the moment a sperm penetrates an ovum, despite the fact that the majority of fertilized ova never adhere to the uterus, and therefore the majority of the human race died before ever being born. Reductionists say, "Don't bother me with facts, my mind's made up." Even their labels are reductionist, as if pro-choice people were against babies, and pro-life people were against freedom. These are handy categories, but they're really not completely true.

The function of the left brain is to analyze, to take apart; the function of the right brain is to synthesize, to put this new information together with other things we know to be true and to see how everything fits, or where other truths challenge the simplicity of our conclusions.

Similarly, no one questions that virtues are valuable, but we must remember that unchecked by other virtues they become vices. Justice without mercy is cruelty; mercy without justice is rank sentimentality. We have clear laws, but we need judges to see extenuating circumstances. For instance, if a woman admits she murdered her husband, that's a clear-cut case of premeditated homicide. But if he's been abusing her and their children for years, it becomes another case entirely. A fair trial is much less clear-cut and definitive than a lynch mob but is quite likely closer to the truth.

Finally, all discoveries arise in the right brain, a hunch we might be able to make something out of this bread mold or these silicon chips; a "feeling" that the theories we've counted on for so long are not quite good enough anymore; what if there *were* a reality faster than light! A lie detector very often gives an indication of someone's truthfulness, but I'd go with the assessment from the person's mother every time. Just as the savvy left brain turns over conclusions to the right brain for verification, the intuitive right brain turns over its hunches to the analytical left brain to see if they will in fact work.

Getting married, for instance, is hardly a strictly rational act. Nobody sits down and makes a list of all the pros and cons and, if the pro list is longer, makes a commitment. It's wise to make a list like that, at least for starters. Otherwise, two relative strangers join hands together and jump off a cliff—exclusively right brain "thinking"—with a large dollop of lust tossed in for flavor. But I knew a couple who went together for thirteen *years*, yet the woman was still unable to make the leap into marriage. A marriage—or any other significant choice—is a *calculated risk*. Even if we gather and scrutinize as much left brain data as we can, there's still a gap that can be bridged only by a right brain hunch that tells us "this is right."

In brief, anyone who works exclusively with the left or the right brain lobe is working half-wittedly. Exclusively left brain conclusions are reassuringly unambiguous, but nearly always too simplified, while exclusively right brain conclusions usually explode in your face. Without imagination, we become soulless; without reasoning, we become no better than instinctive beasts.

There are (at least) two factors in our society which short circuit both the left and right brain lobes—schooling and the media.

Flexing Our Imaginations

As we saw, too much of today's schooling is almost exclusively left brain. Even poetry becomes analytical test fodder. Many students never actively engage in art, music, or drama. Often, teaching doesn't intrigue students into thinking for themselves, presenting them with problems like Hansel's and Gretel's, puzzling them to go after answers they can call their own, but more often only covers the syllabus. With this type of teaching, students merely ingest the textbook, regurgitate it on the test, and then forget it. The same impoverishment occurs when teachers dissect novels so that reading them becomes a chore and not a passion. When students ask what they can do to ace the SATs (usually in September of 12th grade), I tell them, "Start reading at least a book a week in kindergarten." They think I'm crazy, and they're probably right. Maybe kindergarten is too late. The best thing parents can do for small children is to read to them every night. In the first place, it really is "quality time" together. In the second, it flexes kids' imaginations. In the third, it prepares them for Harvard. Anybody who tells you memorizing lists of words will fool college admissions people is a good example of what's wrong with the school system.

The media not only brainwash us into believing that the simplicities they offer us are the truth, but they also deaden our need to challenge our own imaginations. Commercials and hype convince us, from the time we're old enough to sit up in our Pampers, to silence our critical minds and believe that success means money-fame-sex-power–despite the fates of Elvis Presley and the many other celebrities who died young and unhappy. TV programs also warp our ideas about moral behavior.

On TV, sex most often happens between unmarried people; hardly anyone goes to church; and the predators are always glamorous. The programs also take away the challenge Jim Henson had, lying below the old radio, fantasizing into reality Amazon rivers, gunsmoke-filled ravines, swarthy pirates and hardy frontier women. Now it's all just—*there*—done *for* you, and your imagination turns flabby like an unused muscle.

Reason and Imagination Build Moral Character

Imagination is one of the many human values that got lost between that picture of the cheery babies on the blanket and the picture of the dead-faced grownups on the subway car.

Both reason and imagination are essential for forming moral character, but that task is undercut severely when both reason and imagination are crippled.

Moral reasoning requires that we listen critically (left brain) to what "everybody says" and that we are ready to doubt (right brain) their assertions. In fact, there are two acid tests of whether an action is moral (befitting humans) or not: *Reversibility* and (a jaw-breaker) *Universalizability*, and both hinge, not on imposed laws, but on "what-if" questions for our imaginations.

Reversibility asks "What if someone did this to *me*?" It can be reduced to The Golden Rule: Do unto others as you would have others do unto you. As we've seen, that principle is not the exclusive possession of any one religion or philosophy. It appears in *every* positive Western and Eastern philosophy and religion. I don't want to be cheated, robbed, raped, murdered in my bed. But when I myself have something very tempting to gain from one of those actions, I might be tempted to forget—just as I dread being hurt, so does everybody else. That's what forming a personal moral code involves—working out my own principles before the temptations arise.

Similarly, *universalizability* asks "What if *everybody* did this?" More than a few people overlook their own petty thefts, cheating on quizzes or income taxes, lying to avoid a hassle. But if *everybody* cheats or lies when they have need or opportunity, we all suffer. Society is a web of human relationships, and the glue that holds the web together is trust based on honesty. It's like the physical ecology we share; one soda can tossed out a car window is trivial, but if *everybody* does it, we all have to suffer living in a trash-filled world. Just so, telling one little lie or cheating for a few points on a quiz is trivial, but if *everybody* does it, we all have to share a world where nobody can trust anybody else.

There are no victimless crimes. Buying marijuana seems to affect only the person getting high, but ultimately the source of dope is organized crime. Therefore, every time someone buys a "harmless" dime bag, he or she is equivalently helping out the Mob. "Here," the action says (whether you realize it or not), "I'd like to make a small contribution to your crusade to recruit Midwestern girls just off the bus in Penn Station so they can become addicts and prostitutes." Cheating the phone company or an insurance company jacks up everybody's rates—even the cheater's. Shoplifting does the same thing. That is hardly the perpetrator's intention, but it is inescapably the objective result of the perpetrator's choice.

To make sound moral judgments, independently of others' laws, requires that we reason out moral questions for ourselves. You don't have to *like* the person you refuse to cheat or lie to; you don't have to empathize with him or her; but you *do* have to acknowledge that what you do (even if you're never caught) is *hurtful* to that person—as it would be hurtful to you. And that it is hurtful to all of us—including you.

Laws don't *make* an action wrongful. Rather, the action was wrongful before there were any laws—and would be wrongful even if all the law books were burned—and would be wrongful even if some perverse society said such actions were praiseworthy. It was inhuman for cavemen to kill and eat war prisoners—even though there were no written laws—and it was inhuman for Hitler to murder and work to death six million Jews and eleven million Slavs, even though his insanely-written laws attempted to "justify" it.

There shouldn't need to be any laws against battering your own children or driving 80 miles per hour in a school zone or selling guns to children. Laws are made for people who are too dumb or too self-absorbed or too lazy to realize that for themselves.

A Dilemma

As all members of the board agree, the cut in our funding necessitates curtailment of our after-school activities expenditures. We ask you, as a member of that committee, to offer your suggestions in order to save $75,000. (This does not include coach/moderator salaries.)

TEAM BUDGETS		OTHER STUDENT ACTIVITIES	
Baseball	4,500	Forensics	4,000
Basketball	3,110	Three plays	5,500
Bowling	600	Intramurals	500
Football	10,000	Literary magazine	2,500
Golf	1,200	National Honor Society	1,400
Ice Hockey	1,100	Photo staff	400
Lacrosse	3,000	Newspaper	4,400
Soccer	1,500	Ring day	1,200
Swimming	900	Students Against Drunk Driving	550
Tennis	1,100	Senior prom	25,000
Track	15,000	Student government	2,000
Wrestling	1,800	Service program	2,200
Awards/letters	3,300	Appalachia project	1,000
League dues	15,000	Spanish culture	2,000
Officials/referees	20,000	Tutoring program	5,500
Equipment	8,000	Assemblies	12,000
Weight room	800	Transportation	2,200
Volleyball	1,000	Musical program	2,500
Transportation	20,000	Senior field day	2,000
	$ 111,910		**$76,850**

Grand total: $188,760

A Conversation About Imagination

What's your reaction to the following statements?

A = Agree; ? = Uncertain; D = Disagree.

1. Hansel and Gretel's stepmother was closer to the truth than their father. A ? D

2. The only thing that legitimated Jim Henson's life was that he finally made money. A ? D

3. To show emotion so others can see it is a sign of weakness. A ? D

4. Love is an emotion that does not submit to any kind of rational understanding. A ? D

5. There are almost no truths we can know with unquestionable certitude. A ? D

6. Schooling is almost exclusively left brain, to the impoverishment of students. A ? D

7. To ace the verbal SATs, read at least a book a week, starting before kindergarten. A ? D

8. The programs on TV genuinely present life as it really is. A ? D

9. The people who appear on most talk shows are truly worth listening to. A ? D

10. Left brain thinking without right brain thinking (or vice versa) is half-witted. A ? D

Help me understand what you understand by any of these statements.

1. "Poets do not go mad, but chess players do."

2. Any virtue, unchecked by its opposite, becomes a vice.

3. Getting married is not strictly a rational act.

4. "What if someone did this to *me?*"

5. "What if *everybody* did this?"

6. There are no victimless crimes.

7. Laws don't *make* an action wrongful.

8. Laws are made for people too dumb or too self-absorbed or too lazy to think for themselves.

9. A fair trial is much less clear-cut and definitive than a lynch mob.

10. Schools and the media short-circuit our ability to think honestly.

Questions

 (Mom/Dad) and I want you to live a comfortable life, and—like it or not—that means making "good money." But especially when you first get married, you're going to have to handle your income carefully, and a strictly logical approach (the price tag) isn't enough to make a prudent decision about what to buy. Make a list with me of all the concrete things in our house, in four columns: Essential, Handy, Nice, and Luxury. The fridge and stove are essential, but what about the second TV? Suppose there was a monstrous flood and we lost everything. What would be the things we'd *have* to start over with?

What novel are you reading next in English class? Could I have a first crack at it before you get around to it, so we could talk about it as you go through it? It'd certainly be good for me to keep my hand in. I get all tied up in problems at work and around the house. I need to keep stretching my mind about people's lives, and I'd like to see our different takes on it.

In moral problems, especially in sexual ones, I always used to be hankering for certitude when I was your age. I wanted to know—clear as a math answer—"How far can you go? Where do you draw the line?" That's a question you have to answer when you're calm and objective, well before the actual choice arises. In the actual situation, when your emotions and hormones start taking control, it's very difficult to have your conscience keep a tight grip on the reins. There's nothing wrong with kissing, but how can you tell when it's sincere affection or just the other person indulging his or herself—for whatever "reason"—passion, self-gratification, the satisfaction of being (or at least seeming) desirable, the chance to brag on Monday about "What I got"? You don't solve that strictly rationally. How do you solve it?

Gratitude

People With Honor
Feel the Need to Give Back

Bees sip honey from flowers and hum their thanks when they leave.
The gaudy butterfly is sure that the flowers owe thanks to him.
—*Rabindranath Tagore*

Fidèle

nce upon a time, long, long ago, when having virtue paid off, there lived a steward named Fidèle, his wife, Thérèse, and their son, Mesquin, the only child of their middle age. Fidèle's employer's will left him a substantial sum, so that, with prudence he could insure a comfortable old age.

So Fidèle invested in a cloth shop on the main street, with living quarters above. Slowly the business grew. Their unsmiling son, Mesquin, worked in the shop, sweeping, occasionally waiting on customers, though for some reason only older women, never girls his own age.

After a year, Thérèse encouraged Fidèle to hire an assistant, since Mesquin was going on thirteen and had no proper education. They must prepare him to move in circles for which they themselves could never school him. Secretly, the grimly dutiful Mesquin yearned to escape this embarrassing working-class prison. He would become a gentleman! So Mesquin went off to the abbey to learn letters and numbers, dancing, and the etiquette required of a man of means.

When Mesquin came home from school, Fidèle loved to show the boy his future, firmly secured. On those rare occasions, Mesquin followed his father submissively through the shop, idly touching the fabrics, but with no great interest. At meals, he picked at his food and responded absently to his parents' questions about his life at school. Blinded by love and their own simplicity, his parents had no notion their son found them more than slightly embarrassing.

Fidèle's fortunes suddenly took a tragic turn. Thérèse began to suffer with a cold she could not shake. Then pneumonia, and finally she fell into a coma, during which Fidèle never left her side, day or night, and at last Thérèse passed away.

At the funeral, Fidèle tried to console his son. "Mesquin," he said, "we must dry our tears," though there seemed no discernible moisture in the young man's eyes. "We must assure your future after I myself am gone. No worry about money. But you are now a well-to-do young bachelor, and we must find a suitable wife who can give you a standing in the town."

Mesquin was amenable to that.

Now beyond the town lived the Marquis de Marillac whose fortune had trickled away into the grasp of pawnbrokers, owing to the Marquis's taste for fine living, horse racing, and cards. But he did have one very real if "unpawnable" asset: his lovely daughter, Mariette, whose beauty and accomplishments were well known. Also, the young woman owned a small but elegant house in the town which she had received in her mother's will and which was beyond the Marquis's pawning proclivities. She would do just fine, Fidèle thought, and Mesquin was disposed to agree.

As Fidèle sat uncomfortably with Mesquin in the Marquis's threadbare salon, he saw that he was far wealthier than their self-impoverished host. But he still felt the nagging specter of his host's title, which one day—given the Marquis's ulcers, gout and dyspepsia—would be his son's.

"What are your means?" the Marquis inquired from the depths of his baggy jowls, at which Fidèle noticed the nobleman's linen was quite soiled and the sleeves at his elbows were frayed to the warp.

"In merchandise and monies, I have nearly twenty thousand livres in gold," Fidèle blushed, yet he noticed the Marquis's hooded eyes quicken involuntarily. "Of all this, I give my son half."

"I should think," the Marquis shrugged, mentally adding up his debts, "if you truly loved your son and cared *only* for his welfare, as you say, you would settle your entire substance upon him—and upon his *noble* wife. The classical definition of true love. Surely, you have read Plato."

Mesquin nodded knowingly. He, too, had read Plato.

Fidèle withdrew into himself to ponder. He looked at his son's aristocratic face. Mesquin was all he had ever worked for. He himself was getting old and had few years left.

"Yes," he said. "Yes. For Mesquin. And Mariette. Uh, er, the Marquise."

So Fidèle handed over to his son the titles to all he owned and left himself naked as a peeled birch, without purse or penny, except for what he received from his son. And amid great jubilation, Mesquin and Mariette were married and moved into their small but elegant home.

Mesquin supervised the shops, remotely, but would not think of letting his aged father spend his waning days working for a salary, and since the family rooms above the shops were now needed for storage, he insisted—along with Mariette's dubious insistence—that Fidèle move in with them. He would have a fine room in their home, upstairs, facing the garden.

With no choices other than the workhouse or the streets, Fidèle accepted.

At first, the situation was ideal. Mariette's servants tried to be as solicitous to her father-in-law as they were to the lady herself—especially in her expectant condition—but Mariette's smiling approval seemed somewhat tinged with vinegar.

Finally, Mariette delivered a spanking baby boy whom they named Pierre, after the Marquis, who was much improved in health due to the fact Mesquin had paid most of his crippling debts. *Noblesse oblige*— nobility obligates. Within a few weeks of that blessed event, however, Mesquin and Mariette found need to have a discussion with Fidèle one evening at supper.

"You understand, Father," Mesquin smiled, "with the baby, we will be needing a nurse, of course, and quite soon a tutor. You agree it's never too soon to begin to prepare the boy. Just see how long it took *me* to catch up," he chuckled mirthlessly.

"Of course the nanny will need a room of her own," Mariette smiled. "You have no *idea* how difficult it is to get competent help nowadays. So we will fit out a fine room for you in the attic, with your few books and mementos. We will spare no worry about how much it costs us."

So Fidèle dutifully moved himself to a room in their attic and tried to find ways to differentiate one day from another. He met in the square on sunny afternoons with a few old friends, but he knew they felt him a fool for giving away his substance, his freedom, his pride. He went bent with age, like a man searching for a life he had lost. But he took great pleasure, from some little distance, in his grandson Pierre, who grew to be, like his father, a lad dutiful but dour.

Finally one evening, after the candles had been trimmed and the servants gone to their beds, Fidèle heard Mesquin and Mariette whispering hoarsely in the corridor below his room.

"Husband," Mariette rasped, "we cannot have two masters in a single house. That old man had the nerve to ask the maid if she could find some saddle soap to clean his boots."

"You mean he wanted one of our servants to clean his boots?"

"No, he merely wanted the means to do it himself. Doesn't he know his way by this time to the town stables? And he's a bad example for Pierre. He dribbles. And just manages to catch it with his spoon. Surely you've noticed. I lose all appetite just having him in my house."

"You're right," Mesquin agreed. "I'll see to it tomorrow."

Next day, Mesquin summoned Fidèle into his study, neglecting to ask him to sit. "Father, 12 years we have seen to your feeding and clothing and caring. That is as many years as I worked for you as a boy, unpaid, neglecting my lessons. Now it is time you fend for yourself."

"But—but—" Fidèle tried to speak. "My son, turn me not from your door. It's...it's unfitting. I eat little. I take up little space. I try not to disturb your wife and your household. Let me stay for the short while I have left to live. For the love of God."

"Father, no preachments. I regret this, but my wife is very tender, easily upset."

"But where shall I go? I am esteemed for nothing."

"You have been lucky. Perchance your friends will stake you to a new enterprise."

"Stake? Then why could not you—?"

"Father," Mesquin smiled indulgently, "you know that the business is overtaxed as it is."

"I will get my clothes," Fidèle said.

"Not one suit," Mesquin snapped. "They are worn and…embarrassing. Unsuitable for a clothier's father to be seen in such attire."

Fidèle's jaw set against his tears. "Then give me a horse-blanket from your stable! I will hunch myself into it so no one will know whose father I was."

"If you insist." Mesquin turned to see Pierre had been standing in the doorway all the while. "Pierre, fetch the new covering for my horse from the stable. The best one, mind you."

"Yes, father," he said and took Fidèle's hand. "Come, grandfather, and I will see to it."

Obediently, the old man followed the boy, heart heavy and wrathful. In the stable, Pierre lifted down the best horse covering and carefully folded it in two on the earthen floor. Then he got down on his knees, pulled out his knife, and painstakingly slit the cloth, lengthwise.

"My child," cried Fidèle, "surely you're not that much like your father?"

At that moment, Mesquin entered the stable to see the old man well away. "What are you doing, boy?" Mesquin growled. "Give him the whole cloth. I gave my word."

"No," Pierre said quietly. "How would I repay you for all you have done for me? I will keep this half until I am a man. Then I will give it to you when I turn you from my door."

The boy folded his half of the blanket and carried it carefully with him away.

Oprah Winfrey

 n November 12, 1991, a Black woman sat before an all-male, all-White judiciary committee of the U.S. Senate to testify on behalf of a bill she herself had written with the assistance of former Illinois Governor James Thompson and Senator Joseph Biden of Delaware. She had been moved to this unprecedented act by the rape and murder of a four-year-old Chicago girl, Angela Mena, by a man twice convicted of child molestation and twice released after partial service of his sentences. She wanted a national data bank of offenders convicted of child abuse, available to schools, scouting troops, and other child-centered organizations who hire people to supervise children. And she got what she came for. President Clinton signed the bill into law in 1993.

Why did she bother? After Bill Cosby, Oprah Winfrey was the second-highest money-making personality in the world. Every day, 16 million people watched her TV show. She had been nominated for an Academy Award, received Emmys and the 1989 *Ms.* magazine award as "Woman of the Year." She had interviewed celebrities like Michael Jackson, Paul McCartney, Stevie Wonder, Candice Bergen, Barbara Walters—all far more "important" than Angela Mena. Why? Because she herself had been a victim of sexual abuse as a child. When she was nine, she had been raped by a 19-year-old cousin, and then until she was 14 she was repeatedly raped by her mother's boyfriend and an uncle. And she wasn't going to take it any more. "My mission," she said, "is to use this position, power, and money to create opportunities for other people." She was and is a gifted woman, and that very fact impels her to give gifts herself.

Oprah Winfrey was born January 29, 1954, in the tiny town of Kosciusko, Mississippi. She spoke later of her birth resulting from "a one-day fling under an oak tree." Her father, Vernon, lived 250 miles away and was unaware Oprah's mother, Vernita Lee, was even pregnant until he got a birth announcement with a scribbled "Send clothes." Vernita had intended to name the child Orpah, after the sister-in-law of the Biblical heroine, Ruth, but the midwife was not a great speller, so the girl became Oprah and began what was not to be a very easy young life.

In her earliest years, she lived with her grandparents on their tiny pig farm, while her mother was off someplace trying to find work. "The nearest neighbor was a blind man down the road. No playmates, no toys except for one corncob doll. I never had a store-bought dress. It was very lonely out there." Her grandmother was a tough old lady who nonetheless made Oprah know, without words, that she was cherished, forcing her to learn how to read and write long before she ever went to school. But her grandfather terrified her.

The one haven in her childhood before school was the Baptist church, where she was asked to read from the scripture and to act in pageants with other children. By the time she was three, she had given her first public performance, and to pacify her loneliness she began to read and read, and practiced her Sunday recitals to the pigs and chickens. The adults found her charming, but the other kids definitely did not, sneering "Here come Miss Jesus" at her.

What's more, at home her grandparents expected complete and literal obedience, often sending her out for a tree branch with which to whip her. "You couldn't even cry! You got whipped till you had welts on your back. Unbelievable. I used to get them every day because I was precocious." And yet she also says, "I am what I am because of my grandmother. My strength. My sense of reasoning. Everything." But when Oprah finally attended kindergarten, she was bored silly with the childish games and wrote a letter to her teacher about it. Surprisingly, the teacher agreed and promoted her into first grade and very soon after into third grade.

When Oprah was seven, she became too much for her aging grandmother to handle, so she was sent off to her mother, who earned her living cleaning houses in Milwaukee for about $50 a week, plus welfare payments. Mississippi had been hard, but Milwaukee was heartless, and Vernita was at her wits' end trying to provide for Oprah and for another daughter. So within a year, she had sent Oprah off to her father, Vernon, and his wife, Zelma, in Nashville. Vernon was a hard worker, and had moved up from scrubbing pots to doing maintenance at Vanderbilt University. "Zelma was real tough," Oprah says, "a very strong disciplinarian, and I owe a lot to her because it was like military school there." And the little girl continued to give her recitals—in church, women's groups, banquets. One of her favorites was a poem which could well describe her own life:

"Out of the night that covers me,
Black as the Pit from pole to pole,
I thank whatever gods may be,
For my unconquerable soul."
—*William Ernest Henley,* Invictus

But just as she was beginning to feel at home in Nashville, at the age of nine she received word that Vernita had finally married the father of her third child and wanted her back in Milwaukee for the summer. But when Vernon came for her in August, Vernita refused to let her leave and, since she and Vernon had never married, he had no legal rights in the matter. Oprah was painfully unhappy. Her mother was always working or "out," so she spent her time reading or numbing herself with TV. But while she was at the Lincoln Middle School, a teacher named Gene Abrams noticed that Oprah was always alone in a corner reading a book. He got to know her, and he was so impressed by her intelligence and achievement that he secured her a scholarship to Nicolet, a private high school in a wealthy suburb 25 miles from her mother's home.

She was the only Black student, and yet she became the most popular girl in the school, at least partly because the other children were trying to show off their recently acquired racial broad-mindedness. Oprah visited their homes and, although she was grateful for acceptance, realized what it was like to live in a "real" family and saw herself, in contrast, as an "ugly, poor girl." She became rebellious—lying, stealing money from her mother's purse, "dating everything with pants on." Vernita forbade her to have anything to do with boys, although she herself was gallivanting every night. At age 14, Oprah became pregnant, but her premature infant died shortly after. Her mother, unable to cope with her, finally sent her back to Vernon and Zelma.

Vernon now owned a barbershop and grocery in a friendly, mostly Black neighborhood and acted as deacon in the Faith-United church. He knew what he wanted: an 11 p.m. curfew, no makeup, no halter tops or miniskirts. "Listen, girl," he used to say, "if I tell you a mosquito can pull a wagon, don't ask me no questions. Just hitch him up." And every two weeks Zelma took Oprah to the library for five books, for which she would write reports for her parents. One of the most moving was Maya Angelou's *I Know Why the Caged Bird Sings*, detailing as it did Angelou's own account of her childhood sexual abuse, and Oprah finally understood that her own victimization had never been her fault. She saw, too, that her self-indulgence in Milwaukee had really been a kind of self-imprisonment. Oprah gave up a false freedom for a true family.

As a result of forced desegregation, Oprah was one of the first Black students at East High in Nashville, and because of her positive experience at Nicolet, she was able to bridge the uneasy gap between Blacks and Whites. She also gave dramatic readings of the life of indomitable Black women like Harriet Tubman and Sojourner Truth. She easily won election as president of the student body, and in 1970 was invited by President Nixon to represent her school at the White House Conference on Youth in Denver. At 16, she won the Tennessee state oratorical contest and a partial scholarship to Tennessee State University. The following year, she made the final cut in her first beauty contest, and when the three finalists were asked what each would do with a million dollars, the first said she would buy presents for her family, the second said she would give it to the poor, and Oprah, knowing all the "proper" answers were used up, said, "I'd be a spending fool!" She won, hands down, and when she went to the sponsoring radio station to pick up her prizes, the management was so impressed with her intelligence and the depth and clarity of her voice, they gave her a job reading the news every half-hour from after school to 8:30 p.m.

In 1972, Oprah won the Miss Black Nashville and Miss Black Tennessee contests and a four-year scholarship to Tennessee State, along with an all-expense-paid trip to compete in the Miss Black America pageant in Hollywood. But she wasn't happy. Attending Tennessee State—and living at home—were confining. Beauty pageants were degrading to women, not to mention that she felt she was too dark-skinned and too heavy, and her sponsors were making all her decisions, fitting her out in dresses that were too florid and hampering her easygoing style. But her charm made her a shoo-in —until she came out for the evening gown segment in her old senior prom dress and blew her chances out of the water. All the other losers were weeping, but Oprah showed them a big white grin. As her father said, "That's just the way she is. Oprah makes her own decisions."

While at TSU, she majored in drama (over Vernon's objections), starred in university plays, gave dramatic readings in local churches and—before she had finished her freshman year—was offered a job as a TV newscaster in the Nashville CBS network affiliate, WTVF. She was a natural, easy-going and unthreatening, so that listening to her read the news was like listening to gossip from a next-door neighbor. She and her coanchor went out with a cameraman, shot the footage, wrote the scripts, edited the tapes. "I was a token," she said. "But I was a happy— *paid*—token."

In June, 1976, at age 22, she accepted an offer from WJZ-TV in Baltimore to host a talk show and she found her niche. "I came off the air, and I knew that was what I was supposed to do. It just felt like breathing." After six years there, she moved to *A.M. Chicago* for a yearly salary of $200,000. She knew absolutely no one in Chicago, so she spent her first Christmas working in a soup kitchen for street people.

At the end of her first year, *Newsweek* devoted a full page to her; she made her first appearance on *The Tonight Show*; and in her second year *A.M. Chicago* became *The Oprah Winfrey Show*. That same year, Stephen Spielberg and Quincy Jones offered her the part of the tough-as-nails Sofia in the film of Alice Walker's *The Color Purple*, the story of strong, poor Black women whose courage and fundamental self-respect ennobled them—despite sexual abuse, bullying males, racial cruelty, and—in Sofia's case—police brutality. Oprah Winfrey fitted into Sofia's skin like a hand into a surgeon's glove.

When *The Oprah Winfrey Show* went into syndication, it became the highest-ranked talk show in the country, and if Oprah plugged a book on her show, it would lodge itself on the best-seller lists for months. She formed HARPO (Oprah spelled backwards) Productions to develop films, documentaries, and television movies to raise the American consciousness. Of her talk show, she said, "What we are trying to tackle in this one hour is what I think is the root of all the problems in the world—lack of self-esteem." When she addressed the graduates of TSU in 1987, she said, "Don't complain about what you don't have. Use what you've got. To do less than your best is a sin. Every single one of us has the power of greatness, because greatness is determined by service—to yourself and to others."

When you *make* good, something good in you impels you to *do* good.

Noblesse Oblige

 robably not too many dukes and duchesses (even minor ones) will read these pages, but the words noblesse oblige—nobility obligates—

are true for all of us. Real nobility has nothing to do with bloodlines and the right to inherit despite one's embarrassing limitations. It denotes a solidity of character or spirit that scorns whatever is petty, mean, or dishonorable. Nobility comes from recognizing, with honest gratitude, that one has been blessed and is therefore obligated, in honor, to be generous to the less fortunate.

Trouble is, many (most?) of us take our "giftedness" for granted. In fact, many (most?) of us haven't the slightest idea that we are, indeed, gifted. If so, it's no wonder we might find it difficult to feel grateful.

Turning Guilt into Responsibility

Before continuing, it would be wise to draw some distinctions about "guilt" and "responsibility." Although it is invisible and it can be denied, guilt is real, a fact that comes into existence when someone is culpable for some real offense, when one knows he or she is incontestably responsible for a bad result. I did, in fact, fail to write the essay—the dog didn't really eat my homework; my house didn't burn down; I wasn't falsely arrested by the FBI. But the *fact* of the guilt (and the resultant responsibility to do something about it) is quite different from *accepting* both guilt and responsibility. Being the responsible party and acting as the responsible person are two different things. In my experience, too many people groan "Guilt trip!" when they're put on the spot about their moral (human) behavior—not because the suggestion is unfair—but because it *is* fair. And they don't want to admit it's fair or change their behavior after admitting it's fair.

Being self-absorbed is part of our inheritance from our ape ancestors. In fact, the human invitation is to rise above that animal self-absorption and open ourselves to broader and richer horizons. We can rise above our animal nature, but it's not going to go away. That self-absorption makes me want to feel OK about myself—all the time—even at times when I don't have a real *right* to feel OK. Therefore, when someone gets inside my defenses and upsets my comfy equilibrium with a suggestion that (a) I've done something wrong, and (b) I ought to do something about it, the animal in me bristles, sneers, tries to bat it away.

Of course guilt trips can be psychologically destructive, but *only* when the cause of the guilt is either unmerited or out of proportion.

Dropping a pass, for instance, is embarrassing, but the intended receiver didn't *plan* to bobble it, and the offense is hardly in a league with gassing six million Jews and it isn't as bad as a single murder and isn't even as bad as the casual assassination of someone's reputation.

Contrary to what many people would like to believe, honest guilt is a very healthy reality. Just as hunger in the belly leads us to keep ourselves alive, genuine guilt is a hunger that says, "I'm not really OK at the moment, and I ought to do something about it in order to become a more fulfilled human person." The first step is honestly to judge whether I am, in fact, responsible for some misguided act, then to hold myself *accountable* for it, and then to take steps to rectify it, no matter how much effort or embarrassment it means. To take the first step without the second is deadly. When we half-heartedly admit we've done something wrong—but do nothing—we carry around the unfocused guilt like a toothache we'd like to forget. Unless genuine guilt becomes genuine responsibility, it is useless, or worse, it corrodes the entire self from the inside.

Giftedness and Gratitude

Therefore, in what follows regarding our giftedness and its natural connection with our sense of gratitude for it, there is no intention to make anyone *guilty* about being gifted. With most "gifts" like looks, economic status, family background, and so forth, you are not responsible—someone else gave them to you. Rather, the question is what you *do* with what you've been given and with what you make of your gifts. Other than to pay taxes, no law says Oprah Winfrey has to share with the less fortunate the abundance she achieved with her talents and gifts. The "law" is inside Oprah. It's what ennobles her as a human being.

Sometimes you hear about a "self-made" man or woman. No one is self-made. Each of us stands on the shoulders of countless others. By her own admission, Oprah honestly credits her father, her stepmother, her teachers—even her own neglectful mother—for her success. Without her own indestructible spirit, of course, she never would have become what she became. But without those other people, she never could have done it either.

Therefore, what follows is not a guilt trip. It is an attempt to allow us to see how truly lucky we are and to elicit a sense of honest gratitude and perhaps even a sense of generosity.

If you can read this page, you are gifted. A third of the citizens of this gifted country are functionally illiterate, that is, they are able to read simple things like street signs and brand names but they cannot read the directions on a cake mix box or decipher a map. Someone (do you remember who?) taught you how to read, and other people challenged you to read more and more complex writing, year after year. How many of us ever thought to thank them for such an inestimable gift? You may say, "Oh, well, they had to do it. That's what they were paid for." Nope. They could have had a lot fewer hassles and made a lot more money working in a napalm factory.

Year after year, social studies teachers offer at least a class or two on world hunger, infant mortality rates, life expectancy, average income. Public-service ads plea for donations by reminding us of bloated-bellied children in Africa, displaced families, and refugees. They are, knowingly or not, playing on our guilt/responsibility. What they fail to do, I believe, is take the earlier step of simply reminding each of us how lucky we are. Most of us look around a group like a class or a dance and rarely focus on the people who are dressed more poorly than we are. We usually focus on the ones who are better off than we are, so that envy takes the place of gratitude. And yet the materially poorest person in any American classroom is far better off than the majority of people with whom we share this planet. There is no guilt involved in that statement—it's not children's fault they were born in America rather than in a poorer country. And it's not their fault that their parents were able to achieve more materially than most of the world's parents. They needn't feel guilt, but a sense of giftedness, of gratitude.

Whenever someone asks me, "How ya doin'?" I usually say, "Probably better than I deserve." They, in turn, almost always say, "Well, of course you deserve—" What? I didn't deserve to be born. I didn't exist. How could a non-being *deserve* anything? Now granted— if I'd never existed I'd never have known the difference—but I *do* exist. If I tried to write out all the things and people I love, that give me joy, enrich my life, it would take me a year! Yet why do so many of us waste so much time moaning about what we *haven't* got and completely ignore all we *have*.

As Oprah said, "Don't complain about what you don't have. Use what you've got." If Cinderella complained that she had to leave the ball at midnight, the Fairy Godmother might well have said, "Sweetie, who said you could even *come* to the ball in the first place?"

Almost everyone I've ever taught takes it for granted that their parents, well, *had* to have them. Nope. More than a few people freely choose not to have children. Anyone's parents could have had a nice spread in Florida instead, because in choosing not to discontinue that pregnancy, they committed themselves to earning a quarter of a million dollars to support the child until she or he can support themselves. That's some gift. How do you pay back a quarter million smackerolas? No child could, and no good parent gives a thought to their children doing that. But the honorable thing for the child would be not to take it for granted, as if he had somehow merited it.

Students routinely moan "Guilt trip!" when I ask them to consider their mother's pregnancy. For nine months she endured morning sickness, the inability to get out of a chair or turn over in bed, worry about a person she'd committed her life to—sight unseen. There were no guarantees or money-back returns. Then she underwent hours of self-induced torture and risked death in order for the child to have life. Then, she spent a couple of years wiping up all kinds of disgusting stuff the child produced for her, years more of scraped knees, broken arms, mediocre report cards, innocent pranks with unexpected consequences. All so that, at about age 22 or so, the child can say, "Well, I've found somebody I love better than you, Mom, or at least in a much different way. Bye!"

If that lady asks anything (reasonable) and the child tells her to forget it, that kid's already told everybody just what kind of human being he is. Against the facts, there's no argument.

If anyone is *honestly* grateful, everybody should be able to see it, concretely, in the way he or she *acts*. Anyone would admit (at least in the abstract) that, if an employer gives you an honest day's pay, you owe your employer an honest day's work. But over and above the gift of life, most parents offer their children a college education at a cost of at least $20,000 a year, and even higher for some colleges. That's a pretty hefty salary for someone in his or her teens. Not to give a full eight-hour's work for it every day would be not only wickedly ungrateful, but grand larceny!

Not Obligation, But Honor

The Lebanese writer Kahlil Gibran wrote that if your task is to make a chair, make it as if your beloved were to use it. Although we will consider motivation throughout these pages, perhaps the most profound motivation to get the most out of one's education—beyond a diploma as a job ticket—is the work, sacrifice, hope, forgiveness and trust parents have already invested in the education and in us. If our gratitude and love are genuine—and not merely comforting lies we tell ourselves— there is no honest possibility of settling for "the gentleman's C"— a half-hearted effort of cutting corners, playing the odds, asking for extensions, testing the limits of parents' and teachers' patience. Could anyone play those underhanded games with people they claim truly to *love*? Or even to be an adult?

Not guilt—*gratitude*. Not obligation—*honor*. Not duty—*love*.

What you *do* shouts so loudly that no one can hear what you *claim*.

A Dilemma

"Now will you stop with the grief? I do the best I can. Don't give me that look. There are more important things than grades. I got my girl- friend, my music, my friends to hang out with, my car. This grade thing could give you some positive negativity. You can learn one helluva lot more from experience than you can from a lotta books. Could one of those teachers hold her own drinking beer in a club? Get real. Like Mary Poppins in whorehouse.

"What are grades, anyway? Numbers. And if I get a 64.5 (which I *won't!*), I get the same diploma some kid with glasses and his nose in a book all day whose social life is zilch gets, right? And the stuff they tell you's important? Does my old man ever crack open *Shakespeare*? Hell, he never once turned on PBS. He watches baseball. And he makes six big figures a year, man. Once when I was a freshman I asked him to help me with my math homework, and he looked at me like I was from outer space.

"Yeah, he shakes out the bread to support me, but what the hell. Did I ask to be born? They had their fun, and all of a sudden there I was. So they pay for it. Oh, he gets hot under the collar about the grades. But did he have good grades? My grandfather got him into Princeton, and for four years he drank beer and paid his cousin to write his papers for him.

"Owe? What do I 'owe'? When you have a kid, you have a kid, and that means you've got to take care of it. That's the way things are. And I played football for him because it gave him that big macho thrill. Okay, so I was benched most of the time for missing practice, but I did it, didn't I? I was there every single game. Except two. That was a hoot! *He* was at one game I *wasn't* at! He hadda lie. Told them I was sick, but he wanted to show support for the team. Could you barf?"

A Conversation About Gratitude

What's your reaction to the following statements?

A = Agree; ? = Uncertain; D = Disagree.

1. Mesquin was justified in turning Fidèle out because of 12 years of neglect. A   ?   D

2. The Marquis is an unrealistic character not to be found in the everyday world. A   ?   D

3. An inhuman upbringing excuses a great deal of offenses in later life. A   ?   D

4. Seen in proportion, guilt is a very good thing. A   ?   D

5. The root of all the problems in the world is lack of self-esteem. A ? D

6. Many (most?) of us take our giftedness for granted. A   ?   D

7. If teachers are constantly unprepared, they should be fired. A ? D

8. If students are constantly unprepared, they should be expelled. A ? D

9. If you don't work to capacity, you've no honest right to feel good about yourself. A   ?   D

10. Each of us is probably doing better than we "deserve." A ? D

Help me understand what you understand by any of these statements.

1. No one is "self-made."

2. Most of us look at those more fortunate than we are, rather than at those less fortunate.

3. How do you pay back a quarter-million smackerolas?

4. If anyone is honestly grateful, everybody should be able to see it, concretely.

5. "Don't complain about what you don't have. Use what you've got."

6. When you make good, something good inside you impels you to do good.

7. Although it is invisible and it can be denied, guilt is real: a fact.

8. We can rise above our animal nature, but it's not going to go away.

9. If your mother asks you something (reasonable) and you refuse, you've shown who you are.

10. What you do shouts so loudly no one can hear what you claim.

Questions

⚜ Let's just say one of your grandparents is left alone, reasonably secure financially but in precarious health, becoming more and more dependent on outside help and concern. What do you think we ought to do if that situation arises? I know you have feelings, but let's get out into the open the *reasons* why our family should do anything at all.

⚜ The text hints that there's some kind of connection between legitimate guilt and ingratitude. Let's explore that awhile. Let's say you were dogging it in your studies. How would that be rooted in ingratitude? Sometimes your siblings are a royal pain and you lash out at them. Why should you be grateful for them? Are people being ungrateful when they find it too much effort to vote, toss away litter in the streets, spray graffiti?

⚜ Let's take a drive through the inner city. We can see people's homes only from the outside, but try to guess with me what we have (and take for granted) and they probably don't. Just look around this room and tell me what you suspect they don't have. This is no guilt trip; you're not in any way responsible for our being materially comfortable. But does it suggest anything about the kind of *attitude* we ought to have—toward what we have? Does it also suggest anything about the attitude we ought to have toward kids in the inner city? They aren't responsible for where they are either.

⚜ What do you say about the family setting some particular day, maybe the day after Thanksgiving for all of us to go through our closets and bureaus and pull out everything we haven't worn in a year. We obviously don't need any of it. Then we could give it away to people who really do have need of it. Whatcha think?

6

Respect

Without Respect,
Who Can Differentiate
Us From Beasts?

I am human. I consider nothing human
foreign to me.
—*Terence*

Lao Chen

 nce upon a time, long, long ago, when people were
less cautious, a rich man named Fan Sheng-li lived in a great castle
with enough servants to satisfy his every whim. But he had one problem the most conscientious servant could not correct—he suffered from
a seemingly incurable disease of his eyes. All day they burned, and at
night the pain refused him sleep. He had consulted every doctor, nec-
romancer, sorcerer and quack in the kingdom, to no avail. Finally, he
sent criers through the city offering a hundred gold pieces to anyone
able to relieve his agony.

Meanwhile, an old man named Lao Chen walked the city streets ped-
dling candy made by his wife Mei-ling from honey she harvested from

their meager hives. But Lao Chen couldn't resist small poor children, so he gave away as much candy as he sold, and he and Mei-ling were always poor. His wife had given up trying to talk sense into him and, to tell the truth, she loved him the more for his maddening kindness.

When the old peddler heard the rich man's announcement, he remembered a magical herb his grandmother used when the people in his village suffered eye diseases. He knew he could find it. He didn't even hear the part of the proclamation about a reward. So he packed his baskets and returned to the tiny hut he shared with his wife.

"If you go off on this crazy hunt," Mei-ling scolded, "what are we supposed to eat?"

Sheepishly, Lao Chen held out the basket of candy.

Despite herself, Mei-ling giggled. "Old fool. My teeth are bad enough." She took a single sausage from the cupboard. "All we have. Make it last." She sighed. "My dreamer!"

Next morning, when the guard opened the gates, Lao Chen was the first to leave the city. He searched and searched, his back aching from bending over mile after mile, peering under every bush to no avail. At noon, he sat under a huge elm tree by a stream to savor an inch of his sausage. He noticed an army of ants scurrying about in panic, carrying their larvae on their backs like grains of white rice. Puzzled, he saw that a rock had fallen into the stream and spilled it over into the ants' nest. "We are all one," the old man sighed and rose achingly to his feet. He put the rock on the bank, then with a stick he dug a furrow so the overflow trickled back into the stream.

"Well," he said and sat back down, leaning against the big tree. "I got up too early. I'll take a bit of a nap." And he fell softly into a lovely sleep.

Drifting in a dream, Lao Chen found himself walking through a great silent domed city. Tall gray buildings shafted up into the darkness overhead, pierced here and there by what seemed to be stars. From nowhere appeared a squad of soldiers, visored and armored in black. The captain saluted the old man and bowed. "Our queen wishes to see you," he said.

The frightened peddler could only obey, so he followed along the narrow street and up the steps to a great golden palace and into a magnificent throne room. There, atop a golden staircase, stood a slender black queen, smiling. "You tamed the great flood. Yes, we are all one.

From now on, if you are ever in need, you have only to ask, and my people will come to your aid."

It was on the tip of Lao Chen's tongue to ask about the magical herb. But suddenly he woke up, with a crick in his neck. "A good omen," he smiled and got to his feet and began again probing the underbrush for the magical herb. So focused was he that he lost all sense of time passing. Only the ache in his legs and back finally made him look up through the trees to the darkening sky. Night was coming fast, and with it the cold. He peered around for some kind of shelter, and in the twilight he saw a patch of gray which turned out to be an abandoned hunter's shack. Its roof sagged, and the walls were missing slats, but it was shelter from the night.

As he was about to enter, he looked down and saw he had almost stepped on a centipede. He stooped and put it in the cup of his hand. It had red tufts of fur along its back and yellow dots covered its segmented sides. "Well now, my friend," Lao Chen said, "if I didn't crush you with my foot, I trust you won't sting me. We are all one, aren't we?"

The old peddler gathered sticks and soon had a small fire going. As he sat warming himself, Lao Chen found fresh leaves and offered them to his new friend. The centipede nosed them, then turned away. "Don't like salad?" He reached into his sack for the rest of his sausage. "A meat eater? So am I." And he broke off a piece for the centipede and one for himself, careful to leave enough for breakfast. "Tomorrow I must find the herb to help Fan Sheng-li."

Stretching out beside the fire, the old man pillowed his head on his arm and went to sleep. But even as he slept, he was still searching the forest. Through the trees he saw a red and yellow blur approach, and from the brush emerged a tall slender figure, like a mythic warrior. He was dressed in a great russet fur coat flecked with gold that rippled to his feet, and his many eyes glared down at the tiny old man. But for some reason, in the dream, Lao Chen felt no fear.

"We are truly one," the voice boomed softly. "You saved a creature most giants would have crushed for the wicked pleasure of it. And you seek to help a man you don't even know. I will return the favor. When you wake, walk east toward the rising sun. You will find a pine with two trunks. Within its roots is a magic bead, white and tiny as a pearly tear. Dissolve that bead in wine and have the rich man drink it to heal his eyes." And the figure blurred into green darkness.

When Lao Chen woke, dawn filtered through the slats of the hut. He sat up and rubbed his whiskery face. The centipede was gone. So the old man hiked himself up and, chewing the butt of his sausage, began walking toward the rising sun. But all morning and afternoon he saw only ordinary pines. Wearily, he sank down and sighed. Mei-ling was right—he was an old fool.

Just as he was about to creak to his feet and head home, there it was! A pine tree with two trunks! He stumbled toward it and sank to his knees, clawing needles away. But the ground was hard clay. He sat on his heels ready to weep, when suddenly he remembered his first dream.

"Oh, my lady Queen," he sighed. "We are all one. And I am in need."

Immediately, all round him there were a series of tiny hisses. Dozens of tiny holes opened, and from them boiled endless lines of ants. "I am looking for a tiny white bead," Lao Chen whispered, as if a loud voice might hurt their tiny ears. If they even had ears. "It might be very small. Like a baby pearl."

He sat motionless, watching them disappear down the roots of the tree. In no time, back they were, carrying a bead as tiny as one of their unborn babies. Lao Chen laid his hand on the ground, and four stalwart soldiers carried their precious burden and set it down, then skittered back off to the ground. As the old man looked, the pretty white stone seemed to blush with pleasure, and he put it safely in his pouch. Lao Chen bowed to his helpers. "I thank you, and I thank your lady Queen." And the ants scurried out of sight.

Next morning, tired from walking the whole sleepless night, Lao Chen stood at the iron gate outside Fan Sheng-li's castle. "I am here to help your master's eyes," he told the gatekeeper.

The gatekeeper eyed him, haggard and dirty. "An old beggar like you help my master?

"Rich man or beggar," Lao Chen said, "we are all one."

Reluctantly, the gatekeeper went for the steward, who went to their master. In moments, the two reappeared, leading a finely dressed man whose eyes were shielded by fine linen poultices. "I am Fan Sheng-li," the man said. "I beg you, sir, are you *sure* this remedy will work?"

"I am not sure, sir," Lao Chen said. "But I trust it will. A cup of wine, please?"

When the cup came, Lao Chen upended his pouch, and the white stone fell blushing into his palm. Carefully, he pinched it between his fingers and dropped it into the cup. For an instant, it frothed, then settled. "Now, I think," the old peddler said.

Fan Sheng-li drank and handed the cup away. For a moment, he stood, waiting.

Suddenly, his hands flew to his head. "The *pain*," Fan Sheng-li cried.

"Ah, Lord Fan Sheng-li," Lao Chen nearly wept, "I was so sure—"

"The pain is *gone*," Fan Sheng-li whispered. "The pain is gone." He ripped away the bandages and blinked in the early sunlight. He looked around, puzzled. "Where is the doctor who worked this miracle?" Then he looked at the ragged old man standing at his gate, cringing with pleasure. "You did this?" he asked. "Steward, bring this man inside. He will have breakfast with my family, and he will never work a day again."

"Ah, my wife, Mei-ling, will be waiting for—"

"Then fetch his wife, too. Come, my new friend." And he whisked Lao Chen into his courtyard, thumping his shoulders, beaming.

A sudden breeze caught the bandages from the gateway and flew them, fluttering, away.

Albert Schweitzer

n the last week of August, 1965, in the early morning darkness, the courtyard of the jungle clinic of Lambaréné was thronged with people, speaking quietly in the light of torches and lanterns. African natives, old and young, American and European doctors and nurses, lepers, and summer volunteers sat on the ground, steps, and railings, waiting. Then at dawn, from the distant background, came the methodical beat of the telegraph drums, "The great White doctor is dead."

Thus died one of the greatest-souled—and most puzzling—men of the twentieth century.

Albert Schweitzer was born in January, 1875, in Alsace-Lorraine, a circumstance which would affect his outlook for his lifetime. For centuries Alsace was French, yet in 1870 it was annexed by Germany. Thus, Albert grew up speaking both French and German and was unaware of any animosity between the two; a sense of separatist nationalism meant nothing to him. His father was a Lutheran pastor, and his mother was the daughter of one. His grandfather and three great uncles were organists. Albert was a sickly child, lonely and introspective, who grew into a robust man who lived to a phenomenal old age—90 years. He composed his first hymn at seven, began to play the organ at eight, and by nine he was the substitute organist in his father's church. He had a deep concern for animals; when his playmates went after birds and squirrels with slingshots, he shoved them aside. As a boy he was deeply impressed by a gigantic statue by Frederic August Bartholdi (who created the Statue of Liberty) in the neighboring seaport of Colmar. It depicted a sorrowing African slave in chains, and the image stayed with him for the rest of his life.

By age 23, he had accumulated three separate doctorates—in philosophy, theology, and music—and became dean of theology at the University of Strasbourg, while also teaching philosophy and preaching at St. Nicholas Church. At age 30, his book, *The Quest of the Historical Jesus,* established him as a world figure in theological studies. He followed it with a work on organ building, and then wrote *Bach: The Musician-Poet.*

Then one morning in the fall of 1904, he discovered on his office desk a pamphlet from the Paris Missionary Society giving an account of its work in the Congo. It sought to attract volunteers, especially medical personnel. Before the day was out, Schweitzer realized he wanted to go to Africa—as a physician. Although his friends thought him mad, he put aside three successful careers and, at age 30, began medical studies, which he completed in 1912, followed by study of tropical medicine in Paris. That same year he married Helene Bresslau, who herself studied nursing in order to be his assistant.

The Schweitzers assembled all their equipment and paid for the whole expedition with gifts and with Dr. Schweitzer's earnings as an author, lecturer, and organist. Then they set sail March 26, 1913, for Lambaréné in the Gabon province of what was then French Equatorial Africa. There on the banks of the soupy green Ogowe River, 50 miles from the equator, they settled. The clouds, river, and jungle made it seem a prehistoric scene, a place of pythons and gorillas. Most of the year, the air was like steam, and the river clotted with crocodiles and hippos, who tipped over canoes in the dark. Why Africa? "To help repay the White man's debt to the Black." He had never forgotten that heroic statue of the Black slave in chains. But why that God-forgotten place? Because there was no other doctor for a thousand square miles.

The jungle was not their only challenge, or even their greatest one. The tribal folkways which had fused the native African tribes for ages were beginning to fall apart. European companies offered them a new slavery without chains. Men were lured far from their homes on two-year work contracts and were often paid in alcohol. What's more, the Whites began to convert the natives from beliefs in spirits, charms, and magic to their own God, who had no roots in African culture.

With native help, Dr. Schweitzer literally wrested space from the jungle for his clinic and in the process of building the place from scratch, he added to his four doctorates a mastery of carpentry, masonry, architecture, mechanics, pharmacology, and gardening. In fact, at one time, he and Helene had to fill one another's decayed teeth.

He never meant to establish a "hospital"—the type of gleaming, antiseptic facility advanced societies mean by the word hospital. Rather, he intended to set up a field station for *these* people, people unlike other Africans who worked in cities. He understood their simplicity and their ingrained fears. He saw that patients refused to eat unless a family member had prepared the food, lest someone from another tribe infest it with evil spirits. Therefore, he allowed at least one family member to come with each patient, with the result that his "hospital" became a crowded, smoky, at times caterwauling space. He respected their beliefs, and he refused to impose a foreign culture on them. Schweitzer accepted cases the native fetishmen thought were hopeless and refused to treat, and in most cases he cured them. The Africans were amazed that the White doctor could "kill" a person by cutting him open and then restore him to health. This was great magic.

Then, only a year later, World War I began, far away in Europe. It could hardly seem to affect such a remote jungle spot, but it did. French soldiers appeared and put the Schweitzers under house arrest. It was startling irony. Schweitzer was from a country which had been French for generations, and he had been educated in Strasbourg and Paris. He had put all nationalist squabbles behind him. But French Equatorial Africa bordered German Cameroon where colonial troops were fighting. The native Africans were now recruited—by both sides—and were just as confused: "But you told us to love. And if an African kills a White man, he's executed. Now they want to *train* us to kill White men somewhere far away."

Finally, Helene and Albert Schwietzer were allowed to reopen the hospital, but after three years, they were confined in 1917 in France in one prison after another. Not to let the time lie fallow, he began to sketch out another great book, *Philosophy of Civilization* (later published in 1923), in which he set forth his personal beliefs about "reverence for life," which holds all living things sacred—especially human beings—no matter what their color, nationality, or religion. "I am life which wills to live, in the midst of life which wills to live." Each human being must make a rational decision that the life we share is far more important than any of our differences. Unlike Eastern thinkers, he realized that at times one life must yield to another, but lower life must never be sacrificed *needlessly*. As a physician, he was forced daily to kill viruses and germs, but only because a human life was at stake.

Then in 1922, when Schweitzer was 47, he and Helene decided to return to Africa. Again his friends thought him mad; he was too old. Little could they guess he would serve there for another 43 years. In five short years, the jungle had overrun their first hospital, so they began another about two miles down river. Slowly, buildings arose, a volunteer medical staff began arriving, and the Rockefeller Foundation agreed to supply drugs and equipment. It would never be General Hospital, nor did Schweitzer ever intend it to be. He wanted a hospital the natives were not afraid of, in which they would feel "at home."

The main patients' ward was a long one-story structure, segmented into cubicles, each with a bunk and a mat and a doorway into an open court. Outside each was a cooking fire where their families could prepare meals, smoky, but helpful in driving away mosquitoes and therefore malaria. Since there was no electricity, water in the surgery had to be boiled in pots on stones over open fires. For years drugs and bandages were in short supply. The sanitary facilities were, as John Gunther put it, "picturesque." To the dismay of visiting doctors, Schweitzer did not like intricate modern equipment because it was too difficult to repair in tropical humidity and rusted within a week. Even hot water bottles rotted in a few days.

On any given day, 700 African patients and family members made the clinic a bustling village. None of the doctors or nurses wore uniforms; animals wandered everywhere (leaving odorous reminders of themselves as they went). There were no "Quiet, Please" signs. The doctors and nurses came from Europe, Asia, America, and there were usually 20 or so African practical nurses on duty, many of them males. Schweitzer's facility also gave homes to a leper colony. Only the severest cases were segregated, but the rest wandered freely and worked in the gardens. Oddly, the only fruit which grew in the area were bananas, so the Schweitzers began gardens and orchards in which nearly every kind of tropical vegetable and fruit grew, and the hospital was almost completely self-sufficient for food.

During World War II, Vichy French and Free French troops fought along the Ogowe River, but by mutual consent both held the hospital off limits, and the medical staff treated wounded from both sides. But supplies were always desperately short, and many serious African cases had to be sent away with little more than first aid and a kind word.

In 1952, Albert Schweitzer won the Nobel Peace Prize, and the prize money built the new leper hospital. But notoriety, although it brought in more donations, was a mixed blessing. Articles in several European periodicals criticized Dr. Schweitzer, and finally an ill-researched, ill-written book appeared called *Verdict on Schweitzer* by Gerald McKnight consisting mostly of sneers and unfounded innuendo. McKnight's basic thesis was that, if Schweitzer was not a saint, then he must be a fraud—which is somewhat like saying that, because he liked Wagner, he must be a Nazi. Schweitzer surely had faults, and he was the first to admit them. "I have often been arrogant," he wrote, "and often lacking in love."

His fiercest defenders couldn't deny he was cranky on occasion, demanding, dogmatic, behind the times. He was certainly non-conformist, anti-establishment, anti-nationalist, and thus provoked his opponents. He admitted he was autocratic: "An enlightened despot is able to give the greatest amount of freedom." He did, in fact, treat the natives like children: "I am your brother," he said, "but I am your *elder* brother." His hospital was crude, unsanitary, not up to date. But it was not a "hospital" but a jungle clinic, a village he had built up around a functional medical and clinical facility. And when a new, modern hospital arose on the island of Lambaréné, the natives came to Schweitzer instead. It was also true that, as the years went by, he was an old doctor in a new Africa. It was no longer politically correct to believe many Africans in the bush were not ready for nationalist independence.

"I do not feel obliged," Schweitzer wrote, "to justify myself to the public." If his 90-year life had not proved him worthy, mere words would never prove it. Just as Mother Teresa, Gandhi, and Damien of Molokai were taken to task for their least imperfections, so was Schweitzer. Like them, he was not flawless and each of his foibles—which would have seemed trivial in an ordinary person—became important, even damning. In truth he was, as Gunther put it, "a magnificent tyrant with a heart of gold."

"Just do what you can," Dr. Schweitzer wrote. "It's not enough to say, 'I'm earning enough to live and support my family. I'm a good churchgoer.' That's all very well, but you must do something more. Seek always to do some good somewhere. Everyone has to seek his own way to make his own self more noble and to realize his true worth. You must give some time to your fellow man. Even if it's a little thing, do something for those who have need of your help, something for which you get no pay but the privilege of doing it. For remember, you don't live in a world all your own. Your brothers and sisters are here, too."

A Sense of Other

 little while ago, I read a newspaper piece about police who had arrested a 15-year-old boy for the brutal murder of an old woman. They asked if he felt any remorse. "She's not me," he answered. "Why should I care about her?" To anyone who reads the papers, that attitude is not unique. Such sociopaths, only a few steps beyond complete autism, are totally self-absorbed. They think the only real person in the world is themselves, exactly like Helen Keller thought before her liberation.

Dr. Schweitzer said that, whenever he asked an ambulatory patient to give a bed-ridden patient a drink of water, the native might say, "This man is not brother of me," showing only a slightly larger scope of awareness, capable of concern for those of my tribe but no further. Yet, even in a society as brutal as our own—defensively desensitized as we are against so much inhumanity—any civilized person would at least wince at an egomania which limits awareness and concern to one's own "tribe" or, more tragically, to oneself alone.

It is the primary task of parents and teachers to civilize that self-absorbed beast in us (what Freud called the Id), not only by imposing limits on a child's rambunctiousness, but also by widening the child's radius of awareness—and then his concern for—persons living beyond the tight inner circles of "me and mine."

Yet we can find no basis for respect and concern for others in the biological world. One life form preserves itself by destroying others. The series of fish, each larger than the next, readying to devour the one in front of it has become a cliché for the corporate jungle of monopoly and capitalism. The jaguar stalks the gazelle; the wolf falls upon the lamb; even the perky robin hauls the hapless worm up with its beak—as indifferent as the boy who murdered the old woman.

The Web of Human Relationships

The boy-murderer is a human being—like the pimp, the pusher, the terrorist—but his human potential has never been activated. He is just over the line from the wolf, and most likely destined to stay there. Humans are born with the capacity to be different from beasts because we can reason—but neither reasoning nor acting humanely are mandatory, the way rapacity, living on prey, in a beast is irresistible. We are free to ignore our reasoning capacity and our humanity, even to pervert them. Thus, the most basic responsibility of parents is to assure that their children's human potential is constantly challenged, to make them more and more aware of the web of human relationships that stretches beyond the limits of their own skins to their families, beyond family to work and community, beyond community to the nation, and beyond that to the whole human family.

Again, no civilized person would dispute that. The big question is *how do we teach them?*

Rules and precepts are essential until children are able to reason for themselves. For her own safety, a child has to hear, "No. *Don't* do that. You'll be hurt." But at about the time children begin schooling, they are able to ask (or at least wonder) *why* an action is taboo. And by adolescence many are in open defiance of any taboo, even manifestly reasonable ones. It is no longer enough to know just *that* something is wrong; they must know, honestly, *why*. Further, knowing "this is wrong"—and even forceful reasons for it—is quite different from *internalizing* a moral truth, from feeling the "*I*-myself-ought" within it and making it a part of one's own personally validated conscience.

A cynical (or at least practical) motive for young people to behave morally at that stage is (a) it avoids the hassles—and the punishments, and (b) being good pays off. But at those levels of motivation, we are only a few rungs up the moral ladder from inhuman humans. Although most research says it is unrealistic (not to mention unfair) to expect youngsters to leave secondary school brimming with altruism, integrity and principle, we nonetheless can legitimately expect that they move further away from self-protectiveness into at least a developing sense of empathy and fellow-feeling for others. But parents and teachers have to plow before they plant. Before they can expect fellow-feeling, they have to find strategies to make young people realize and accept that the other *is* in fact a "fellow," and —even earlier— that the other person is even *there*!

It is for that reason I suggested that the *sine qua non* virtue—the primary virtue—was the faith in family which makes children confident within themselves, and that the second virtue was the curiosity which makes them restless to reach *beyond* the self.

Infants are innately curious and empathetic. Even within hours of birth, a baby's cries will set other babies crying in a kind of vocal support. Even while nursing, infants can sense if the mother is tense or upset. Yet they are still self-absorbed. The mother is merely an extension of the self who almost always responds as dependably as the infant's own fingers. Only later does the child get some inkling that the mother is "other."

When a child starts to toddle sometime in his second year, he also is beginning to form a hunch about himself as separate, and empathy gets somehow devalued in a process of staking out that self. Now his desires, which had always been catered to before, begin to be thwarted, by parents with their "no-no"s, and by other children. In the process of developing a sense of self, toddlers' toys, clothes, and stuffed animals are seen as extensions of themselves. To part with those possessions is almost like giving up a piece of themselves. The child isn't being selfish, just making a declaration of himself as a separate being.

Even as late as four, a child can still be self-centered: "See, Mommy, the sun follows me wherever I go." They think another shares their viewpoint and that what interests them automatically interests the listener. Again, they are not selfish, just prisoners of their own viewpoint because they're mentally incapable of more—as yet. But keep in mind that 15-year-old murderer who never got beyond that self-imprisonment. Opening our horizons beyond the self is what genuine learning is all about.

A sense of fairness and tolerance of others (both of which fall short of empathy and concern) depends on the child's understanding and acceptance that the other person, child or adult, *is* a fellow—who fears the same things, longs for the same things, is hurt by the same things. Children can accept that they have to take turns and share and scribble thank-you notes to Grandma, but they submit to it in the same uncomprehending way a toddler accepts that it's okay to bite the breadstick but not the electric cord. The one brings smiles, the other scowls. That's as far as it goes. To internalize the *reasons* for fairness takes more work, yet until that occurs within the child, she will merely conform, and usually only when an adult is around to enforce it. Parents and teachers have to prepare children to act humanly even when no one's watching.

As we have seen, a child has to develop reversibility, to get into the other person's skin and walk around in it awhile. To understand what is fair and polite, a child must have the mental ability to consider another person's viewpoint, which occurs only when a child is about five or six. Meanwhile, parents and pre-school teachers can help wean children ever so gradually from their attachment to "my way," to develop a sense—however vague—of the *worth* of another, a worth that needn't be earned and which demands a yielding to that right. Often the strongest persuasion is the child's unexamined conviction that fairness is important to the parents. Loving the parents and wanting to be like them makes a child want to internalize their values.

The Latin root of the word "respect" is *respicere*, "to look at." Even tots can be asked to look at another person: "Ooh, who's that?" Role-playing helps, too: "Show me how Jimmy walks." "She got upset when you took her bunny. Can you guess why? What do you think might make her feel better?" "Remember when Scotty grabbed your red Power Ranger yesterday? Tell me what it felt like inside."

Although having siblings can be a royal pain—intrusions, "borrow-ing," clashing tastes, tattling—one has to suspect that having at least one sibling is worth the torment in the long run. In the first place, siblings offer unarguable proof that, like it or not, there are others in one's life. But in the second place, unlike other children during play years and schooling, siblings provide a more or less constant need to learn toler-ance and compromise—otherwise the whole family is going to end up in separate padded rooms. Those abrasions are really opportunities to grow as human beings, provided the parents see them as such and use them imaginatively. By the time kids are in school, parents should be able to say to two squabblers, "Look. The two of you sit here at the kitchen table, and when I come back in 15 minutes, you tell me how you've settled this, OK?"

Children and adolescents also have to internalize a realization that their parents are "fellows," too, that they also have feelings, get tired, say things they'd like to take back. "Honey, I'm so tired right now I feel I could drop over"—and the body language says more than the words. Parents also have to say, "Look, I made a mistake. I grounded you without thinking enough about it." Admission of weakness is a sign of strength—and of confidence in the child's love. It also shows the child that she can admit when she's making a mistake and expect forgiveness, too.

Adolescents especially have to be told that even when a parent is objectively wrong (about other ethnic groups, intruding with coaches, being over-protective), the parent still deserves respect—not for what the parent believes in this particular case but for who the parent *is*. No matter what the parent's faults, he or she is a person without whom the child wouldn't have existed. Without this child, the parents would be a quarter of a million dollars better off, but they decided the trade-off was worth the loss. A child may not particularly *like* a parent at the moment, but simple justice (if not gratitude) demands that he or she respect them.

"Do unto others as you would have others do unto you" isn't just the exclusive belief of the Judeo-Christian ethic. It is a matter of human survival. You will find it echoed in Confucius, Lao-tse, Babylonian hymns, in Greek and Roman writing, Native-American and Samoan lore, and in just about every folk tale from every civilization for the past 3,000 years.

The Bedrock of a Child's Well-being

The most crucial factor in teaching children respect for others is the parents. First, the children have to have a "gut-certitude" that their parents care about them—no matter what—even when they're disciplining them. That in turn hinges on the parents' own self-image, self-esteem, confidence, emotional vulnerability, patience, and perhaps most important of all: the perspective to see this particular infuriating moment in its proper proportion. That means it's essential that parents—no matter what their devotion and concern—have time to themselves to find some peace and balance, and also have time alone with one another to work on their marriage, which is the bedrock on which the children's search for a self is founded.

Hard as it might be to accept, the purpose of adolescence is to prepare young people to become good spouses and good parents—people who will each be a personally validated self. No one can provide clearcut models, like blueprints, but children's education is to help them sketch out their own lives. If a prospective spouse and parent has achieved that, all is well. Because all the rest is improvisation.

A Dilemma

"Why'd you throw me outta class?"

"Danny, look. I asked you three times when you were tickling Andy, 'Danny, just stop. Danny, will you grow up? Danny, get out.'"

"I didn't do *anything*!"

"You distracted me from what I was trying to do. You completely ignored me as another human being. All you think about is yourself. You got me angry."

"I'm not in charge of your anger."

"Yes, you *are*, Danny. When people are friends, their friendship says, 'OK, I give you permission to tick me off more than a stranger can, because we're friends.'"

"You're my teacher, not my friend."

"That's because it all comes from one side."

"I don't know what you're talking about."

"I *know* you don't! That's why this is the third or fourth time we've talked. I didn't have to do this, you know. I could have said, 'What the hell, let him waste his life.'"

"I'm not wasting my life."

"You *are*. You've got an A mind and C grades. Everything you hand in is top-of-the-head, no thinking beforehand, no outline. Sheer swamp gas."

"The other kids in the class think you've got it in for me. Like a vendetta."

"We just got off the point. I was talking about the fact that you're dogging it."

"I'm *not* dogging it. I'm doing my *best*!"

"You're *not* doing your best."

"How do *you* know that?"

"Because I've been at this, Danny, since before your parents knew one another."

"Gimme a break."

"From the *truth*? You're really sick, do you know that?"

"Get offa my back."

"You really are. You're psychologically incapable of saying 'I'm sorry.'"

"Right."

"Then why can't you just say, 'I'm sorry for fooling around in class'?"

"I didn't do *anything*!"

A Conversation About Respect

What's your reaction to the following statements?

A = Agree; ? = Uncertain; D = Disagree.

1. If you refuse to mind your own business, you live a more interesting life. A   ?   D

2. If you want to be useful, you have to be used. A ? D

3. Native Africans in cities were ready for freedom; those in the bush were not. A ? D

4. "My country right or wrong" is not the claim of a good citizen. A ? D

5. Schweitzer's slovenly clinics were a disgrace. A ? D

6. Genuine heroes and heroines need not be flawless. A ? D

7. People who leave their lockers open have no right to complain about thefts. A ? D

8. Using racial or ethnic slurs is really only a minor, careless bad habit. A ? D

9. Having at least one sibling is worth the torment in the long run. A ? D

10. Parents deserve forgiveness for being imperfect. A ? D

Help me understand what you understand by any of these statements.

1. "Rich man or beggar, we are all one."

2. Schweitzer refused to impose a foreign culture on his patients.

3. All living things are sacred.

4. "It's not enough to say, 'I'm earning enough to live and support my family.'"

5. "Remember, you don't live in a world all your own. Your brothers and sisters are here, too."

6. "She's not me. Why should I care about her?"

7. We find no basis for respect and concern for others in the biological world.

8. "Do unto others as you would have others do unto you" is a matter of human survival.

9. "I am human; nothing human is foreign to me."

10. The most important factor in children's well-being is the solidity of their parents' marriage.

Questions

- The founder of Boys Town said, "There's no such thing as a bad boy (or girl)." What he meant was that he'd encountered mixed-up boys, ego-bruised boys, battered boys, even crazy boys—and boys he personally couldn't get through to. But he'd never met one who was bad through-and-through, irredeemable. Think about people you know at school. Try to come up with a couple we can talk about, ones who seem bad through-and-through. Use your imagination. Why do you think they're like that? There has to be a reason. Everybody (even Hitler) has to feel somehow justified in acting the way he does. How do you think those people justify the way they are? How did they get that way?

- In the early '40s, in a startling number of camps around Europe, men and women of the German SS ordered and assisted in the systematic extermination of six million Jews and 11 million Slavs, either by direct gassing or by slow starvation and overwork. A great many of them had no personal grudge against their victims; they were just "doing a job," following orders. What's more, they were people who would never even think of kicking their neighbor's dog. Some of them spent the work day routinely exterminating human beings (many of them children) and then went home to play Mozart on the piano. What do you think got lost inside them?

- Making that moral situation smaller and bringing it closer to home, be honest with me (and more importantly with yourself), are there any people at school or in the neighborhood you sort of "eliminate?" Not literally kill, obviously, but sort of "wipe out" of reality, at least in your own mind. There's something "wrong" about that. I can't precisely put a finger on why, but let's talk about it a bit. Maybe we can both learn something.

Empathy

Opening Your Wallet
Is Not the Same
As Opening Your Heart

Pity may represent little more than the impersonal concern
that prompts the mailing of a check, but true sympathy is the
personal concern which demands the giving of one's soul.
—*Martin Luther King, Jr.*

Silas

 nce upon a time, long, long ago, when hypocrisy
was more common than today, there lived a man named Silas, a
wizened little fellow with musket-ball eyes who had always been the
first one abused in childhood games. Silas ran what he liked to call a
boys' refuge, taking in runaway and abandoned boys at a reasonable
subsidy for each from the count of the shire. Each day, Silas rented out
the boys for another modest fee to artisans and merchants in need of
unskilled help. No reason for the children to waste the day in idleness—
what's more, they learned a trade. Meanwhile, they were assured of a

roof over their heads, a bit of clothing in the interest of modesty, and two healthy bowls of porridge each day.

One stormy night, after Silas had come from the boys' loft where he had silenced their whining with his thorn stick, he sat by candlelight for a bowl of warmed-over breakfast porridge. Rain thrashed the roof, whipping in silver curtains outside the windows, when suddenly there came a knock on the door. Silas ignored it. Some fool who lost his way deserved the lesson of his lack of foresight. The hammering continued. So he rose, grumbling, and hobbled to the door.

There stood a man even older than Silas, clad in a long, faded purple cloak. Within the hood was a face chipped from granite framed in thick white hair. Two eyes of infinite sadness glistened from under long brows curled up into tiny crescents.

"Please," the old man said, "could I beg of you—?"

"No!" And Silas slammed the door to return to his porridge before it lost its steam.

But the hammering began again. Silas sat huffing. He knew if he didn't let the old fool in, he would not get the sleep he needed to be a compassionate provider to his charges. So he got up, hissing, and opened the door, returning to his meal and letting the stranger enter or be hanged as he chose. Without looking up he realized the old man had shut the door. Then he sensed him shuffling to the table and sitting on the very edge of the chair across from him. Silas looked up and saw the hound dog eyes on the sticky porridge. For a moment, he hesitated. Then, with another snarl, he shoved the bowl across and rose to get another, hotter bowl.

"Oh," the old man rasped with a sad grin, "this is entirely too generous. I could never—"

"Eat what you can," Silas hissed, "and throw what's left back into the pot."

For a moment the only sounds were the scraping of the two wooden spoons and the wash of the rain. The old man sat back with a sigh, his gruel hardly touched. "You are most kind."

"Where are you traveling?" Silas asked, to break the silence.

"I'm on a quest," the old man said.

"Quest?"

"I'm looking for …someone."

"Who?"

"I'll know him. When I find him."

Silas ground his teeth, realizing he had opened his door to a lunatic. But the old man hadn't enough gristle to brain his benefactor and make off with his considerable gold.

"Where are you from?" Silas asked.

"Oh," the old man said quietly, "many places. Many places."

Silas looked at him irritably. "What are you called?"

"Ahashuerus."

Silas scowled. "What sort of name is that?"

"Latin. An approximation of my name: Asher Ben Sirah."

Silas's jaw dropped. "Then you're a—"

"Yes. A Jew. Or I was." He smiled weakly. "I suppose one never stops being a Jew."

Again the silence fell round the two men. Silas wanted to go to his bed, but he was curious about this ancient puzzle. "You say you've been 'many places.' Where were you last?"

"London. Before that, Paris, Nuremberg, Rome. I have tried Rome many times."

"Rome? Did you see the pope in Rome?"

"Oh, yes. From a long way off."

"And he was not your man?"

"No," the visitor said sadly. "And I've seen more than a few popes."

"How many?"

"How many have there been? I couldn't say."

Silas scowled at him, sure he was hallucinating. And yet the man seemed so all-fired calm. "How long have you been on this—this quest?"

The man sighed. "It seems like forever."

"Well, where did you begin?"

"In the Holy City." He closed his eyes. "I was a sandal maker. Thirty years old. There was a great to-do in the town at that time. Some upcountry rebel stirring things up. He was really quite foolhardy, railing at our leaders. Called them all sorts of harsh names, like 'hypocrites.' And of course the people are always looking for someone to snarl from behind."

"Did you ever meet this hothead?"

"Once. But not really."

"Whatever that means. So?"

"The crisis came with the march into the city. They bowed down to him as if he were a new king. Really the last straw, we thought. He was arrested. Then he did the unthinkable."

"Yes, yes. Go on."

"He claimed he was a god."

"The man was insane," Silas barked.

"Yes," the old man said. "That seemed quite clear. So he was tried and condemned to death. But as luck would have it, the platoon escorting him to his execution passed down our street. People jeering, throwing trash, prodding him with staves. I almost felt sorry for him. Then he fell. Right in front of my shop. He had been pretty badly mauled. The cross-piece for his crucifixion just brought him to his knees."

"Merciful God!" Silas gasped. "They still *crucify* felons in your country?"

The old man went on, eyes burning. "He looked up at me and said, 'Could I rest here a moment?' I was completely repelled. I batted his hand and said, 'On your way, heretic!' The man groaned and locked his eyes on mine. 'Yes,' he said, 'I am on my way to my rest. But you will wait, forever restless, until I return.' So they hauled him to his feet and booted him on his way."

"And that was that," Silas said.

"No. Just the beginning. Of course, the man died and they buried him in some cave. There were rumors about the cave being empty, which we all knew was sheer rubbish. The place was riddled with caves. They merely went to the wrong one. So we got on with our lives."

"This quest, then," Silas said. "You don't mean you're looking for this mad felon."

"Yes," the old man said softly. "Looking and looking."

"But the man was dead!"

"So we thought," Ahasuerus sighed. He saw the light of false dawn pearling in the window. The rain had stopped. He stood. "I must be going. Thank you for your kindness."

"But wait," Silas said, rising too, "who was this felon? Who are you seeking?"

The old man turned with his hand on the latch. "Surely you know." And he was gone.

Silas slumped back into his chair. Of all the nonsense. No one could live that long. And he had sat up half the night listening to the crackpot. There was a knock on the door. "That old man be damned," Silas grunted and prepared to climb up to his bed.

But the knocking continued and Silas, biting back his rage, flung open the door. It was not the old man at all but an old woman, looking like a nest of sodden rags, wrinkled as a walnut. "Please," she muttered, "could I rest here just a moment? I'm—"

"And I'm about to take my own rest," Silas barked and made to close the door.

But something clutched in his chest, a reminder. He opened the door and saw the old woman's back bent as she hobbled up the path.

"Wait!" he said. "All right. Come in." And she limped to the table and sat, looking at the old man's uneaten porridge. "Finish it," Silas snapped. And the old woman dug in greedily.

It would be misleading to say that from that day forward Silas began putting raisins and currants into his boys' porridge, that he installed pot-bellied stoves in their loft, that he searched the villages for warm clothing, and began giving them part of their wages as an allowance.

But every time there was a knock on his door, no matter how late at night or how weary he was, Silas rose to answer it.

Eleanor Roosevelt

 icture a pretty little girl with lovely sad eyes—pretty except for having a receding chin, with buck teeth protruding from pudding cheeks—born to the most glamorous couple in New York in the gay '90s. Eleanor Roosevelt's young parents, Elliott and Anna, were the toast of the city's social life and their glamour was overpowering to the homely little girl, a mockingbird misplaced among nightingales. Even as a child, she was so solemn and painfully shy that her own mother poked fun of her, calling her "Granny." But Eleanor adored her charming, irresponsible father, though she was puzzled by his moodiness and depression and was fearful of his frequent drunkenness. She hardly ever saw her popular parents and was tended by servants, which made her even more withdrawn.

When she was eight, her mother presented the family with a little brother, Elliott, Jr., and a year later another brother, Hall. But finally at her wits' end with her husband's alcoholism, Anna Roosevelt insisted that he be hospitalized and separated from the family for a year, until he could prove he had been cured. Eleanor longed for her father and resented her mother for keeping them apart, yet when Anna was bedridden for days with excruciating headaches, the little girl sat for hours by her bed, massaging her mother's aching temples. "Feeling that I was useful was perhaps the greatest joy I experienced."

But her mother caught diphtheria and in December, 1892, she died. A girl of ten, Eleanor felt grief at her mother's passing but far less grief than the joy she felt knowing that her beloved father would come home. Yet even after her death, Anna prevented this—her will stipulated that custody of the three children be granted to her stern mother, Mary Ludlow Hall, who had never accepted Elliott. Eleanor felt more alienated than ever, especially when her brother, Elliott, succumbed to scarlet fever only a year after her mother's death. A year after that, her father died from a fatal fall during a drinking bout. But all the tragedies she endured as a lonely child evoked in her a profound sense of kinship with all lonely, deprived, and excluded children—a kinship—which would form the fabric of her life.

Eleanor submerged herself in her books, which did not enhance her attractiveness as she moved into her teens. Worse, her severe grandmother dressed her in shapeless dresses that did nothing to improve her now gangling figure. One of her few escapes, besides reading, were her visits to her uncle Teddy Roosevelt's rough-and-tumble family, which allowed all kinds of child's play unthinkable at her grandmother's Spartan household. But those moments of real family life were few.

Finally, a door opened for Eleanor when her grandmother sent her to Allenswood, a girls' boarding school outside London, England. There, Marie Souvestre, the headmistress, took a special interest in this overly tall, overly reserved girl. In February 1901, she took Eleanor on a trip to

France and Italy, which she found "a revelation," a world she never could have dreamed of. So exhilarated was she that she wanted to return for a fourth year at Allenswood, but Grandmother Hall adamantly refused, insisting she return to make her official debut into New York society—an event she dreaded. At age 18, she was taller than nearly any boy she danced with, and she was helpless at the chitchat expected of young girls, preferring to talk politics—which withered her chances even further. "I didn't quite realize beforehand what utter agony it would be."

Another relative who seemed to offer her hope was her father's sister, Anna Roosevelt Cowles. During visits to her house in Washington, DC, Eleanor found all sorts of interesting, well-read, concerned people like herself and not least of these was Mrs. Cowles' brother and Eleanor's uncle, President Teddy Roosevelt. Eleanor saw how much the president valued her aunt's advice on affairs of state, and she saw that a woman could in fact affect national affairs, not only with the great people, but also with the obscure people—people with whom Eleanor felt such a pained kinship. She joined the Junior League, a group of wealthy young women working for the poor in hospitals and settlement houses, offering child care and skills to immigrant women. Working in the slums of New York, she found the squalor and want not daunting, but challenging. Indignant at the sordid conditions, low wages, and long hours in the sweatshops—even for children aged four or five—Eleanor made it her task to visit businesses and report to the Consumers' League about their inhuman practices. "I was frightened to death," she wrote later, "but I wanted to be useful."

Meanwhile, in the far more intimidating round of parties, teas and dances, she renewed a lifelong acquaintance with a distant cousin, the dashing and intellectual Franklin Roosevelt, who was finishing at Harvard and seemed to value an aspect of Eleanor which lighter minds ignored. Finally, in December, 1903, he proposed. She was astonished, as was Franklin's domineering mother, Sara, who prevailed upon her only child to delay the engagement a year, hoping for someone better. But the following year, when Franklin entered Columbia Law School, they announced their engagement. In March, 1905, they were married, with President Theodore Roosevelt giving away the bride, and that summer they honeymooned in Europe.

When the couple returned to New York, Eleanor was happily pregnant, but her joy deflated when she found her mother-in-law had rented and furnished an apartment for them, complete with servants she had chosen, just two blocks from her own home. The Roosevelts' first child, Anna, was born in May, 1906. To Eleanor, the baby was "just a helpless bundle, but by its mere helplessness winding itself inextricably around my heart." Precariously, she began to trust love. In ten years, she gave birth to five more children, four of whom survived: James in 1907, Franklin, Jr., in 1909 who died within a year, Elliott in 1910, a second Franklin, Jr. in 1914, and finally John in 1916. The family spent the year in New York and summers at Campobello Island in Canada.

But it was not ideal. Responsibility for the children frightened Eleanor, who was unsure she could do what was best for them. Worse, Sara Roosevelt built them a home in Hyde Park, New York—a home connected to her own, so she could walk in at any time, day or night. Her dictatorial nature more or less "took over" the children. Trapped between such an unflinching mother-in-law and such an ambitious husband, Eleanor became more and more withdrawn and inaccessible.

In 1910, Franklin was elected to the New York state legislature, and the family had to move to Albany—and away from Franklin's mother. Three years later, he was appointed assistant secretary of the navy, and they moved to Washington. Eleanor realized the wife of an up-and-coming politician could no longer sit in the parlor reading. She dutifully began socializing, visiting other politicos' wives and cementing relationships. When World War I began, she joined the Navy Relief Society and served meals to soldiers passing through Washington's Union Station. For the Red Cross, she visited hospitals, where she campaigned for further funding to care for battle-scarred veterans. She began to believe—because she saw the results—that she could make a difference, not only as a support for her husband but as an individual woman.

When her husband ran as vice president on the Democratic ticket in 1920, she campaigned vigorously—not only for the Democrats—but for women to exercise their newly won right to vote. When the ticket was defeated, the Roosevelts returned to New York, and Franklin took up law practice. Then, while the family was on vacation at Campobello, Franklin fell victim to polio.

The couple was unyielding. Franklin resolved he would one day walk again, and he did, though only with the help of heavy iron leg braces. And Eleanor resolved she would take his place until he could be active again. She threw herself into Democratic politics, leaving behind her aristocratic background and taking up the cause of those in society who seemed to have no voices or chances. She joined the Women's Trade Union League to organize women to campaign for a 40-hour work week, abolition of child labor and minimum wages. She campaigned for Al Smith for president. Then she campaigned for her husband when he became well enough to run successfully for governor of New York. Later, in 1932, in the midst of the Depression, she campaigned for Franklin again when he ran for president of the United States. Suddenly, the little goose had become a queen, but it would not be like the storybooks.

In the White House, she moved furniture herself, operated the elevator for herself, invited anyone who chose—White or Black, rich or poor—to tour the house for which their taxes paid the rent. She allowed only female reporters at her press conferences; she began a monthly column in *Women's Home Companion*, inviting anyone in the country to write in about their concerns. In her first year as First Lady, 300,000 responded. She began giving radio talks and lectures. Asked if her husband's illness had affected his mind, she answered unflappably, "Anyone who has gone through suffering is bound to have greater sympathy and understanding." She herself proved that.

She invited Blacks to the White House, from sharecroppers to Black college presidents, to inform the government of their frustrations. Invited to a meeting in Alabama where it was illegal for her to sit with her Black friends, she set her chair in the middle aisle between the two groups. In 1939, when the Daughters of the American Revolution denied Constitution Hall to Black singer Marian Anderson, Eleanor resigned her membership and worked behind the scenes for a free concert in front of the Lincoln Memorial, which 75,000 people attended.

As World War II began, Franklin was elected to an unprecedented third term, due largely to Eleanor's speech at the Democratic convention, calming explosive factions and urging unity. Although the U.S. had resolved to remain neutral, the Japanese attack on Pearl Harbor, December 7, 1941, rendered that impossible. While FDR made a diplomatic tour of free

Europe, Eleanor made one to servicemen in the South Pacific. The commander, Admiral William "Bull" Halsey, was none too pleased at first but quickly changed his mind when he saw that this woman was not merely paying a quick photo-opportunity courtesy call to each hospital. Instead, she went to every ward, every bed, and met every wounded man personally. She had four sons in the service herself, and for these broken boys her presence was almost like a visit from their own mothers.

As the war began drawing to a painful close and only 82 days into his fourth term as president, Franklin Roosevelt died in Warm Springs, Georgia, weary and wasted, looking far older than his 63 years. When Vice President Harry Truman came to see Eleanor at the White House, he asked if there was anything he could do for her, but she said, "Is there anything I can do for *you*?"

When the war ended four months later, Truman took her at her word, appointing her a delegate to the newly forming United Nations, where she headed the commission drafting a Universal Declaration of Human Rights. She also worked for the million refugees in internment camps all over Europe, many of which she visited. Truman also used her as a goodwill ambassador to Lebanon, Pakistan, India, and the newly emergent third world, where thousands of people greeted her at each stop. Typically, she thought they had shown up out of respect for her late husband, not out of respect for her. When she spoke at the 1952 Democratic National Convention, the chairman called for order: "Will the delegates please take their seats? Several million people are waiting to hear the First Lady of the World."

When President Eisenhower accepted her resignation from the UN when she was 73, she agreed to an invitation from the *New York Post* to travel as a correspondent to the Soviet Union, during which time she had a two-and-one-half-hour interview with Nikita Khrushchev, after which he said, "At least we didn't shoot one another." But she said, "Either all of us are going to die together or we are going to learn to live together, and if we are to live together we have to talk."

On November 7, 1962, Eleanor Roosevelt died in New York City. As she had told reporters on her 77th birthday, "Life was meant to be lived. Curiosity must be kept alive. The fatal thing is the rejection of it. One must never for whatever reason, turn his back on life."

Kinship

*very year when we ponde*r in class what being part of a family means, I show Robert Redford's film, *Ordinary People.* I've seen it now probably about 30 times, but every time I switch the tape off at the end, after the son has finally been able to tell his father he loves him and the father has told him he loves him, too, I always end up with tears in my eyes. So this year, I mentioned this, and from the class (all boys) came mock groans and hoots of "Awww!" Apparently, to feel deeply for a stranger—or at least to show it or admit it—is very "un-cool."

I pulled myself up to my inconsiderable height and glared. "You guys really *scare* me, you know that?" They sobered up pretty fast. "Are your self-defenses so strong you can't even allow yourself at least a bit of fellow-feeling for a man and a boy whose wife and mother has just walked out on them, who just cling together in shared pain?"

One kid sneered, "Well, you can feel sorry for somebody without breaking down in *sobs*." He exaggerated my reaction so he could reduce it to something absurd, and therefore not have to censor his own callousness in any way.

What bothered me was the need of so many of them to mock genuine sentiment, honest fellow-feeling. Then I began to wonder if their seeming hard-heartedness was only one small part in a kind of "general defensiveness" that's almost essential today, at least in big, overcrowded, noisy, dangerous cities. Locking oneself inside a Walkman is another way to block out the chaos. Walking corridors and sidewalks with invisible blinders on is another. Focus on the subway ads and on the elevator numbers rather than on "sharing" the space with the others, who are there, but who are in no really meaningful (inconvenient, intrusive, even hurtful) way. If you refuse to notice them, they may not go away, but they'll become less real. There's just so much one can deal with; if you let in all the stimuli, you'd blow all your mental circuits. Best to zip up the old cocoon and let the rest of the world roll by, unnoticed and incapable of upsetting.

Television and films have a similar effect. By the time little kids reach kindergarten, they've seen more deaths—real or fictional—than a veteran in the army of Julius Caesar, to the point that psychiatrists say the kids can't tell the difference between real pain and acted pain. A great many of the blockbuster movies bristle with explosions and mayhem until those scenes are no more able to move—or shock—anyone than the explosions in a video game. On the other hand, we're also besieged with public service announcements showing African children with great glistening, mournful eyes and flies drinking up their tears, making us feel helplessly soul-bruised to the point where it just becomes too much. We flick the dial, turn the page, render ourselves amnesiac about it. It's just too much overload for anyone to cope with.

This general "soul-numbing" is understandable, but also impoverishing. At the core of *Ordinary People* is the need of the mother, Beth, and the son, Conrad, to have "control." The elder brother, Buck, died in a boating accident. At Buck's funeral, Beth and Conrad were the only ones who didn't cry. They couldn't allow themselves to. And Conrad felt such inexpressible guilt at having survived the accident that he attempted to cut his wrists. The father, Calvin, reaches out to both of them, but they can't allow him access to their pain, nor can they allow themselves to identify with his pain. But as Burger, the psychiatrist in the film, says, "If you can't feel pain (your own or another's), you're not going to be able to feel anything else." The cocoon may very well be protective, but it is also very small and smothering.

Empathy, Sympathy, and Compassion

Empathy, sympathy, compassion. Different words, but made up of similar parts: em-, sym-, and com- are Greek and Latin roots meaning "with." Both "path" and "passion" mean "suffer." So all three words mean "to suffer with." They denote a reality inside a person that *resonates* with the anguish inside another human being, *identifies* with it. In a sense, they're all "victim" words, and since few of us seek to be victims, they can be scary even to consider. Empathy, sympathy, and compassion go far beyond what my uneasy student meant by "feeling sorry for"—a pity which can be very remote, cool, only slightly warmer than indifference. It also goes beyond respect, which we can honestly offer to another person without any personal involvement or cost. Respect is the first step on the road to justice; empathy is the first step on the road to love.

All of us want to love and be loved—or at least we claim we do. And yet, if we genuinely want the goal and we are honest with ourselves, we also must genuinely want the *means* to the goal. For instance, if I claim to want an education, that should be evident in what I do, large and small, from putting in a full 40-hour week to writing outlines. Without that concrete evidence, my claim is a lie I tell myself—and worse—a lie that I believe.

The same is true of loving. If I claim (even in just an unspoken way within myself) to be a loving person, I should be able demonstrate this simply by my concrete behavior and responses. If I claim to love my parents, that claim is undercut if I grouse when asked to take out the trash, refuse to be truthful with them, deny them an honest day's work for an honest day's pay. I might like to *think* I love them, but my actions prove pretty convincingly that I'm lying—to myself. Real loving costs. If it doesn't, using the word "love" is a self-delusion.

Similarly, we can be stingy with our love, restricting it in a very unloving way to a very narrow, insulated group, which is also self-impoverishing. If what makes humans different from animals is that we can keep learning and loving, then the more things we learn and the more people we love, then the more our lives—our selves—are enriched. The only obstacle to that enrichment is our own fear about being "taken in"— hoaxed, made to look foolish. But if you never let yourself be taken in, you'll never see the inside of anything.

Empathy Enriches the Receiver and the Giver

Nine times out of ten, when you offer someone your trust, that person will honor your trust. The same thing is true of offering your empathy for another's suffering; it enriches not only the receiver but also the giver. True enough, one time out of ten you'll offer your trust to some-one and get scorched. We all have the scars to prove that. But to avoid that one scorching, ("better safe than sorry.") we give up those nine other potential friends, even though everything about them seems to indicate they can in fact be trusted. And when you allow yourself honestly to be moved by someone else's anguish, you risk being laughed at, as my class laughed at me. But I'd rather be laughed at by a group of tough-souled boys than become a tough-souled old man in order to achieve their dubious approval.

Take the case of the panhandler. Everyone reading this page has probably been ambushed by at least a few. The standard, practical response is: divert your attention and pass them by. They're almost certainly going to spend whatever you would give on booze or drugs, right? Especially if they're disheveled and smell bad? You can almost convince yourself you're doing them a *kindness* by denying them help. But just for a moment, remember what Atticus Finch suggests in *To Kill a Mockingbird*: get inside their skin and walk around in it awhile. How did this person get where he is now? Quite likely he wasn't always this way. Would anyone really *want* to surrender his dignity, his self-esteem, to put out his paw and beg from strangers? And looking at it from a broader perspective, what's he asking for? No more than the cost of a single telephone call. (You can see why gratitude came before empathy in this book, right?)

If you sincerely want to be a caring person and you're honestly afraid this money he asks for food is really going for drugs, buy him a sandwich or a banana. If (as can happen) he sneers at that gift and really is a phony, *you'll* at least have proven that you're not. The question here really isn't whether the beggar is in authentic need but whether you are authentically kind. Personally, I'd rather be bilked by nine beggars in a row than pass by the tenth who was really needy. And if you give someone a gift certificate at Christmas, do you often say, "Now, be sure to buy something I'd approve of, right?"

Taking the First Step Toward Empathy

The first step toward the empathy that enriches both receiver and giver is to *notice* them. Granted, if you don't notice them, they are far less likely to cause you grief. But not noticing *guarantees* they'll never become your friend. When I walk through the school corridors, I purposely try to focus on as many faces as I can in the chaos of changing classes. I never once have done it without seeing someone who, by his build, must be at least a junior, and I've never noticed him before. In three years! Whenever I cross the university campus, I always try to catch eyes with everybody I pass and say, "Hi," and almost invariably they say, "Hi," back. A small thing, but it's a start. And it's a lot less lonely.

Volunteering is another way to get your empathetic juices stirring. All of us know the queasy reluctance we feel visiting someone in a hospital or a nursing home, the same aversion most people feel at the outset of their first service project: "Those old people will smell, and they'll paw me and make me feel awful. Those handicapped kids will drool and won't understand and fight me off." But I've rarely seen anyone who sincerely tried at a service project who didn't come back saying, "I went to give *them* something and, without my even realizing till now, they were giving *me* something. Something important." Right. A sense that you are not negligible, that you can, in fact, make a difference, a small difference maybe, but a meaningful one.

As for all those painful pictures of needy children, we can avert our eyes from them, too, refuse to notice them, but again in denying them we are denying ourselves. Take just one fact about them: UNICEF, the United Nations Children's Fund, reports that each *day* 1,000 children go blind because they have no access to 20 cents worth of Vitamin A. And even if they did, their parents couldn't afford it. Think of that. For the cost of one compact disc, I could save 65 kids from lifelong blindness! You can't crusade for all of even the worthiest causes, but to be a person of character, you ought to choose just *one*.

Yet another way of developing a sense of humanity (character) is simply to go through your closet and drawers and pick out anything you haven't worn in a year. Obviously, you have no remote need of it, and it could save someone's life—or at least give him or her a momentary lift. And even in a worst-case scenario, where the Salvation Army driver steals all the best stuff and fences it for money—in the first place, you'll never know that, and in the second place, your compassion and generosity have done something very good inside *you*.

Novels, plays, and films can help evolve our empathetic powers, too—if we're not too well-defended against them. *Shane, The Elephant Man, A Man for All Seasons, Death of a Salesman, Our Town*—these were all written by great souls capable of reaching down into the human heart and coming back with something that speaks to our own hearts, if they are open. From a play whose name I can't remember comes a line

I can never forget: "Coward, take my coward's hand." That says what true empathy is.

Finally, empathy helps to develop the very humanizing virtue of forgiveness. If anyone has pesky, intrusive young siblings, it's easy to fly off the handle at them. But ask kids to get inside their skins, try to remember what it was like when you were their age–confused, feeling left out, not quite understanding, self-centered—in fact, lacking precisely the virtue we're exploring here—empathy. When a parent snaps or overreacts, the other parent ought to ask kids to see their reactions from the inside, rather than just from their own (quite limited) point of view. Some day, you'll probably be a parent yourself. How would you act differently? Or would you?

Many people sneer that empathy is a "sucker" virtue, and perhaps it is. Yet all of us want to believe our lives are in some way useful. Yet to be useful, we have to be used.

A Dilemma

Think of someone you can't stand, someone the very thought of whom makes you wince. Now, close your eyes and imagine it's the time of a full moon and, like Wolfman, you're slowly, slowly turning into that person. Your face is gradually transforming into his (or her) face, the skin, the cheekbones, the eyes and nose and mouth. Your body is elongating (or shrinking) into the exact shape of his body. Feel what it's like inside there. Feel the heart thumping, the pulse, the tension in the muscles. In your imagination, hunch the shoulders inside that new skin. Try to feel at home, at least physically, inside that other person.

Roam the innermost pathways of that person's thoughts. How do you guess he relates to his family, to his pals (if he has any), to work, to "the crowd"? What would you imagine could genuinely *hurt* him? What would you imagine would give him a sincere thrill? (Don't simplify. Like an actor preparing for a role, you are trying to inhabit a character, not be a caricature.) Where is this person "coming from?"

Now think of a single time when that person has ticked you off, by what he said or did—or didn't say or do. Relive the situation as if you were the perpetrator. Why did he/you act that way? Try to "feel" the twistings, the hurt, the ego bruises that made him lash out—or sneer at, or ignore, or demean "you?" Is it possible that, at least in that person's mind (which you now inhabit), there was some firmly felt justification for it? (Remember, you're not looking at and feeling this situation from the point of view of your own hurt feelings, but his.)

Rest there awhile. Feel what he (or she) feels about "you."

Now what?

A Conversation About Empathy

What's your reaction to the following statements?

A = Agree; ? = Uncertain; D = Disagree.

1.   Open-hearted hospitality is more important than "unbothered" security. A ? D

2.   Bookish people are uninteresting to people with more important concerns. A ? D

3.   Those who have never suffered are the most boring people in the world. A ? D

4.   Women should be allowed into combat and given combat pay. A ? D

5.   The only emotion allowed to real men is anger. A ? D

6.   Locking oneself inside a Walkman blocks out most of life. A ? D

7.   I honestly believe my actions demonstrate that I'm a caring person. A ? D

8.   Most often when you trust others, they will reward your trust. A ? D

9.   Better a live slave than a dead hero/heroine. A ? D

10. People who beg on the street brought their situation on themselves. A ? D

Help me understand what you understand by any of these statements.

1. "I was frightened to death, but I wanted to be useful."

2. "Anyone who has gone through suffering is bound to have greater understanding."

3. "If we are to live together, we have to talk."

4. "One must never, for whatever reason, turn his back on life."

5. "If you can't feel pain, you're not going to be able to feel anything else."

6. "Empathy, sympathy, compassion" are all "victim" words.

7. If you never let yourself be taken in, you'll never see the inside of anything.

8. To avoid that one "scorching," we give up nine potential friends.

9. You can't crusade for all causes, but a person of character has to choose one.

10. "Coward, take my coward's hand."

Questions

 Let's talk about the author's experience with his class and *Ordinary People*. Were you ever really moved by a movie to the point of getting quietly choked up? Is that something anybody should be sort of "ashamed" of? When you turn the pages of a tabloid newspaper, what's your honest reaction to "Mother Kills Baby and Leaves It in Dumpster" or "Drive-by Shootists Slay Six"? Does it shock you in the slightest way? Do you think that lack of reaction is a necessary shield in a world filled with too many shocks? There's a trade-off there, though. What do those Teflon defenses cost us?

 What about the panhandler mentioned earlier? You've certainly had that happen to you, right? I suppose most of us dribble out a few coins once in a while (to get away from being cornered). But forming a personal sense of character doesn't happen on the spot, when your reactions are more or less instinctive. It happens in times like this, when you're able to think calmly and more clearly. Try to tell me what your personal "policy" ought to be in dealing with down-and-out people who ask for money. The question of a single beggar in an hour or so is one thing. But what about the second and third?

There are all kinds of crusades out there. You don't have enough (allowance/salary) to help all of them, or even a few. But let's make a list of all we can come up with and see which *one* you could give, say, the price of a movie ticket to once a month. For starters, there are those children going blind or starving, AIDS victims—and especially their babies, the homeless, cancer research, and so forth. If you can just pick one and do something about it, the problem becomes less overwhelming and you don't feel helpless anymore.

Finally, think for a minute. Is there anyone you really ought to forgive? It's pretty useless—in fact, damaging—to carry around a grudge for very long. It doesn't inflict any punishment on the person who hurt you. Only on you. How could you get rid of it?

Kindness

Empathy Makes Your Heart Reach Out. Kindness Uses Your Hands

The unfortunate need people who will be kind to them. The prosperous need people to whom to be kind.
—*Aristotle*

Honoria and Perfidia

 nce upon a time, long, long ago, when courtesy was not yet condescension, there lived an impoverished Count Carlos, whose lands had been ravaged by a religious war between two factions, neither of whom could have explained the principles for which they had fought.

The lack of living taxpayers left Carlos with monumental migraines. A widower, he had but one daughter, Honoria, beloved of the village because of her wondrous skills in making creams and potions for all their ills. But she was painfully plain, not easily foisted off in marriage on some noble with ready cash. Despite her healing skills, even rich hypochondriacs were uninterested.

But Honoria's value became inconsequential upon the Count's own marriage to the outrageously wealthy Dona Peligrosa, whose late husband had supplied arms to both sides in the recent hostilities. She captivated Carlos, as did her ravishing daughter, Perfidia.

After a few months, Honoria realized how embarrassing she was, so she asked leave to depart, to find her way in the world. The Count waved her on her way, and Peligrosa cheerily ordered her a sack with brown bread and hard cheese, lest the girl perish too soon.

Honoria roamed the dark forest, hoping to find a castle and employment. As the day waned, she found herself hemmed in by briars and was about to turn back when she spied a small well. Weary and thirsty, she pushed her way toward it and opened her sack of simple food. About to take a bite out of her hard cheese, she heard a swish in the well, and out popped the head of a monk, fringed with ginger hair, smiling on the wavelets his arrival had produced.

"Good heavens!" Honoria cried. But the friar's smile was so sweet she had to stifle a grin.

"Sure an' forgive me, m'lady," the head said. "I am Friar Dwyer, decapitated on a pilgrimage from Ireland, therefore perhaps," he blushed, "a martyr. Depending on who won."

"I have no idea," Honoria said. "I think it was a tie."

"Oh," the Friar said, distracted by the bread in her hand.

"I have plenty," she said and popped a morsel of bread into his bobbing mouth.

"Ah," the friar said, "something besides moss and bugs! I pray you never go hungry."

Suddenly another head bobbed up, wrinkled as an albino prune, grinning, with the brightest gold hair she had ever seen.

"My goodness!" she giggled. "Is this a graveyard, then?"

"Oh, no, lady," said the head. "Alfiero the Miniero. Zee Friar an' I, we are on opposite sides of zee recent . . . *conflicto*. So I see he eez Friar, so my enemy, no? So I of course lops off 'ees 'ead and drops eet een ziss well."

"Fine clean blow, Alfiero, me lad," the monk said, "for which I'm grateful."

"Zen comes Romero zee Jardiniero, an' 'e lops off *my* 'ead." He winced and twisted.

"Is there anything wrong?" asked Honoria.

"Zee *gold* in my 'air, señorita. Come straight from mine, and zee wet in my 'air makes it *mucho* 'eavy, like a weeg of nettles."

"Can I comb it out for you?" asked Honoria.

"Oh, miss, take a 'ead in yer lap? Not for a lady."

Honoria lifted the dripping head from the pool and reached into her sack for her comb.

Alfiero purred, "Ah, my lady, keep zat devil gold. An' I pray eet never run out on you."

Just then still another head popped out of the pool.

"Well now, my lady," smiled Friar Dwyer, "this is our other friend, Romero the Jardiniero. He, uh, from the purest of intentions, slew our friend Alfiero the Miniero here, and in turn—"

"—was *hacked* by some *stable* boy," Romero huffed, "not for the *cause* but for my *shoes*! And I was only on my way to have my *beard* trimmed. It's probably down to my knees now. If I still *had* knees. Distressing."

"I'll trim it," she said, fetching a scissors from her sack.

"Oh, *would* you? I'd be *ever* so grateful."

So, carefully floating Alfiero's head back, she lifted out Romero's head and snipped his beard in half and rounded the edges nicely.

"Oh, my *lady*," Romero said as she laid his head back, "may your cheeks bloom with *roses,* your breath with *lilac*, and your hair curl like *hyacinth*. And may you wed into *royalty*."

Honoria's dishpan hands flew to her unlovely cheeks. There was something happening to her skin, her whole body. She peered into the pond and saw a lovely young girl gaping back.

"*There!*" said Romero. "Lovely without, as lovely within."

So, grinning, the three ducked under the water. And Honoria found her way to the capital city. With Alfiero's gold, she set up a small shop where, with the help of a poor boy named Pepe, she began to sell the potions and possets she had made for her father's people all her life.

Soon, her business was thriving. Then one day, a handsome young man in richly made clothes stumbled in, clenching his jaw, hardly able to see with the pain in his tooth. Honoria sat him down and reached for a bottle. "Drink this," she said, "to deaden it," and the young man complied. "That will have to come out. Pepe, the pincers." And in a wink, out she popped his tooth. The prince (for so, of course, he was) opened his eyes. "I . . . it's all gone! And I didn't feel a thing! And you're . . . you're the loveliest thing I have ever seen. Ever."

Well, to curtail an overly long narrative, Prince Felipe and Honoria fell instantaneously and deliriously in love and were quickly married in sumptuous splendor.

Her new royal family was eager to meet Honoria's father, so with great pomp a whole entourage showed up outside Count Carlos's gate for a surprise visit. Peligrosa and Perfidia ransacked their closets like invading Vandals trying to one-up the opulent, mysterious princess. Imagine their consternation when they found she was their very own belittled Honoria! And imagine their envy when they heard of the three saints who had prayed she might never go hungry or need gold and have both beauty and a royal spouse. The two women huddled in the kitchen.

"You go into that woods," Peligrosa rasped, "and find those three saints. Don't come back till you're promised at least an emperor. Someone to put that proud minx in her place."

"But how will I *know* these saints?" Perfidia scowled back.

"You've seen their pictures in church. Big gold plates nailed to the backs of their heads. Wait. Take this basket. Sandwiches and a bottle of your stepfather's finest Malaga wine."

So off Perfidia went, fuming at having to walk, and found the bushes blocking her way. Clothes shredded, she finally slumped at the well to wash her cuts. She was in one foul mood.

Up bobbed the head of Friar Dwyer, smiling, and Perfidia recoiled. "God in *heaven!*" she screeched and bopped his head with her stepfather's finest Malaga wine. "I'm looking for *saints*."

Friar Dwyer scowled. "Any saints down there?" he hollered, and instantly the heads of Alfiero and Romero popped up and received each his own bop with the bottle.

Friar Dwyer whispered, "May your breath smell like onions and anchovies. And sulfur."

"And your hair will fall out," whispered Alfiero the Miniero.

"Till a good—*very* poor—man loves you," gloated Romero the Jardiniero.

And they were gone.

Perfidia shrieked. Her golden hair cascaded onto her ragged shoulders! She ripped her ruined skirt and tied it round her shining pate and tried to wash her foul mouth in the well. Finally, she rose unsteadily and made her way to the thorny barrier, shaking with fear.

Days later, heartsore from begging of people who fled her appalling breath, she sank down outside a small shop, and wept. Suddenly, she heard a soft voice beside her. "What is it, miss? What's—?" The person sniffed. "Oh, I see."

"I'm sorry," Perfidia scrubbed at her tears. "I'll leave."

She looked up and saw a homely young man in a soiled apron. "I'm Pepe," he smiled shyly. "The apothecary. Wait there."

He returned with a green bottle and a bowl. "Rinse your mouth," he said. Suddenly her breath felt fresh again. Squatting with a basin of water, Pepe said, "Let me wash your face. Such a pretty face." And so exhausted was Perfidia she endured his kindness. "Now, your hair."

"*No!*" Perfidia cried. "You've done enough. Why do you trouble with a wretch like me?"

"I'm a wretch, too, miss. And it really is such lovely yellow hair."

"Oh!" growled Perfidia. "I see. All this—this *kindness* was to mock my bald head!"

"Oh, no, miss," Pepe said. "See your reflection in the bottle."

Perfidia snatched the bottle and stared. Her fingers flew to twist the blonde curls. Tears puddled in her eyes, and she stared through them at the simple face of young Pepe. "Oh, Pepe," she murmured. "Oh, Pepe!" And she buried her face in his slender shoulder and wept.

No need to say more. The rest is very dull. And wonderful.

Mother Hale

 very year, at least 5,000 infants are born in the U.S. to mothers addicted to heroin, methadone, cocaine and other hard drugs— more than half of them in metropolitan New York City alone. Through no choice of their own, these babies are born with a savage craving for crack from the very first instant they breathe. Whether the mother seeks help with her addiction or not, the infant goes through the same agony of withdrawal as a long-time addict: weeks of diarrhea, vomiting, terrifying images, twisting in torment, red-faced and screaming, often manifesting their need for drugs by inflicting bloody scratches on their bodies and crying inconsolably.

In the 23 years between 1969 and her death at age 87 in 1993, Clara Hale saved 500 of these babies. Everyone who knew her called her "Mother Hale." And rightly so.

In 1923, after graduation from high school, Clara Hale and her husband, Thomas, moved from Philadelphia to Harlem. He ran a floor-waxing business; she cleaned movie theaters after the last show so she could spend her days with their growing family; Lorraine, born in 1926, Nathan in 1927, and Kenneth, adopted in 1929. She had been no stranger to hard work or bad breaks. Her father was murdered when she was an infant, and her mother supported the family by taking in boarders and cooking for longshoremen. Her mother, she said, gave her "the foundation of all I've done: to love people, to be proud of myself, and always to look people in the eyes."

Thomas died of cancer in 1932 when Clara was only 27, leaving her with little money and three children under age six. For several years, she supplemented her income from theater cleaning by cleaning people's apartments during the day. But reluctant to leave her own youngsters, she started baby-sitting working mothers' children for two dollars a week each, then she kept children the whole week for mothers who were live-in maids, and she eventually became a licensed foster mother.

For 27 years, her five-room walk-up apartment on West 146th Street was home for seven or eight foster children at a time. "I didn't make a whole lot," she said, "but I wasn't starving. And the kids must've liked it because once they got there, they didn't want to go home. My daughter says she was almost 16 before she realized all those other kids weren't her real sisters and brothers. I took care of 40 of them like that. They're now all grown up. They're doctors, lawyers, everything. Almost all of them stay in touch. And now I have about sixty 'grandchildren.'"

In 1968, at the age of 63, Clara Hale thought it was time for her to "just kinda take it easy." But a year later, her daughter, Lorraine, who had attained a Ph.D. in child development, was driving along 146th Street and noticed a drug-addicted woman sitting on a crate, nodding in a stupor with her two-month-old baby about to slip out of her arms. Impulsively, Lorraine stopped, jumped out of the car, roused the woman and gave her Clara's address as a place "where you can get your baby help." Next morning, Clara called Lorraine and said, "There's a junkie at my door, and she says you sent her." Mother Hale took the baby, and soon a steady stream of addicted babies found their way to her door. "Before I knew it, every pregnant addict in Harlem knew about the crazy lady who would give her baby a home."

Within two months, she was caring for 22 addicted babies, packed wall-to-wall in cribs in her five-room apartment. Working overtime or at two jobs, Mother Hale's three children provided the sole financial support for a year and a half, until Percy Sutton, then Manhattan Borough president, persuaded the city, state, and federal governments to undertake the costs. Additional funds came from individuals such as singers Lena Horne and Tony Bennett. John Lennon gave Mother Hale $30,000 and his widow, Yoko Ono, continued to send her $20,000 annually after Lennon's murder in 1979.

The treatment was hardly complicated. "We hold them and touch them. They love you to tell them how great they are, how good they are. Somehow, even at the young age, they understand that. They're happy, and they turn out well." Until the week she died, Mother Hale awoke each morning to give six o'clock bottles to the addicted infants who shared her room. She cleaned up their vomit, changed their diapers, fed them lunch and dinner, napped when they did. When they cried out in the torment of withdrawal, she walked the floor with them, talked, sang. But she gave them no medicine, not even aspirin. "I don't want them to get in any habits, so they go cold turkey." She cuddled them, rocked them, cooed to them, knowing that "one day they'll smile at me." Ninety percent of her children recovered, and if their mothers successfully completed drug rehabilitation, most returned to them, both better for the excruciating experience.

Percy Sutton also began the search for a house that would suit Mother Hale's escalating needs and found a vacant five-story brownstone at 154 West 122nd Street, which was gutted and rebuilt with a federal grant. It opened as Hale House in 1975, only six years after that first addicted mother showed up at Mother Hale's door. The first floor has a playroom for pre-school activities, a kitchen, a dining room covered with mirrors. "I want my kids," she said, "when they pass by those mirrors to see themselves and say to themselves that they look nice." The second floor has a nursery for detoxified babies, usually about ten days old, who, during their period of withdrawal, stayed with Mother Hale in her third-floor bedroom before moving downstairs.

After weeks—or even months—of withdrawal, when the infants could sleep through the night, they moved from Mother Hale's bedroom to the floor below, where trained child-care workers watch over them until their mothers can take them home. Older children share rooms on the fourth floor. While they undergo rehab, usually for 18 months, mothers must visit their babies regularly. The aim is to reunite mothers and children, and of the 500 children who lived in Hale House during Mother Hale's life, only 12 were offered for adoption. Mother Hale stoutly maintained all her life: "This is not an orphanage."

Before her death, Hale House expanded to include housing and education for mothers after detox, apprentice training for children beginning to get into trouble, and a home for mothers and infants infected with AIDS. Those born with AIDS faced a drastically shortened life of suffering, which Mother Hale and her helpers vowed to make as easy as they could make it.

Lorraine took over administration of Hale House, leaving her mother free to deal directly with the children. There were several child-care workers and three sleep-in aides to spell her in her job, which was, she said, "just to love the children." Other staff members today include a house parent, a social worker, a teacher, a cook, and a maintenance worker. A part-time health staff provides medical and dental care along with a local clinic. At the beginning, the staff worked for only about $175 a week.

Mother Hale's generosity was not limited to children. Her daughter told a reporter, "Anybody can come to my mother for a handout, and she'll give it. She gets paid a salary, and she gives it all away. We finally got her to open a checking account at the age of 76. Every month, I write 30 envelopes to different causes she supports."

President Ronald Reagan invited Mother Hale to attend his State of the Union address to Congress on February 6, 1985. "When the president called, I was sick, but I went anyway. I wanted the kids to see and know it. The doctor said I shouldn't travel, because I might have a stroke. But I told him, when the president calls, I go." She was seated in the visitors' gallery of the House of Representatives when President Reagan looked up and hailed her as "an angel . . . a true American hero." Everyone present—senators, representatives, members of the Supreme Court, and the cabinet—rose to their feet in a standing ovation.

"Everyone comes into this world to do something, and I found what I was meant to do. I love children, and I love caring for them," she said. "I'm not an American hero. I'm simply a person who loves children."

Empathy makes your *heart* reach out. Kindness uses your *hands*.

Reaching Out

he *first week of September, 1997,* everyone's life overflowed with pictures of a serenely beautiful young woman unselfconsciously kneeling at the feet of AIDS patients, or wrapping her arms comfortably around a little Bosnian girl whose legs had been blown off by a land mine, or cradling a dark baby gazing up in awe at her flawless white face. There were also pictures of a tiny, wrinkled old nun, her face radiating tranquility, doing essentially the same things—cuddling infants, consoling lepers, easing the final journey of the dying.

There couldn't have been two more different faces, the one youthful and satin-skinned, the other age worn and leathery as a purse. Their backgrounds could not have been more different—the one a woman of rank and privilege—the other a woman who had vowed away all money to care for lepers in the gutters of Calcutta. Yet each shared that physical and psychological ease with broken bodies and spirits, each radiated a glow of genuine caring that touched hearts all over the world and made them genuinely mourn the two women's deaths that occurred within the same week. And I found myself saying, "What a wonderful aura unaffected kindness gives to a face."

Charity and courtesy can be faked; kindness can't. Witness the contrast between idly (or grimly) dropping a coin in a beggar's cup or a waiter's smarmy fawning and the natural, motherly ease of Princess

Diana of Wales and Mother Teresa of Calcutta—caressing hurt children, whose eyes show the awed acceptance of such kindness.

Whenever I ask students what makes "a really good friend," they often answer that a good friend is someone you can count on to "be there" when you're in need. That's pretty vague. When you're in pain, confused, hurt, lost, the walls of your room are "there," but they are not very heartening. Your old faithful dog could "be there," too, and she might even whimper in empathy, but she's no real consolation. When a good friend is "there" for you, it means you can *feel* their empathy, even if they can't "solve" your problem with words. At a wake, for instance, when there is nothing anyone can say to make the pain of loss go away, a friend can only put his or her arms around you, and that touch says, "I'm here with you. I don't know what to do either. But you're not alone." But families or friends who have a barrier against touch and tears will find their lives far more difficult than will families who are more comfortable with physical vulnerability.

Touch Is a Touchy Subject

Touch seems much easier for girls than for boys, and certainly easier for mature women than for men. Surely part of the reason is from *nurture*, from the way we're brought up. People just "expect" young girls to be more caring, to play with dolls like little mothers, to grow up to be nurses or teachers. They also accept the male stereotype that boys never cry, never show tenderness, and surely never, never touch anyone, especially another male. It's OK to have a huge "group hug" when you've scored the winning goal, but in any other situation . . . well, you don't want to give anybody the idea you're queer, right? There also seems some unwritten law that, when a boy gets into the later years of grade school, fathers have to stop touching them. And even if a genuinely loving father wants to show real physical affection for his sons, the sons repel it. Again, it's OK to roughhouse, but not to caress.

They are stifling stereotypes, smothering girls' human impulse to challenge and boys' human impulse to share compassion—but neither is likely to go away. All one hopes is that some adult mentor can convince young people how truly stupid and impoverishing these stereotypes are.

But another reason females are more comfortable with touch roots itself, I think, in *nature*, from the physical way we are made. Psychologists believe that, because girls grow up (usually) with a person of their own sex, they define themselves and acceptable behavior by bonding with their mothers, while boys who grow up (usually) with a person of the opposite sex define themselves and acceptable behavior by separation from the mother, setting up psychological and physical ego boundaries. Also, they find that, even before stereotypes can be drummed into them by media and peers, little girls who build scenes with blocks and human figures will build—almost exclusively—warm, inclusive interiors with welcoming doorways. In contrast, little boys—almost exclusively— build exteriors with turrets and defensive battlements, and ruins usually occur only in boys' play. Girls seem by nature to be more inclusive; boys seem to be more resistant to enclosure.

Boys and Girls: Equal, But Not the Same

The only outward difference between males and females is their genitals, girls with interior genitals and boys with exterior genitals. Other than that, females and males are absolutely equal and deserve equal treatment. But although they're equal, they are not the same, any more than a cow is a bull or a mare is a stallion. Both males and females are intelligent beings, but they are also embodied beings, and the body does have an effect on one's psychology, one's attitudes, one's view of the self and the world. Skin color, loss of a limb, a wasting disease have a stunning impact on the mind and soul, but they do not make us less human. Often, in fact, they have precisely the opposite effect. But the body does alter a person's viewpoint.

The same, I think, must be true of our physical sexual differences. I cannot help but think that, by nature and not by custom, females and males view life from different angles—not unequal, mind you, just different. I cannot believe there is not a marked psychological difference between a person who has accustomed herself to the monthly bleeding of menstruation and a male who has not. There must be a difference in her sensitivity to pain and to her compassion for others who undergo suffering. This does not mean only women would make good nurses, but it does imply they might be naturally better at it—and perhaps better at being doctors, too. Further, I believe a woman who has actually conceived, carried, nursed, cared for, cleaned, fed, and coddled even a single child is profoundly affected by those experiences, and is sensitized in a way no male—no matter how well-intentioned—could ever be. All women don't react to either menstruation or to childbearing in the same way—but no *man* has ever had even the opportunity.

There are probably some females reading these pages who do, in fact, need a bit of "softening up," putting *down* their defenses against open-heartedness, open-handedness, reaching out to touch someone in need. But my educated hunch tells me there are far, far more males who need it. The women's movement has made giant strides in convincing males that the sexual stereotypes are not only insulting to women but are also psychologically impoverishing to men. More men nowadays share tasks more simple-minded ages restricted exclusively to females (if not slaves): cooking, cleaning, diapering, and so forth. It's now a staple of advertisements to see a hunk with his infant asleep on his bare chest. And every male should be grateful for that liberation to be a fully human being—and fully male.

But what would be a "typical" father's response to his son's shame-faced admission that he had gotten his girlfriend pregnant? (a) Rail and curse, threaten, abuse; (b) offer "the" answer: "This is what we're going to do, young man," (c) collapse into a swamp of self-recrimination: "How have I failed?" or (d) put his arms around his son and grieve with him. This is the test of genuine love: "For the moment, your shame is more important than the shame you've brought on me." To repeat, the family who is uncomfortable with touch will have a harder time facing life.

Often, the only way to elicit a sense of fellow-feeling strong enough to overcome our fear of reaching out is to generate situations that will make people *feel* their lack of it and how mean-spirited and impoverished their lives are without it. I start off a class on prejudice asking someone to describe Archie Bunker (a ploy that probably won't work for very many more years). They wade in gleefully, talking about Archie's impregnable bigotry, certitudes about Blacks, Poles, "Cat'licks" and Jews, based on pure hearsay without a shred of objective evidence. We can laugh at Archie because we like to consider ourselves open-minded, believing in "live-and-let-live."

Then I snap the trap. OK, then what about fat, pimply girls with glasses at a dance? Are you open-minded about them? Unprejudiced? (Snickers.) How about boys who are not athletic? Did you ever think of saying, "You mind if I show you how you can throw that better"? (Embarrassed shrugs.) Then the kicker: How about ho-mo-sex-u-als? (Cold, stiff-faced silence.) "If you're looking for a bigot, don't turn around. One's sitting inside your head."

I admit I was exactly the same at their age. I came home one day in my senior year, and my mother informed me I was escorting Sylvia Smith to her senior prom. Sylvie lived in the neighborhood; I'd gone to grade school with her. She was pale as a peeled potato, with frizzy red hair and granny glasses, and there wasn't a curve on her body that I could discern. So of course I informed my mother I was most certainly *not* going to squire Sylvie to her ball.

A flashback: my mother was a woman who, when I skipped a piano lesson to go to the Saturday kids' matinee (two features, two serials, cartoons), appeared in the back of the packed theater hollering, "Where are you, Bill O'Malley? I know you're there." Then, muttering about spending good money on those lessons, she strode down the aisle, into the row, and hauled me out by the ear in front of 500 hooting kids out into the harsh light of reality.

Thus, it goes without saying that I did, indeed, escort Sylvie to her ball.

By now the students are really guffawing: "Ol' Hotshot O'Malley!" And it got worse. I didn't have my night driving license. So my *Dad* had to drive us. (Belly laughs.) And it got worse. We got there on *time* so we were—desolately—alone together. I tried every conversational ploy I could think of, just short of the causes of World War I. Nothing. And it got worse. My *pals* started to arrive, elbowing one another, snickering. Besides all that, I am one world-class dancer; Sylvie, alas, was not. The shine was gone from my shoes within minutes. So about 11:30 p.m. I said, "Well, it's getting late," and I called my Dad and took her home.

My students are rolling in the aisles. Then I say, very quietly, "What a selfish son of a bitch I was."

Dead silence. Suddenly, they *feel* it. They understand.

It was her first date, her first formal dress, her first night out from a very rigid family. And for three hours, I had thought of nothing but myself. The kids are really with me now. Because they've been there themselves. What would happen, I ask, if you went up to an unattractive girl and asked her to dance? What would it take—15 minutes of your life? And she'd go home thinking, "Hey, maybe I'm *not* Miss Godzilla after all!"

After all these years, I can anticipate their objections: she'd think it was a trick, condescending; my pals would think I was an idiot; she'd become a leech on the phone all the time. All of which misses the point: you'd have made someone happy. You'd have been kind.

We have enormous power to give life or give living death, but most of us are unaware of the effect we can have on other people by our kindness or by our cutting remarks. This lesson doesn't have the same effect on students as Helen Keller's encounter with the pump, when her whole idea of life exploded, but it is a definite crack in their defenses.

Another more obvious, protracted, and long-lasting lesson in empathy and confidence is a service project. Many students hate it —that is, fear it—but no one short of a sociopath can spend an hour a week— needed by an impaired child, reading to a blind person, trying to make a nursing home resident smile—without growing as "a good person." As we saw, empathy and kindness—honestly feeling for others and reaching out to them, makes *both* people richer.

In Kurt Vonnegut's *God Bless You, Mr. Rosewater*, a woman asks a gentle, generous eccentric to give her child a commandment to live by, and he says, "There's only one commandment: Goddammit you've got to be kind."

A Dilemma

"Hey, Ted, mind if I sit down and watch practice with you? How's the leg?"

"Sure. Go ahead. Doctor says the cast comes off next week. But I gotta wait another week more before I can practice."

"Mind if I ask you a question?"

"Shoot."

"Yesterday I asked Pete Henderson to be editor-in-chief of the yearbook."

"Oh. Yeah."

"Now people are telling me the seniors don't like him."

"Yeah. He's a d--k."

"Huh? I mean, I know what a d--k is, but why is he one? He seems like a nice guy, smart, willing to work."

"He's just a d--k. He's been a d--k since sophomore year."

"But—but can't somebody *change* in two years?"

"I dunno. I haven't had anything to do with him in two years."

A Conversation About Kindness

What's your reaction to the following statements?

A = Agree; ? = Uncertain; D = Disagree.

1. "The prosperous need people to whom to be kind." A ? D

2. Being hurt is an invitation to learn compassion, fellow-feeling. A ? D

3. I can genuinely understand what motivated Mother Hale's life and envy it. A ? D

4. President Reagan "used" Mother Hale, but she was willing to be used. A ? D

5. Males who easily hug male friends are quite likely gay. A ? D

6. Extraordinarily athletic females are quite likely "butch." A ? D

7. By their very nature, boys are more analytical and girls more intuitive. A ? D

8. Female (physical) sexuality might make them more naturally compassionate. A ? D

9. The author's criticism of himself over Sylvie is an overdone guilt-trip. A ? D

10. When a friend is hurt, sometimes touch is the only way to ease their pain. A ? D

Help me understand what you understand by any of these statements.

1. Empathy makes your heart reach out. Kindness uses your hands.

2. Charity and courtesy can be faked; kindness can't.

3. Just to "be there" for a friend is not enough.

4. Families uncomfortable with touch will have a harder time than those able to be vulnerable.

5. "For the moment, your shame is more important than the shame you've brought on me."

6. Sexual stereotypes are truly stupid and impoverishing.

7. The body does have an effect on one's psychology, attitudes, views of the world.

8. We have enormous power to give life or give living death.

9. Honestly working at a service project can't help but make one a better person.

10. "There's only one commandment: Godammit, you've got to be kind."

Questions

 Touch is a touchy subject. Can you think of a single good reason why, at a certain age, fathers should stop touching their sons offhandedly and sons should resent it when they do? Teachers are another matter, especially with so many shocking stories of teachers (in all kinds of combinations) abusing their trusted positions. On the other hand, there are also painful stories of teachers wrongly accused of sexual advances by overly sensitized students who mistook a casual touch for something aggressive. This is a tough one. Does it help to see such moments in the light of everything else you know about such a teacher? Or is every kind of casual touch reason for quick judgment and possibly a lawsuit? Is our safest recourse always to presume the worst?

Sexual stereotypes die hard. If you were a parent and your son came home and asked to take ballet lessons or your daughter informed you she was going to become a fighter pilot, would you have cardiac arrest? Why? Should a boy be "ashamed" that he writes poetry or a girl that she's a better baseball player than her brothers? Why? Would everybody be shocked if a girl went up to a boy and asked him to dance? Why? Could a boy think of his best male friend, somebody he'd risk bodily harm for, and say (even in the quiet of his own head where no one else could hear), "I love him?" Why?

Let's talk about the Sylvie story. The author didn't realize how selfish he'd been until years later. Would it have been unreasonable to expect him to have his later sensitivity when he was still a teenager? What were the things inside him that held him back in the actual situation? Do you feel the same hesitations about, say, talking to some lonely kid at lunch? How much does what other people think hold you back from being kind?

Responsibility

Shouldering Our Burdens

Responsibility, n. A detachable burden easily shifted to the shoulders of God, Fate, Fortune, Luck, or one's neighbor.
In the days of astrology, it was customary to unload it on a star.
—*Ambrose Bierce*

Rory

 nce upon a time, long, long ago, when everyone knew his neighbors, there lived a sprightly hunchback named Rory, jester to Duke Derek. Unfazed by the odd gift on his shoulder, Rory was a lad who made the most of what he had, coaxing out the many souls within his lute. No matter the mood, soon he had everyone dancing and laughing. Even the dour duke.

Many's the neck Rory saved merely by enthralling the duke with a tune after a death sentence and, when asked his reward, requested the man's head, unsevered. And every time Bedwyn the barber shaved their throats, they prayed for Rory a long and mischievous life.

One evening, Rory dined with Tancred the tailor and his dumpling wife, Trina. It got quite late, but the three sat, choking back "just one more" pint, howling at Rory's jokes and japes. "Here, Rory," Tancred howled, reaching for a fat trout, "a last morsel." And he slipped it into Rory's mouth just as Rory roared at his own last joke. The jaws clamped shut, and he swallowed.

His eyes flared, his cheeks reddened, and his wiry hands flew to his distended throat.

"There was no *bones* in that fish!" Trina shrilled. "I boned it meself!"

"Well, you can see there *was*, woman," Tancred snarled. "Now for the love of our necks, clap his back!" So the two belabored Rory's hump till he rolled beneath the table. "We've killed him," Tancred gasped. "The duke's favorite. We'll swing by tomorrow noon."

Trina's mouth pursed into her pudding cheeks. "Wait," she said. "Wrap him in the table cloth, and we'll carry him off to the doctor's house. Dump him at the door and just walk away."

So they did. When they reached the doctor's, a party squalled in the house above, so they crept up the stairs, thumped poor Rory at the door, and hightailed it off into the night.

In the din, the doctor thought he heard a knock, so, somewhat impaired by the ale, he flung open the door, sending poor Rory down the stairs, head knocking on each of the ten steps.

Instantly sobered, the doctor bustled down and listened for a heart-beat, no simple task, owing to the ringing in his own ears. No doubt. He had murdered some wretch left at his door. He parted the tablecloth, and his eyes ballooned. Rory the Jester! The apple of the duke's eye!

"What is it, Henry?" he heard from his wife Mavis overhead. "Why that looks like... Merciful God!" and her hand flew to her letter slot lips.

"Hush!" he snapped. "You'll have all the neighbors to witness. Grab his arms."

"What are we doing?" Mavis whispered hoarsely.

"We're taking him to the duke's. Bend over and sniff him."

"Ooof!" she spat. "He smells like a brewery latrine!"

"We haul him up the roof of the cookhouse and toss him off into the trash. He sneaked in, slipped off the roof, and broke his neck. I'll testify that when I'm summoned to take him away."

So the two humped down the lane to the river to the back of the duke's estate.

"We'll be shot for poachers," Mavis whined.

"Zip your lip," he snapped, "and get up on the cook house roof. I'll pass him up to you."

So with much grunting and splitting of seams, they manhandled the corpse onto the roof with a terrible thud, heaved him off, slithered down the thatch, and back for a much-needed drink.

Moments later, the cook peered out into the darkness, his bloodshot eyes narrowing. "Who's... there?" he whispered. "I have a fry pan here, and I'll brain you if—"

"Conrad," his wife bawled from bed, "come back in. It was just the cat."

"Hush, Cloris! I *heard* someone. Tinkers come to pilfer the duke's scraps."

At that moment, Rory's body, listing slightly on the precarious piles was spilled over by the fat-rumped cat which leaped from above onto his hump and off to the ground, spitting.

In an instant Conrad was upon him, wielding his frying pan. "Hiss at me, will you, you miserable thief!" And he belabored his head and shoulders with the pan—one, two, three.

"Conrad," Cloris whispered, peering muzzily, "did you get him?"

"I did indeed," he said smugly. "All right, man, up!"

But the white bundle did not move.

"Maybe he's—" Cloris whimpered.

"Nonsense. I hit him no harder than you always hit me."

The two stood open-mouthed.

"It's—" Cloris murmured.

"I *know* who it *is*!" Conrad snapped.

"Gate locked," she mewed. "So he climbs the house and falls. An' broke his head."

"Three times?" Conrad hissed. "The duke will say, 'Conrad, *you* done the deed. Now, get ready to keep him company. And your hornet-tempered wife, too!'"

"*I* didn't do nothing! And I am *not* hornet-tempered."

"We'll lug him to the tavern. Someone's clobbered there every night. Move, woman!"

So they hauled the body along the river to the tavern. Conrad signaled Cloris to help him hoist the body up into the lowest branches of the tree by the door. "Just set him loosely. He'll fall. That's how he died." And they skittered off into the night.

A moment later, Bedwyn the barber bade his pals goodnight and slammed out into the dark. Just enough to dislodge Rory from his perilous perch, crashing down on the barber's head.

Bedwyn leaped to his feet like a bantam rooster, fists cocked. "All right, you balmy fool," he croaked, and he belly-whumped his attacker through the tavern door and dumped him before his startled and tipsy companions.

Just then in strode the portly village bailiff. "Time for you boys to—what the devil …?"

The flap of tablecloth fell and revealed the duke's jester. The duke's favorite. The duke's treasure. The duke's darling. The last best hope of everyone in town.

"Well, then," the bailiff said, "Bedwyn, my lad. And I fear you'll dance in the air by noon."

Next morning the hapless barber faced Justice Waspish, a hawk-faced personage not given either to wasting time or second thoughts. When he had heard the barest details, he rose to his feet. "Call the hangman," he said and headed for the square, the whole village following.

At high noon, poor Bedwyn climbed the scaffold stairs, clutching his wretched bag of barber tools to his skinny chest, to remind the crowd of services he had done them all, trimming their beards and pulling their wretched teeth. But immobile Rory lay at Bedwyn's feet, like proof.

"Wait!" came a shout, and Conrad the cook lumbered forward, trembling. "I can't let an innocent die. *I* put Rory in the tree. He was in the trash. I only hit him a bit with a fry pan."

"Fine," said the justice. "Hang the cook!"

So the bailiff pulled the rope from Bedwyn, who collapsed in a heap, and he widened the noose for fat-necked Conrad.

"Wait!" came another cry, and the doctor pushed up the steps, trembling. "*I* dropped Rory off the cook's roof. I found him outside my door, and he went tumbling down the steps."

"Fine," said the justice again. "Hang the doctor!"

So the bailiff pulled the rope from Conrad's fat neck, and the man deflated down next to the barber. The bailiff tightened the rope and slipped it round the doctor's dewlaps.

"Wait!" came yet another holler, and Tancred the tailor elbowed up the stairs. "*I* killed Rory," he sobbed. "I shoved a piece of fish down his throat, and he choked on a bone."

"Fine," said the justice. "Hang the tailor!"

So the bailiff pulled the rope from the doctor's neck, and he fainted dead away next to Conrad and Bedwyn. And Rory. Then he looped the noose over Tancred's neck.

"Wait!" came yet another shout from the crowd, which was becoming a bit restive at the lack of closure in this little drama. But it was Duke Derek himself who pushed up onto the scaffold.

"They tell me," the duke growled, "my good jester Rory's been murdered. *And* they tell me four different men confessed." So Justice Waspish told him the whole pitiful tale.

The duke's fat face pinched in mourning. But suddenly he bent over and stared at the gaping corpse. "Quick," he snapped, "get me the barber's bag." So the bailiff hustled the bag over to him, and the duke poked in it and pulled out the long pliers Bedwyn used to pull back teeth. He inserted it into the open mouth and pulled back, beaming, holding up the fish bone.

Rory groaned and turned over. "Oh, my *head*!" he burbled.

"Yes," said the duke, straightening. "Every time the poor sot was almost conscious again, you idiots knocked him senseless again. The next time the bailiff finds a drunk, every pub will lock its doors for a month." And with the help of his four murderers, the duke took Rory home.

But at that moment, all those standing sheepishly about, including Justice Waspish himself, began to feel a powerful thirst, and the whole crowd headed as one for the tavern.

César Chávez

ne week it was lettuce. Next week it might be picking fruit— so much better than working with the short hoe that bent your backbone like a bow too tightly strung When he was only ten, César, his parents, and siblings woke every morning at 3:00 a.m. to meet the labor contractor whose bus rattled them along dusty roads to work the fields until 4:00 p.m., when they would rattle back to a one-room shack in a labor camp. One light bulb, no furniture, no water. In a week of 12-hour days, the family hoped to make $20, barely enough after the shack rental and food to bus them a hundred miles north to the next agricultural valley, following the crops. One thing you could be sure of—you could be sure of nothing.

César Estrada Chávez was born in Yuma, Arizona, on March 31, 1927. During the Depression, his father, Librado, ran a grocery store, an auto repair shop, and a poolroom 20 miles north of Yuma. César learned from his mother "never to turn away anyone who came for food, and there were a lot of ordinary people who could come and a lot of hobos, at any time of the day or night. Most of them were White." Yet in school many of the Anglo children called Chicanos "dirty Mexicans," mocked their accents, and took any chance to bully them.

Librado had overextended himself and, worse, gave credit to too many friends and relatives strapped for cash. The family was finally penniless, so in August 1937, the family crowded into their old car and headed for California in hope of work. Growers valued Mexican labor because they were docile, able to endure the fierce heat and backbreaking monotony of field work with the crippling short hoe, and eager to work—at any wage.

California was no paradise. Labor contractors often owned the camps where the migrants lived in tents or tar paper shacks, deducting workers' rent from their pay at exorbitant rates, charging inflated prices for supplies at the camp store. They recruited too many workers, then lowered the wage promised; charged Social Security, then pocketed it; assessed short weight on the workers' boxes, then kept the difference themselves.

In 1944, at age 17, César joined the Navy, but two years later was back in the fields, and in October 1948, he married Helen Fabela, with whom he had eight children. They settled in the Mexican barrio of San Jose, California, called Sal Si Puedes ("Get out if you can") where he finally found a more secure full-time job working in a lumber yard. And in Sal Si Puedes, César Chávez came face to face with his destiny.

The pastor of the barrio church was Fr. Thomas McDonnell, sent by the Archdiocese of San Francisco to work with farm laborers, visit the camps, minister to the workers' spiritual needs, and make them aware of Church teachings on social justice and labor. He gave César the papal encyclicals on labor, books on labor history, and Louis Fisher's *Life of Gandhi*. Chávez was so impressed by the life and work of that ascetic messiah of non-violent protest that he went on to read anything he could find about him. Gandhi preached of the need for complete sacrifice of oneself for others, of the need for self-discipline in order to achieve a higher goal than the self.

Another influence was Fred Ross, an organizer in San Jose for Saul Alinsky's Community Service Organization (CSO), established to help Mexican Americans organize and exert a unified pressure on the exploiters, to confront institutionalized power. The CSO focused on issues in the urban barrios: civil rights violations, voter registration, community action, education, housing. "As time went on, Fred became sort of my hero. I saw him organize, and I wanted to learn."

César began working full-time for Ross, at a salary of $50 a week. His job was first to get to know people and help with their needs, then to expect those he helped to become helpers themselves. "You must become a servant of the people. When you do, you can demand their commitment in return." From modest dues ($3.50 a month) in César's own newly established Farm Workers' Association (later the United Farm Workers), he and Helen set up a credit union from which members could borrow in emergencies, and Helen became its administrator, working out of the garage of their cheap rental home in Delano, California. He found his most important source of support from ordinary poor workers, not from the middle class, who were at best suspicious of him, and at worst branded him a communist for inciting unrest among the poor. His most potent means of calling attention to inhuman treatment were boycotts, marches, and political lobbying. Meanwhile, he was reading anything he could find on farm labor organization and came to a critical realization: Don't try to do two things at once; organize *before* you think of strikes.

Gradually, they were joined by others as single-mindedly dedicated as themselves, among them Rev. Jim Drake, a Protestant minister, and the woman destined to be his alter ego, Dolores Huerta, a housewife with small children, just completing a college degree, who was nothing like the stereotype of a Mexican mother. Dynamic, assertive, fast-talking, she became an indispensable lobbyist. César's cousin, Manuel, designed the Association's flag: a fierce black eagle symbolizing the workers' brutal situation, emerging from a white circle of hope, surrounded by a blood-red field signifying what justice would cost. Their motto: Sí, Se Puede (Yes, it can be done).

But not done easily. Members signed up, then lost interest, or courage, or the $3.50 for dues had to go to more pressing needs. Finally, César hit on a method of recruitment: hold a family barbecue, free, but sell enough beer to cover expenses—and sign up anyone who showed up. By 1964, the union had a thousand dues-paying members and more than 50 local chapters. The following year, FWA held its first successful strike against flower growers in McFarland and won a wage increase. Then, it held a strike in Porterville against outrageous rents, this one using college volunteers.

The critical moment came in early 1965, in Delano. Workers had been brought in from Mexico to work the vineyards even more cheaply than the local Filipino- and Mexican-Americans. Chávez called a meeting. The hall filled with Blacks, Puerto Ricans, Filipinos, Arabs, Anglos, Mexicans, shouting, "*Huelga*! Strike!" Picketers lined the roads outside vineyards, trying to cajole the scabs to join them instead of taking their jobs. Foremen raced pickups along the roads, choking picketers with dust, spraying them with pesticides. The police never intervened.

But picketers found the point beyond which no human could allow himself to be degraded. "When a man or woman takes a place on a picket line for even a day or two," Chávez said, "they will never be the same again. They have confirmed their humanity. Through non-violence, they have confirmed the humanity of others... We can turn the world, if we can do it non-violently. We will not let ourselves be provoked by our adversaries into behaving hatefully. We draw our strength from the very despair in which we have been forced to live. We shall endure."

César went to California college campuses to recruit volunteers, not with wild rhetoric but with sincerity, humility, and searingly objective facts about dehumanization. An NBC-TV special mounted by Fred Friendly and Edward R. Morrow, *Harvest of Shame*, focused the attention of the entire country on the farm workers' anguish. Walter Reuther, head of the United Auto Workers, pledged his support. Chávez organized a 250-mile march from Delano to the state capitol in Sacramento. Hundreds joined them along the way; by the time they reached Stockton, there were 5,000 people singing, chanting, waving. Then, in April, when news came that New York bartenders refused to sell Schenley products which were made from grapes picked by imported labor, the major employer gave way and agreed to a contract with the UFW.

But in the late '60s, America had become a snake pit of resentments—over the Vietnam War, racial injustice, the government's toadying up to vested interests. Governor Ronald Reagan appeared on television urging viewers to ignore the boycott and support the growers. President Richard Nixon ordered the Defense Department to send two million pounds of grapes to Vietnam. The mood of violent response to injustice spread to the UFW, and Chávez had to go up and down picket lines taking weapons away from angry pickers. Finally, he declared publicly that he would begin a fast, as Gandhi had done, until his followers had firmly recommitted themselves to nonviolence. It lasted 25 days, and ended with a mass for 4,000 workers—and the national media. On July 20, 1970, 29 grape growers assembled near Delano to sign union contracts with the UFW, pledging a wage of $1.80 per hour plus ten cents an hour to the workers' health fund.

But when the UFW's table grape agreements came up for renegotiation in 1973, the growers signed with the Teamsters Union, prompting 10,000 farm workers in California's valleys to walk out of the fields in protest. César called for a worldwide wine and grape boycott and by 1975, a Harris poll showed 17 million American adults were honoring it. More than 15,000 people followed Chávez on a 110-mile march from San Francisco to the Gallo winery in Modesto, and in May, 1975 the California Agricultural Labor Relations Act was the first law governing farm labor in the continental U.S., and the dues-paying membership of UFW soared to 100,000.

During the 1980s, UFW produced a film called *The Wrath of Grapes*, with graphic footage of birth defects and high rates of cancer from pesticide poisonings among farm workers and consumers, more than with any other types of produce. In July of 1988, César began a fast in protest of pesticide use, during which he consumed only water. Dolores Huerta warned reporters, "This is a spiritual thing for him. This is not a publicity stunt." His fast lasted 36 days. Eugene Nelson described the kind of person who would do such a thing as "a man with a healthy sense of his own worth and with a corresponding intense drive to see that he and his kind are treated as equals; yet, he has a disarming simplicity, down-to-earthness, and interest in the ordinary things of life." He was an honest man, dedicated to his family and the community of farm workers, demanding equality, respect, and justice, especially for the poorest of them. Like other UFW officers and staff, he never made more than $5,000 a year.

"There has to be someone who is willing to do it," he said, "who is willing to take whatever risks are required. I don't think it can be done with money alone. The person has to be dedicated to the task …. I am convinced that the truest act of courage, the strongest act of humanity, is to sacrifice ourselves for others in a totally nonviolent struggle for justice. To be human is to suffer for others." Luis Solis-Garza put it well: "He had a fire inside him."

César Chávez died in his sleep April 23, 1993 at the age of 66. At his funeral in Delano a week later, 35,000 people from all over the world gathered to honor him. His 27 grandchildren went up to the coffin and laid on it a carving of the UFW eagle and a short-handled hoe.

Spine

icture a young man, apparently physically fit, being dragged along the street by a big sloppy dog and waving his cane helplessly in the air. "What's wrong with your legs?" you ask. "Nothing," he replies, "my parents gave me this cane to control the dog." You snicker, "Well, why don't you give him a thump on the rump and teach him how to behave, show him who's boss?" He shrugs sheepishly. "Well, uh, you see, I hate to curb his spirit."

That clumsy little parable describes each of us. The big sloppy dog is what Freud called the Id ("The Thing"), the beast in us that adults try patiently to convince us to control. The stick is the Superego ("The Over-Me"), all the rules and "no-no"s and norms imposed on us from our weaning days forward, taped unquestioned from parents—and equally unquestioned from the media. The purpose of adolescence is to assess, honestly, what elements in the Superego are valid (i.e., based on the objective nature of things) and what are not (i.e., "values" and taboos that have no foundation in the natures of things) Attitudes that aren't valid might include "Beware of Blacks; sex is just a recreational activity; money will make you happy; everybody on welfare cheats." Then the task is to take control of your Id-Beast into your own hands and decide for yourself what is dehumanizing and what is not.

"Spine" is what forms when someone does this; it's a solid column of reasoned principles that are our own and from which we will not deviate, no matter how scary the undeserved punishment nor how alluring the possible rewards. There is no doubt that commitment to a set of tested principles limits anyone's freedom. But if you're open to *any* suggestion, you're not really free at all, you're just a spineless fool being dragged along by a big, sloppy dog.

Freedom is a wonderful thing, but it's like money in your pocket, nice to know you have, but of absolutely no value until you give it up—commit it to something you want *more* than you want the money or the freedom. You can stand in front of five attractive options, with no outside intimidation whatever, free to take any one of them, but if you don't *commit* your freedom to one choice (and, at least for now, give up the other four), your freedom is useless and you just stand there, free and frozen.

Freedom and Discipline

The "Id-beast" is like fire, powerful, but without control it runs wild, burning up everything in its way. César Chávez said, "We must remember that the highest form of freedom carries with it the greatest measure of discipline." Freedom and discipline seem like total opposites, yet either one, without the other to balance it, is utterly dehumanizing.

A reminder about the difference between personality and character. Personality is a set of habits we developed before we were three, in response to parents and siblings: extrovert/introvert, rational/intuitive, etc. No personality type is better or worse than any other; each has its assets and liabilities. And because they are habits formed before we could make judgments, we are in no way responsible for their existence—though, as we shall see, we are responsible for what we do about those habits. Character *is* spine: a personally validated set of moral (human) principles. Unlike personality, however, character is hard-won. A person of character takes charge of his or her own Id-beast, honestly and without self-deception critiquing all the important dos and don'ts, and values imprinted on their Superegos by others. A person of character is in charge of his or her own angers, jealousies, moods—and is not their victim, much less their slave.

Blaming Faults on Our Personalities

Nor is a person of character a victim of his or her own reactive personality. "I was brought up to be reserved, not aggressive," "I'm impulsive, that's just the way I am," "I guess I'm just a procrastinator." All those self-serving statements seem to let the speaker off the hook, as if shyness or impetuosity or stalling on responsibilities were incurable diseases of which one is a victim, like a diabetic or epileptic. They blame their faults on their personalities, rather than blaming their personalities for their faults and changing their bad habits.

Moreover, we all have scars left on our souls by the mistakes of others: "My parents broke up; my mother's an alcoholic; my Dad died when I was four." All true, all tragic. And the speaker isn't responsible for what happened. What the speaker *is* responsible for is what he or she *builds* from the rubble others have left.

Making Excuses

There are more than a few ways of evading character, spine, commitment to being an autonomous human being. One is *scapegoating*, blaming everything on parents, the economy, skin color, unfair teachers and so on. But from now on, *I* take responsibility for what I've done wrong. "I am what I've done, and who I am makes no excuses."

Another rejection of responsible adulthood is *minimalism*, settling for getting by, avoiding punishment, cutting corners whenever you can get away with it. But anyone with aspirations to an adult self couldn't live with a self so cheap, contemptible and unworthy of respect.

Still another avoidance of maturity is *withdrawal*, believing that, because the world is unfair, the shrewdest ploy is to poke your head into the sand and let the rest of the world go by. But how does that blind tranquillity differ in any real way from being dead?

Playing a victim with no legitimate cause is, of course, cowardly. Marion Barry, mayor of Washington, DC, who was caught smoking crack with a prostitute in a hotel, said, "Bitch set me up!"

A father of a boy busted for drugs at the University of Virginia blamed the police for not investigating drugs at some *other* university. Dan White, who murdered the mayor of San Francisco, argued that he was a victim of temporary insanity brought on by eating junk food. Lawyers claim women who murder their children should be excused because of hormonal imbalances. A New York man threw himself in front of a subway train but, because the train stopped short, courts awarded him $650,000, because he was only maimed and not killed. Something is pretty wrong here, but commonplace. We hear too often, "Well, with parents like mine—" or "Nobody gives Blacks a break," or "If I weren't so short—" What will *you* build from the rubble?

In order to achieve character, to lay claim to an adult self, we have to develop a healthy relationship with guilt. Except in mentally unstable people, guilt is a very healthy attitude, if it is grounded in the facts. A lot of people consider themselves "innocent until proven guilty," innocent even in their *own* eyes. That is world-class self-deception. But as in the story of Rory's "murderers" in this chapter's folk tale, you can never be free until you face the truth, clear-eyed, submissive, honest.

Responsibility means being dependable, being someone others can count on, even when the chips are down. We all expect parents to be dependable, at home and at work, otherwise life is chaotic. But what's true of adults surely has to be true of anyone claiming to be a "becoming-adult," at home and at work. More and more, he or she has to acknowledge—and *own*—the obligations that being conceived, being born and being cared for by parents naturally impose on a person of honor. More and more, he or she has to begin taking on the same tasks they have always presumed the parents would "take care of"—cleaning, cooking, laundry, driving.

But shouldering responsibility is also necessary "at work," and for most youngsters "at work" means at school. Most students I've known who have A minds and C averages say they're lazy. Nobody's lazy, just unmotivated. If I told a class that Cindy Crawford and Brad Pitt were down in the cafeteria, I imagine most of them could overcome their inertia and amble down for a look. All you have to do is check a weekend dance to prove nobody's lazy, they just lack a convincing reason to do what they're asked to do.

The reason is that schooling for most students (except for the motivated ones) has no immediate payoffs. And the "stuff" you study doesn't even seem to have any payoff in the future! Do parents read poetry? Do future lawyers need physics? Does *anybody* get paid for doing verbal analogies? If anyone ever needs all that useless information, that's what *libraries* are for. Be honest, no one is ever going to use that "stuff." The point is not the "stuff" but what *processing* the stuff does to the nimbleness of one's thinking processes. Every subject is trying, with different data and different approaches, to teach students how to *reason*: how to gather, sift, outline, conclude, critique. It's what the mind is for.

Therefore, every time you fudge on honestly gathering the data, you lessen your attractiveness as a job candidate. Every time youngsters fake an outline, they weaken their skills at reasoning and thus their skills as decision makers. They'll almost surely get "some" job, but they'll be following orders, not making decisions. Every time they just check the grade and ignore the comments teachers make on papers, they resist growing up. Each compromise with their own inertia is trivial in itself, but if they get into the habit of selling out, it's a tough habit to break. Students believe some fairy godmother will show up in their college dorm, tap them with her magic wand and, ping! Discipline, drive, determination, and a dream! Good luck.

There are many solid motivations we can offer to overcome youthful "laziness" in the face of unpleasant work: fear of the cost ("My parents will *kill* me!"), hope of reward ("My grades will get me into Harvard."), family loyalty ("My parents support me to the tune of about 20 grand a year; I owe it to them."), future marriage and parenthood ("Do I want my spouse and kids to think I'm dumb?") But most important and fundamental is not the control of others but control of *oneself*: character, pride, "self-ownership."

Character means having the spine to challenge one's own inertia, moods, sluggishness. It means denying immediate gratification for a long-term goal: being an attractive job candidate and a capable spouse and parent. The TV, the guitar, the stereo, and the telephone all kill time, get us through, distract us, but they also sap our strength, like a natural athlete or musician too dulled to practice. It'll cost—big time— count on it.

One overcomes inertia and begins building character one… step… at a time. Aristotle said that you learn by doing. You learn responsibility by *acting* responsibly, just as you learn carpentry or art by starting small and stretching your abilities with constantly tougher challenges. That's how education differs from schooling: education keeps stretching one's reasoning powers with ever more complex data. But the data isn't the goal; the goal is stretching the mind.

Looking around a classroom at this point, I see a lot of grim faces that say, "Damn! The old fool's starting to make sense again, and I don't like it. When's the bell gonna ring so I can forget about all this? Why can't he just let me be a kid? Well, because I don't want to be treated like a kid anymore. But ... I'll pull myself together in college." Right.

The first step is to resolve that, yes, I have this inescapable obligation to make myself a learner, a decision maker—an obligation imposed by gratitude to my parents, by the expectations of my future employers, by the hopes of my future spouse and children. The next step is to make a schedule, a sheet with seven columns of 24-hour days, fill in all the inescapable things—sleep, meals, classes, practice, work, and most youngsters will probably find they have about 70 hours free! But most adults work a 40-hour week, while most students spend, say, 25 hours a week in class. That's 15 hours less work than a grown-up has (and all young people want to be treated as grown-ups). Guess where "they"—teachers—got the idea of assigning three hours' homework every day? The third step, of course, is to stick to the schedule.

But a motive beyond job and even beyond spouse and family is that each of us has only one "go 'round" in life. Each of us wants to make a difference, and yet (judging by people's choices) too many people are saying: "Oh, I'm nobody." But that's a self-fulfilling prophecy. If you *feel* like a nobody and *act* like a nobody, you'll *be* a nobody—treading water, treading water, treading water. And then you die.

César Chávez was a nobody, but he refused to act like one. So did Oprah Winfrey and Mother Hale. And they made a difference.

A Dilemma

"Look, girls. When you signed up at try outs, you signed a sheet. I've got it right here. It says, 'If I'm picked for the show, it will be my primary after school activity. I'll rearrange all my other activities, appointments, college visits, etc., around the play schedule, and I'll be there on time, lines memorized, ready to work. I consider this a commitment.' Then you signed your name. Your name's your *word*, girls. How good's your word?"

"But it's our senior *trip!*"

"One week before the show? How do I explain that to the kids who were dumb enough to change their plans for the only weekend rehearsal we have, the first time we put the whole show together? Are you being fair to them? Are you being honorable to them? You've had the schedule for six weeks. When did you find out about this senior trip?"

"Well … last September."

"So you gave me your word with no intention of keeping your word?"

"But we're only in the *chorus.*"

"But that's like saying, 'We're not important.' Don't you see I'm making all this fuss so you'll understand you *are* important? I could have said, 'Oh, well, they're not important. Let 'em go. Who cares?' But I do care, don't you understand that? More about your sense of honor and responsibility than I care about the show. Hell, it's my *85th show.*"

"What—what are you going to do?"

"I don't know. I'm so angry right now, I don't know what I'll do. Shall we ask the rest of the cast what I should do? What do you three think I ought to do?"

A Conversation About Responsibility

What's your reaction to the following statements?

A = Agree, ? = Uncertain, D = Disagree.

1. Someone who makes the mistake of getting drunk is responsible only for that. A ? D

2. César Chávez would have lived a happier life if he'd found another line of work. A ? D

3. There is no such thing as an unjust profit. A ? D

4. The only ground for moral choices rests with oneself and one's family. A ? D

5. Any family that produces eight children deserves whatever they suffer for it. A ? D

6. Writing a letter to a member of Congress is a waste of a stamp. A ? D

7. Commitment to principles severely limits your freedom. (Careful on this one.) A ? D

8. I personally am in charge of my angers, jealousies, and moods. A ? D

9. Pleading victimization is most often an act of cowardice. A ? D

10. My principal motive in school is just getting a diploma. A ? D

Help me to understand what you understand by these statements.

1. Gandhi preached the need for complete self-surrender of oneself for others.

2. Sí, Se Puede. (Yes, it can be done.)

3. "We draw our strength from the very despair in which we have been forced to live."

4. "There has to be somebody who is willing to do it."

5. Freedom is like money in your pocket.

6. "The highest form of freedom carries with it the greatest measure of discipline."

7. They blame their faults on their personalities rather than their personalities for their faults.

8. Wisdom is making peace with the unchangeable.

9. What's true of adults must be true of those claiming to be becoming-adult.

10. Nobody's lazy. Just unmotivated.

Questions

⚜ Rory's the center of the folk tale only insofar as he's an "object" that focuses all the people's shenanigans. What is each of them trying to do? When you try to cover yourself by lying or laying off the blame, what in your experience usually happens? What kind of momentary "solution" did having a drink offer the villagers?

⚜ Tell me something that really, really bothers you—at home, in the neighborhood, in the city, in our country. Something that bothers you so much you'd be willing to put yourself on the line to the same extremes César Chávez did. If there isn't anything like that, can you tell me why not? I really care about that "why not." If there is an injustice that gets you that mad, what do you think you and I could do about that—not wishful-thinking, something real, something concrete? Maybe we might not change things much, but at least we'll know that we tried. Maybe we'd change something important in ourselves.

⚜ When (Mom/Dad) and I gave you the car keys for your first "solo flight," that was really scary. I mean, *really* scary. Try and tell me what you guess was going through our minds. All the crazy made-up scenarios of the worst things that could happen. Can you imagine what a tough thing it is to want to give you the freedom to be independent of us and the stronger yearning to keep you safe? When you bend (or break) your curfew time, do you believe you can be truly honest with us and be sure neither of us is going to fly off the handle, ground you for a year, send you to juvenile hall? Would you be willing to agree to a rule that you assign your own fitting punishment—when we all concur you did wrong?

⚜ Would you be willing to sit down with me and draw up a seven-day, twenty-four-hour-a-day schedule that I'd monitor for a week or two and then turn over to you? It'll be a truly liberating experience. I promise that.

10

Honesty

Without Honesty There Can Be No Trust

Opinion is a flitting thing,
But truth outlasts the Sun—
If then we cannot own them both—
Possess the oldest one.
—*Emily Dickinson*

Melanie

 nce upon a time, long, long ago, when one's word was worth one's life, there lived a lovely girl named Melanie, daughter of a prosperous merchant. An only child, Melanie was the joy of her parents, who spoiled her with outrageously expensive toys. But she was often lonely, so she contented herself with imaginary friends and playing solitary games with them.

One day Melanie was playing in the woods, tossing in the air a ball made of gold, a gift from her doting father. She tossed it, clapping front and back to see how many times she could clap before catching the ball. But the ball went too high, and she lost it in the bright sun. She waited, hands clasped atop her head, fearing a golden concussion.

She spotted the ball bouncing brightly across the rocks into a deep forest pool. Bump, bump, kalumph, splash! Her heart froze. What could she tell her father? Quickly she ran to the edge of the pool and peered in. Fathomless blackness.

"Oh, *pooh*!" she pouted and collapsed in a small bundle, tears trickling down her cheeks.

Then her eyes popped as she heard a sound that went "*Bork*!" And then a voice like someone with a heavy head cold said, "Alas, my lass, what's come to pass?"

"What?" said Melanie, sitting straight as a bookend, eyes alert as a startled fawn's.

"*Bork*! Ah, my girl, my pearl, something bad's made you feel so sad?"

Melanie looked down, and there at her knee squatted a frog, wraparound jowls puffing.

"Good heavens," she gasped, "you're a frog."

"Erikoax-koax's my name." He chuckled. "But if that's too hard for you, Erik by itself will do. It's a dreary day this, and I'm glad you came. And would you mind, miss, what's your name?"

"Melanie," she said absently, trying to make sense of this.

"Ah!" he sighed, "A name from a delightful dream. A crystal, sprightly moonlight beam!"

"Do you always speak in those ghastly rhymes?"

"I'm sorry, miss, if you find it repulsive. I'm awfully afraid I've become compulsive. But I can't complain of a fault so small. I'm lucky of course to be talking at all."

Melanie looked straight ahead. "I can't believe this," she said to herself. "I'm talking to a frog." She leaned down to glare at him. "And you're talking back. It's so—bizarre!"

"Bizarre depends on who *you* are, your point of view. But very few of my fellow frogs can match my face, my form, my style, and surely not my wit or guile. I'm quick, considerate, patient, zealous. And yet it makes the others jealous. I have to understand that, only … it really does get rather lonely. A feeling I am sure you've known. I saw you playing all alone."

"Oh, my ball!" Melanie cried. "What am I to do? It was hideously expensive."

"I can get it for you in a trice. *Bork*! But surely you know, there'll be a price."

"My amethyst clip?"

"I could not use your pretty clip. But I'd be glad of some … companionship."

"Companionship? Make you a pet? Frogs are boys' pets. And usually not for long."

"I'll fetch your golden ball, and all you have do is take me home with you. Let me eat from your plate without disdain and sleep each night on your counterpane."

Melanie's face crunched. He was, for all his boasting, only a frog and easily hoodwinked.

"All right," she said with a huge sigh, but a crafty look in her eye. "I have no choice."

So Erik the Frog scissored into the depths and in less than a trice was back with the ball in his mouth, and booped it—*Ptui!*—right into Melanie's hand.

"Oh, my ball! Oh!" And off she ran without so much as a thank you or even a goodbye.

"Melanie?" Erik croaked. "Miss? Your … promise?"

That evening Melanie sat at dinner with her mother and father and her pinch-faced governess, Madame Prunella. At her father's feet crouched his hound, Whip, and above his shoulder hunched Streak, his hawk, and whenever her mother wasn't looking, her father slipped hound and hawk bits of bread and butter. The hawk spat the effeminate victuals out, with the result that her father's brocade coat was unknowingly bedecked with sodden white pips.

Suddenly, there was a racket of whumping brooms outside the dining room, punctuated with several unmistakable "*Bork*"s. But also some kind of song: "Ah, Melanie, it's cruel of you to dismiss me thus. You can't forget what your promise was."

"Oh, that hateful *frog*!" Melanie ground her teeth. "He must have followed me home."

"Frog?" her father snorted. "Do you have acquaintance with … with some frog?"

"Imaginary friends again," Madame Prunella pursed. "I said so, sir. Never say I didn't."

"It's—it's only a frog I … met today by a pond."

"Met? You … *met* a frog today? And you, uh, spoke to him?"

"My golden ball fell in a pond. And this frog promised to get it if I'd let him eat from my plate and sleep on my pillow. So—so I promised. A dumb frog can't take me to court, can he?"

"But, Melanie, a promise is a promise. Even to a frog. We will see this wondrous frog," her father said and signaled the footman who put the thing down next to Melanie's plate. The hound sat up and wept down in his throat, and Streak, the hawk, evinced a sudden interest.

So for the rest of the meal, Melanie ate from one side of her plate while the obnoxious amphibian nibbled from the other. By and by, Erik looked up at Melanie and said, "It was simply a marvelous spread, but I'm—reasonably sure it's nearly our bedtime."

Melanie threw a hapless look at her father, but his eyes said, "A promise—"

So, taking the repulsive blob between thumb and forefinger, she slowly climbed the stairs to her chamber, set him reluctantly on her pillow, and scrubbed her palms on the hips of her dress.

She scuttled behind the screen, slipped into her nightgown, then slid under the covers as far away as she could from the awful intruder. But quietly, in a surprisingly sweet voice, Erik began to sing. "Once on a time, not very long ago, there lived a prince whose story you should know—"

The tale of a young prince from far away. The song lilted on, lulling Melanie to sleep.

Next morning, Erik was gone. Melanie rose with a lightness tinged with sadness. She had never heard the end of the prince's story. Or even the middle for that matter.

But next evening as the family sat down to supper, in hopped Erik. Hop, hop, hop, and with one final spring plopped on the table next to Melanie's plate. "But—" Melanie stammered.

"I hope that I have not offended," Erik said, "I thought the promise was open-ended." And with that he engaged her father in conversation on the price of fleeces. Then he talked to her mother about servants, and Madame Prunella on the disgraceful loss of good manners today. He charmed even foul-tempered Streak, who seemed more interested now in Erik's stories than his caloric value.

That night, somewhat less cautiously, Melanie carried Erik up to her bed chamber sitting in the palm of her hand. Melanie giggled as she donned her nightgown behind the screen, and she crept comfortably into the bed as Erik began to sing:

"The prince was brave and tried his best, but he caught the eye of a wicked sorceress. Spurned by the prince, the wicked woman swore he would spend his life as a wand'ring troubadour. Banished from home, the prince began to roam through foreign lands without a—"

Melanie struggled against the weight of her eyelids, but she drifted off into a dream.

Next evening, Erik's stories were even more diverting, then Melanie carried him up to bed, cupped in her hand next to her bosom, and she quickly changed and got into bed.

"The proud young prince refused to yield his soul, and he sang his rhymes and passed his money bowl, till it soon became a tidy treasure which gave the sorceress a deep displeasure. She changed him next to a mangy mongrel dog. And when that failed, she made the prince a frog."

Melanie looked at him sadly. "That's why you can speak."

"Yes, my dear, now the time has come. Only you can free me from what I have become. It won't be easy, but you must do it quick. No, don't be queasy. Just fetch the candlestick."

Melanie rose from the bed and picked up the candle Madame Prunella left lest she wake.

"Now, take the base," Erik said, shivering, "and smash it on my face."

Melanie pulled back in horror. "I *can't!*"

"Relieve me of this curse. If we should fail, it never could be worse. Please!"

Tears streaming down her face, Melanie raised the heavy candlestick over her head and brought it down on the frog, again and again, sobbing more deeply with every blow. Finally, she fell back. The candlestick tumbled to the floor, and the light guttered out.

Then suddenly, a tinder struck in the dark, and there stood her handsome Prince Erik, smiling through his own tears. "Free!" he choked. "Free! Love, I'll go back to that awful fen, ere I ever rhyme two words again."

And that was that.

Will Rogers

ill was one quarter Cherokee Indian whose ancestors had trekked in the winter of 1837-38 along the "Trail of Tears," when the government forced Cherokees from their ancestral home in Georgia to the "Indian Territory"—the western border of what is now Arkansas and the northeast corner of what is now Oklahoma. After service in the Confederate army, his father, Clem, settled his family on a homestead on the banks of the Verdigris River, three miles east of the town of Oologah, Oklahoma. The last of eight children, Will learned to ride as soon as he could walk and learned all the skills of a cowpuncher: breaking horses, roping, branding cattle, mending fences. But he didn't absorb much book learning. In ten years at six schools, he estimated he probably got as far as fourth grade, and yet he became a world famous vaudeville star, newspaper writer, journalist, advisor and representative of presidents, lecturer, film star. A diploma might be reassuring, but it's no substitute for discipline, drive, determination, and a dream.

What fascinated Will Rogers was rodeos— bull-dogging steers, riding wild horses, doing fancy tricks with a lariat, which he became as skilled at as he was at dodging school. Like the Indian Territory, the rodeo was a place that had no patience with sham or pretense; a man was judged by his skill and reliability. But also cowboys were known for a wanderlust that made them serene on long cattle drives from Texas to Kansas. At age 18, Will surrendered to his itchy feet, and ran away from military school, first to a ranch in Texas, then to San Francisco and New York City. Then at age 23, he and a cowboy friend set out for Argentina, working ranches for no more than room and board. When a cattle buyer offered a job on a cattle boat headed for South Africa, Will jumped at it. He spent his time breaking broncos for British soldiers who "had about as much chance of staying on top of some of those renegades as a man would sneezing into a cyclone."

In December, 1902, in Johannesburg, Will joined Texas Jack's Wild West Show as a trick rider and roper and took the first step in what would be a lifelong career. The following year he went with the Wirth Brothers Circus through Australia and New Zealand, and finally returned to the States to join Colonel Zack Mulhall's Wild West Show at the St. Louis Exposition in 1904, then to Madison Square Garden in New York City. There Will made his big decision—he wanted to go into vaudeville.

Variety shows featured singers, dancers, comedians, jugglers, magicians, acrobats, and Will figured his roping would be a unique addition. Unfortunately, too unique. It had never been done before. He tramped from one agency to another, till finally he got a tryout at Keith's Union Theater in June 1905 where, without saying a word, he did fancy rope tricks like "The Crinoline," where he began whirling the rope in a small circle overhead, gradually widening it and widening it until he circled far out into the audience. For a finale, a horse and rider suddenly erupted onto the stage, and Will threw two ropes, lassoing both the horse and the rider.

Then he began to talk, usually to cover up a dropped rope or an error in timing, just a man talking to himself, oblivious of the audience. "Swinging a rope is all right," he'd say, "when your neck ain't in it. Then it's hell." His casual, drawled humor began to catch on, and within a year he was traveling with a show through Europe. But before he had left for South America, he had begun to fall in love with a young woman named Betty Blake, and in 1902—despite her hesitation about the vagabond life of vaudeville—they were married. And after the birth of their first two children, Will, Jr., and Mary Amelia, Betty persuaded him to buy a house in Amityville, New York, where he could be near the city but where the children could have a less hectic life.

Finally, in 1916, impresario Florenz Ziegfeld hired Will for his night club, and since many of the audience came back night after night, Will was strapped for comic material, until his wife suggested he get ideas from the daily newspapers. Suddenly the comic had become a humorist. Will broke into the big time with a place in the Ziegfeld Follies, now concentrating less on the roping and more on the homespun humor, seeing how his audiences warmed to the truth—spiced with a bit of exaggeration. *The New York Times* described his act, "He begins talking in his Oklahoma drawl, and all the while chewing gum and playing with the ropes. When he begins to make the ropes writhe like snakes and strike the bull's-eye time and again with his quaint homely wit, you are as proud of him as if you had done it yourself."

A turning point in Will's style and confidence came when he played before President Woodrow Wilson at the Friars' Club Frolic in Baltimore. He had always poked fun at politicians, but when he began fooling around about Wilson's sending General Pershing into Mexico to apprehend the bandit, Pancho Villa, "everybody in the house before they would laugh looked at the president, to see how he was going to take it. Well, he started laughing, and they all followed suit." If you can poke fun at the president and get away with it, anything else is fair game.

On the last day of 1922, *The New York Times* wrote: "The famous cowboy monologist, Will Rogers, has undertaken to write for this paper a weekly article of humorous comment upon contemporary affairs," and gradually his column was syndicated in papers all over the world. His readers chuckled as he deflated the pompous and self-righteous—politicians and businessmen. In 1926, *The Saturday Evening Post* sent him on a tour of Europe for a series of articles which also became a book, *Letters of a Self-Made Diplomat to His President*. In 1932, he traveled throughout the Far East, and eventually went around the world three times. As early as 1919, Will had appeared in several forgettable silent films, but in 1929, he began to appear in a string of talkies, most notably *A Connecticut Yankee in King Arthur's Court* and *Steamboat 'Round the Bend*. In 1926, he made his first radio broadcast, then signed a contract for a weekly show.

Will Rogers was in the tradition of the cracker-barrel philosophers, wise old codgers who sat in the local store on a cracker barrel and doled out wisdom. Like Artemus Ward, Josh Billings, Mr. Dooley and Mark Twain, he assumed a posture of ignorance in order to prick pompous balloons. Nothing dishonest or hypocritical escaped his critical eye, and he became a symbol of the Common Man, a man of horse sense who was never deceived by political duplicity or misled by fads or unsound causes. Of the devastating treaty imposed by the Allies on Germany after World War I (which eventually brought Hitler to power), Will said, "The terms of the Armistice read like a mortgage. But this Peace Treaty sounds like a foreclosure."

Although Will didn't drink himself, he resented Prohibition, government making people's personal choices equal to crimes like robbery or assault. He pictured a prohibitionist who "presents a Medal to himself because he's going to *meddle* in everybody's business but his own." He was always willing to tell the truth, and always told it with a twinkle in his eye. Addressing the International Bankers Association in 1922, he said, "Loan sharks and interest hounds! I have addressed every form of organized graft in the U.S., excepting Congress. So it's naturally a pleasure for me to appear before the biggest. You are probably the most disgustingly rich audience I ever talked to, with the possible exception of the Bootleggers Union Local No. 1, combined with law enforcement officers."

Congress provided him ample material: "They are having what is called a filibuster in the Senate. The name is just as silly as the thing itself. It means that a man can get up and talk for 15 or 20 years at a time, then he is relieved by another, just to keep some bill from coming to a vote, no matter whether it is good or bad.... Why if a distinguished foreigner was to be taken into the Senate and not told what the institution was, and heard a man ramble on, talking that had been going on for 10 or 12 hours, he would probably say, 'You have lovely quarters for your insane, but have you no warden to see they don't talk themselves to death?'"

Having read about the decline and fall of Rome, Will was prepared to be impressed when he traveled there. He wasn't. "The Colosseum," he wrote, "has been a grand old building, but they stole enough off it to build everything else in Rome. Between reading something and actually seeing it, you can never tell till you see it just how big a liar History is. I didn't know before I got there that Rome had Senators. Now I know why it declined."

Will reacted to dishonesty like a compass reacts to iron. When the papers published the tax amounts paid by the super-rich, (which seemed pretty paltry compared their lavish lifestyles), he wrote, "Don't feel discouraged if a lot of our well-known men were not as wealthy according to the taxes as you thought they ought to be. They are just as rich as you thought. This publication of amounts had nothing to do with their wealth. It was only a test of their honesty, and gives you practically no idea of their wealth at all."

Ironically, it was Will's restless curiosity that led to his death. He had always been a great proponent of airplanes and had barnstormed with General Billy Mitchell and Charles Lindbergh. With his friend, Wiley Post, a pioneer of air travel who was just back from an around-the-world tour, Will set out to explore a possible air route from Alaska to Siberia which would avoid the dangers of a long flight over the Pacific. They were flying from Fairbanks to Point Barrow, the westernmost point on the American continent, but their plane never arrived. A lone Eskimo fisherman saw the crash and reported: "Mans with sore eye (Post wore an eye patch) start engine and go up. Engine spit, start, then stop. Start some more little. Then plane fall just so." With his hands he indicated a bank, a fall on the right wing, a nose dive into the water, a complete somersault. Then silence.

Truth

 he *glue that holds together* our web of moral relationships (society) is trust. When I ride a bus, I need to have at least some trust that *most* of my fellow passengers are not packing guns and knives, or at least won't use them. A quarterback must trust that his linemen aren't going to flop down and let the opposition mangle him. When we fly, we trust the pilot; when we dine out, we trust the chef; when we flip on a light switch or pick up the phone, we trust that unseen people have done their jobs. Without a reasonable basis to trust, we become a nation of justifiable paranoids.

But trust dovetails right into honesty. If I know from experience someone is dishonest when the cost of honesty is relatively trivial (a couple of points on a quiz), I have cause not to believe them when the punishment is extreme (losing your license for a year). If, however, they always come right out and admit they've screwed up when they have, I will probably believe them when they say they're innocent but the evidence suggests they're guilty. A habit of honesty is always in one's own *self-interest*. Nobody can "find you out" if you always tell the truth. And the truth is always easier to remember.

Honesty, Trust, Truth

Just as trust dovetails into honesty, honesty merges into the truth. As we saw, the truth is "out there" before it's in my head. What I say is legitimate and true only if objective evidence backs it up. Therefore, if the fabric of society depends on trust, and trust depends on honesty, and honesty demands the truth, one might say, without exaggeration, that the whole purpose of education (vs. schooling) is to teach people to *see and speak and live the truth*.

Not merely to see the truth but *yield* to it, even when the beast in me wants to blot out the truth, deny the truth, change the truth into something false but more palatable. Truth is the only antidote to narcissism, to self-absorption. Swiss psychiatrist Carl Jung made clear that all neuroses—anxiety, obsessional thoughts, compulsive acts—are always rooted in an inability or refusal to yield to the objective truth. Yes, my husband left and *won't* come back; yes, I *did* lose my leg; yes, I *was* mean to my friend; yes, I *did* copy her homework. Facing the truth, head-on, is often very painful, yet the neurotic games we fabricate to avoid the unchangeable truth are always more bitter, more confusing, and more self-destructive than yielding to the truth would be in the first place

Any talk about human (moral) relationships is silly if "everybody's opinion's as good as everybody else's." Anyone of the opinion the earth is flat and cyanide is harmless is *wrong*, pure and simple. Anyone who says Jews, Blacks, or other ethnic groups are less human than others is wrong. Anyone who claims fire doesn't burn or rape doesn't defile is wrong. What gives me the right to say that? The objective facts—the truth. If "the truth" changes whenever it becomes inconvenient, then "the truth" has no meaning.

Whenever we play a game, we want some rules—the alternative is chaos. We may argue whether the rule was broken—"My foot was *not* over the baseline"—but both parties agree on *the rules* for fair play. The rules for fair play in the game of Society is the truth: the way things are made and how I can validly use them. As we saw in the introduction of this book, rocks, apples, bunnies and people tell me what they are and how I can honestly use them. They are *objectively* different—I don't tell *them* that, they tell *me*—and those objective differences determine how I can validly treat them.

Try a few examples. A human baby is objectively more important than a whale baby. (The human baby could become Jonas Salk; the best the whale baby can become is Moby Dick.) The human mind is more important than the human body (faced with the choice of losing a significant part of your mind or a significant part of your body, which would you choose?) Human sex is more meaningful than animal sex (If it's no more than a healthy animal act, why not do it on the front lawn, the way dogs do? Why not tell the girl's brothers about it? Do animals get hurt and jealous when a sexual relationship is betrayed?).

In the present ethos, that last assertion about human vs. animal sex needs more defense. When I bring it up in an all-male class, the constant response is: "C'mon. If she wants it as much as you do, who's getting hurt?" In other words, her *desire* for sex must make it right. (What about the bank robber's *desire* for wealth, the cocaine addict's *desire* for oblivion, Hitler's *desire* for power. Did their *desires* make their actions right?) Recall the boy who said, "Look, if you like one another, it's just *natural*. If you're thirsty you turn on the faucet and get a drink. If you're horny, you call your girlfriend." To him, she's no more important than a glass of water, a momentary satisfaction.

The first step toward wisdom—and true freedom—is to call a thing by its right name, to be honest with yourself. If a sexual action is not in the same class as a mother's unselfish love for her baby, but is just a self-indulgence, don't call it "making love." Call it by the other word. It may be uncomfortable, but it will be the honest truth. You can fool everybody else, but surely don't fool yourself, about yourself.

Aristotle said we learn virtues by doing them, and he could have said the same about vices. The first little lie is painful, but the next one is easier. Soon, it's even hard to be aware that we are, in fact, lying. We have a nearly infinite capacity to kid ourselves, to assure ourselves we're honest when we routinely cheat if we have need and opportunity; to tell ourselves we are loving when we destroy other people's reputations without a thought; to pride ourselves on being loyal when we don't give our parents an honest day's work for an honest day's pay. They tell a story (perhaps too good to be true) about British playwright George Bernard Shaw sitting next to a voluptuous blonde at a dinner. He twitches his moustache and asks, "I say, would you sleep with me for 100,000 pounds?" She blushes demurely and responds, "Well, I rather think I would." He snickers, "Would you sleep with me for five pounds?" She pulls herself up and snarls, "*What* do you think I *am*?" He snickers again and say, "We've settled what you *are*. Now we're just haggling over prices."

People often object that telling the truth, being honest, is sometimes too hurtful—not just to the speaker but to the one spoken to, and that is a just objection. When a friend asks how you like her dress, and you think it's dreadful, the only kind reply is something playful like "You make anything look great." If she pushes further, answer, "If you like it, that's all that counts, right?" If she starts getting hotter, then she deserves the truth. She asked for it.

There is also an old moral chestnut, "*non expressio falsi, sed suppressio veri*— meaning, "not expression of a falsehood but withholding of the truth." It is the basis of the Fifth Amendment, "I refuse to answer on the grounds it might incriminate me." Prosecutors have to prove your guilt by other means—by law they can't expect you to convict yourself when they're unable to convict you. In the ludicrously tragic McCarthy hearings, witnesses were asked if they were now or ever had been communists. Many "took the Fifth" simply because they believed the questions were not only irrelevant to their loyalty as American citizens, but were an abuse of their civil rights. If a stranger asks you how much money you're carrying, it's none of his business.

In Elizabethan England, when harboring a Catholic priest was legally treason, those guilty of doing so, simply answered, "no," when asked if they were hiding a priest, since they believed, in their deepest conscience, that the law was immoral and therefore the questioner had no moral right to a true answer. More than once they defended themselves in court with a hypothetical case: "Suppose I were hiding the Queen from assassins. Would the court force me to tell the inquirers that I was not?" The same argument could defend those who hid runaway slaves in the antebellum South or Jews in Nazi Germany. No matter what a country's laws, it is also immoral to threaten a lawyer, psychiatrist, or minister of religion if they refuse to breach a client's, patient's or parishioner's confidence.

But readers of this book are not likely to face such dramatic challenges to their truthfulness. In the ordinary course of life, we owe each other the truth. Without honesty, we can have no trust, and without trust the whole web of society slackens and ultimately falls apart. Surely if parents can't trust what their children tell them (and vice versa), the family disintegrates. That is just as true of a school, which wastes its time playing cops and robbers—a colossal waste of everybody's time and brain power. Truthfulness is essential for the community, for the marketplace, for government. What a contrast in the years from my Norman Rockwell-era youth to the MTV culture of today—so much depressing cynicism has eroded our enthusiasm for commitment, for a sense of belonging to something bigger than ourselves.

As with any other virtue, honesty builds one step at a time, with the small things—I will never again lie to myself, especially about myself. I will never again lie to my parents or teachers or friends, or especially to anyone to whom I'm sexually attracted. Unless you can be trusted when the possible punishments or rewards are trivial, you can't be trusted at all.

No one ever said the truth would make you happy, they just said it would set you free.

A Dilemma

"Look, I came to you because you're my friend. My smartest friend. And because I know you'll keep this in confidence.

"I worked damn hard in grade school to get a scholarship here, and I've worked damn hard for the last four years. I'm one of the top three girls in my grade. That's not bragging. It's the truth. But all the other girls who care about their education come from rich families. They could afford that $400 SAT prep course. No way my parents could. It's an unfair advantage, isn't it?

"Well, you know Richie Cousins. You know, the computer geek with the pocket protector? Well … and you've *got* to keep this quiet … he hacked into some mainframe and got this year's SAT questions. And, well, he shared them with me. Because he said he admired me, and he thought I got a raw deal, what with the other girls having the unfair advantage. I'm pretty sure he was hoping it would lead to, well, something else. But if he thinks that, he's crazy.

"Anyway, I crammed those questions like a bandit. I knew it so well I had to *force* myself to make three mistakes, so it wouldn't look too … fixed. Well, I got a 1550 combined score. Don't look so shocked. It's really true. Without Richie I'd have gotten maybe, 1400 or so. But having the exam aced it.

"But … but now I'm feeling *really* conflicted about this whole thing. Because, well, I got a call from admissions at Harvard yesterday afternoon. They've offered me a full ride. I might even have gotten in on my own, but I could never have paid. And I know I'd never have gotten this scholarship offer.

"What do you think I should do?"

A Conversation About Honesty

What's your reaction to the following statements?

A = Agree; ? = Uncertain; D = Disagree.

1. A promise is a promise. Even to a frog. A ? D
2. Those who poke fun at public figures are self-righteous hypocrites. A ? D
3. A habit of honesty is in your own best *self*-interest. A ? D
4. A human baby is more important than a whale baby. A ? D
5. The human mind is more important than the human body. A ? D
6. Human sex is more meaningful than animal sex. A ? D
7. "Taking the Fifth" is an act of cowardice. A ? D
8. Lying is a relatively easy habit to break. A ? D

9. Acting against the laws of any legitimate government is automatically immoral. A   ?   D

10. If national security is involved, the state can justly force breaches of confidence. A   ?   D

Help me understand what you understand by any of these statements.

1. The glue that holds society together is trust, and trust can't exist without honesty.

2. The whole purpose of education is to enable us to learn how to see, speak, and do the truth.

3. Talk about relationships is silly if "everybody's opinion is as good as everybody else's."

4. "C'mon. If she wants it as much as you do, who's getting hurt?"

5. The first step toward wisdom—and true freedom—is to call a thing by its right name.

6. "We've settled what you *are*. Now we're just haggling over prices."

7. If someone really pushes for an unpleasant truth, give it to them. They asked for it.

8. If family members can't trust one another to tell the truth, the family disintegrates.

9. Unless you can be trusted when the punishment is trivial, you can't be trusted at all.

10. No one ever said the truth would make you happy, just set you free.

Questions

⚜ Have you ever been in an argument, especially with (Mom/ Dad) or me when suddenly a light popped on in your head, and you said, "Rats! They're *right*!"—but you kept *on* arguing? Why? It certainly wasn't that you really wanted to find the truth, right? What kept you going? Probably the fact that "winning" was more important—or at least not having the *appearance* of losing. (I'm not saying this because I've never done it myself!) You don't want to look stupid. And yet, the longer you argue when even *you* know you're wrong, the stupider you look! Talk to me about that.

⚜ In the middle of President Clinton's second term, the nation was smothered with a nit-picking investigation about his alleged sexual misconduct that seemed to go on forever. The special prosecutor (rightly or wrongly) was as relentless as Javert in *Les Miserables*. When the evidence finally became inescapable, the President of the United States defended himself about weaseling his way past a grand jury by saying, "It depends on how you define 'having sex.'" What do you think would have happened—to his own reputation, to the office of the presidency, to the confidence of the nation, and the moral state of society—if, as soon as the accusation had been made public, he had gotten on national television and made the same apologetic and remorseful speech he finally was forced to make (even after his first nationally aired, half-hearted admission?) What does that say to you?

⚜ More than likely, you're going to be a parent yourself some day. What would go on inside you if you found your teenage son or daughter were sexually active? How would you handle it? Would you expect them to be honest with you? Honest with themselves? Why?

11

Perseverance

"To Give Light, You Must Burn"

Only with winter-patience can we bring
The deep-desired long-awaited spring.
—*Anne Morrow Lindbergh*

Berenice

nce upon a time, long, long ago, when commitment was commendable, there lived a King named Bruno who had a daughter, Berenice. The joy of his life, loyal as she was lovely, cheerful as she was charming, bright as she was brave. And a perfect pawn for an alliance with an even richer and stronger king. Such, he thought, was the purpose of beautiful daughters.

Now among the many suitors, only one stood out in Berenice's emerald eyes—Prince Hugh, son of King Cosmo, from the ratty little kingdom next door. Unfortunately, King Bruno refused. Unbudgingly. "There's more to life," he thundered, "than thumping hearts!" Rather, he decreed, she would marry King Bismol, whose treasury was uncountable. "So he *is* thin and can't see four feet in front of his face! So he *is*

slightly deaf and lisps a bit and already wore out seven childless wives. Essentials like money come *first*!" King Bruno bellowed.

But Berenice stood before her father, chin pertly poised, and said, "Hugh, or no one."

"Then *no* one!" he cried, and on the instant decreed a tower be built and Berenice walled within till she reacquainted herself with her senses. So the tower was built with a year's supply of food, and intractable Berenice and her maid were entombed within. If she could last a year without going mad or committing suicide or murdering her maid, the king might accept this Hugh.

At first, the two women did little but moan and lament their stuffy fate. But after awhile, to cling to sanity, they began to embroider, to tell one another stories, and to play music on their lutes—and in general, to make the best of a bitter bargain. King Bruno would not break them.

For the first few months, young Hugh circled the tower, calling yearningly to Berenice, but the windowless walls were so thick she could not hear. And as winter crept across the hills and his legs turned to iron from knees to toes, Hugh headed for home in despair.

Days dragged by within the walls, without a sound from without. But as the supply of food declined, Berenice and her maid knew the year was coming to an end. Yet what if the royal provisioners had miscalculated? Day after day they waited for the hammer blow that didn't come.

So one day the two decided to start chipping at the mortar with their knives, wondering why neither had thought of that before. After what seemed like days, they finally loosened one stone. Then another, and another, until finally they broke out into the daylight.

They stood up outside and blinked around. What had happened? The whole land was devastated. Trees splintered, crops torched, not a soul in sight. Thinking they might have better luck if they separated so at least one might live, Berenice and her maid went their different ways.

The princess struggled along the road home, but when she arrived, there was nothing but toppled towers and a stagnant moat. Out she stumbled back to the road again, sleeping by night beneath a bush or boulder, boiling bitter nettles just to stay alive. Day after day, bitter nettles.

Late one night, she came to a castle and begged at the kitchen to be hired. The wall-eyed cook squinted her up and down, nodded, and immediately sat her down and filled her with thick pea soup and told her to rest for the night. There'd be plenty of work on the morrow, for the King's son was to be wed that very day. "And who is this prince?" Berenice asked.

"Prince Hugh, son of King Cosmo," the old cook huffed and led her to the hayloft.

Next morning, Berenice listened eagerly to the cook as they shaved carrots and potatoes. King Cosmo was gruff and greedy as King Bruno. A hulking lad like Hugh, brooding over a princess certainly dead? No! He was to marry Queen Hulda, King Bismol's last brief bride.

"They say she's so ugly she wears a veil to spare old folks having strokes."

Two months before, Old King Bismol had declined a yearlong wait for Berenice and harnessed himself instead to Hulda, a lady of formidable wealth. The very morning after the nuptials, the servants found the old man dead as lead in her bed, and she smiling like a cat with cream on her whiskers. Poison was not out of the question. Yet it was also possible one peek behind the lady's veil was enough to make the old duffer decamp into the hereafter.

But King Cosmo's son, Prince Hugh, was willing to go along with the whole affair if the witch would end his woes as swiftly as she had her previous spouse. Suicide by marriage.

"Best take up the biddy's breakfast, Berenice," the cook said. So Berenice carried the tray up to Queen Hulda's chambers and rapped softly on the door.

"*In!*" a voice howled, like a standpipe sucking air.

Berenice pushed in with the tray. Queen Hulda sat under a veil as thick as a tapestry.

"This is your lucky day, my proud beauty," Hulda hissed. "You will take my place at the church. Monstrous tales already spreading! The contracts have all been signed, and the rest is mere formality. You will be merely a proxy. They do it all the time. I will not have this prince lift my veil and run away! My ... my last marriage was brief enough!"

So Berenice, suppressing a smile, bedecked herself in the queen's bridal finery and jewels, and rose to take the arm of an archduke who was to lead her to become a stand-in bride.

Everyone below gasped at this gorgeous creature, having heard she was grisly as a gorgon. When she entered the royal hall, she saw Hugh's eyes go wide.

Hugh whispered to Berenice, "You remind me of a girl I once loved and will always love."

"Twice lucky," Berenice whispered back and smiled.

As they neared the church, Berenice saw a nettle plant and thought of all the nights when bitter nettles had kept her alive. "Bitter nettles," she whispered, "I am the one true bride."

"I'm sorry," Prince Hugh said. "What did you say?"

"Oh," Berenice smiled, "I was thinking of a girl I once knew. Her name was Berenice."

Prince Hugh stiffened. "Did you know Berenice?"

"Most of her poor, sad life," she said, and moved along.

On the steps, Hugh stopped. "I want you to have this." And he clasped an emerald the color of her eyes around her neck. "This was for my one love, and perhaps you are she."

They entered the church, and the priest joined their hands and pronounced them husband and wife. The bells clanged, and the procession returned to the palace for a riotous celebration.

But Berenice excused herself and climbed to Hulda's chambers. The anxious queen tore the clothes from the girl's back and draped herself in them, winding her head in a veil so thick she could hardly see. And Berenice put on her own gray smock and returned to the kitchens.

That night the bride was led to Prince Hugh's apartments, veiled like a military secret.

"What did you say to that nettle plant we passed along the way?" Prince Hugh asked.

"Nettle plant?" Hulda huffed. "One doesn't *speak* to nettle plants."

"Oh, but you did. If that wasn't you, then you are not the true bride."

"Excuse me," Hulda said and sidled to the door. "I must see my maid." And she raced to find Berenice. "*What* did you say to that confounded *nettle* plant on the way to the *church*!"

"I said, 'Bitter nettles, I am the one true bride.'"

And off Hulda sped, for Hugh was even handsomer than she had heard.

"I remember," she said to Hugh. "'Bitter nettles, I am the one true bride.' Er, uh, something to that effect."

"Yes," Prince Hugh exulted. "That was it! "But where is the emerald I gave you?"

"Emerald?" Queen Hulda snorted. "What emerald? I *never* forget emeralds."

"I gave it to you at the church door." Hugh sprung back in mock terror. "Who *are* you?" And he drew the veil from her horrid face. "*Hah*! You are not the girl I married in the church!"

"Technicalities," she smirked and closed in on the prince. "All the papers were signed. I got a scullion to take my place while the religious formalities were fulfilled."

Prince Hugh hurled her from him. "I want to *see* this maid!"

So Queen Hulda whirled from the room and hurtled down to the kitchen. She shouted to the gagging footmen that the servant, Berenice, had tried to kill her and must be strung up in the courtyard at once! So the terrified footmen dragged Berenice, screaming, into the courtyard.

Upstairs, Prince Hugh heard the hurly-burly and ran quickly down the stairs. "*Stop!*" he cried and the footmen set Berenice free, and Queen Hulda backed into the shadows like a spy.

"Berenice," Hugh said quietly, and the scullery girl ran into his arms. "Can you think of a place worthy of Queen Hulda's habitation for the rest of her life?"

"Not the tower," she smiled. "Set her to teach the nastiest children in the realm. She will know all their tricks. And they will either change her or be a punishment worse than death."

"Ah, my wise bride!" Prince Hugh hugged her to him. "No man more fortunate than I."

"Worth the wait?" she smiled.

"Ah, yes," he said. "Ah, yes!"

Viktor Frankl

s a teenager in the Vienna of the 1920s, Viktor Frankl did brilliantly in his studies, including a course in Freudian psychology. At 16, he wrote a two-page paper on mimicry and, on a whim, sent it along to the master himself. To his amazement, Freud loved it, forwarded it to the editor of his *International Journal of Psychoanalysis*, and wrote to the boy, "I hope you don't object." Frankl said later, "Can you imagine? Would a 16-year-old boy mind if Sigmund Freud asked to have a paper he wrote published?" Three years later, he was walking through a Vienna park when he saw a man with an old hat, a torn coat, a silver-handled walking stick and a face he recognized from photographs. "My name is Viktor Frankl. Have I the honor of meeting Sigmund Freud?" he asked, whereupon the gentleman said, "You mean the Viktor Frankl at Czernin Gasse No. 6, Door Number 25, Second District?"

After receiving his medical degree from the University of Vienna in 1930, Dr. Frankl headed a network of low-cost counseling centers, and when Austria plunged into the Depression, he had the opportunity to study out-of-work men and women suffering from severe psychological as well as financial depression. Without jobs, their lives seemed useless, so he advised them to take up volunteer work and dwell less on their feelings of inadequacy, and in a remarkable number of cases, the therapy worked. Two years later, at the Am Steinhof Psychiatric Hospital, he directed treatment of more than 3,000 suicidal women over a period of four years. With these severely depressed people, he took the dramatic step of asking: "What's stopping you from committing suicide right now?" When the women began to tell him what held them back—my child, my fear of God, my novel, my sister—then the doctor had something positive to work with, to motivate them to choose life rather than to escape from it.

He began to see that the two great schools of Viennese psychiatry had no ways to cope with such a radical sense of meaninglessness. The school of Freud rooted all neurotic behavior in unresolved sexual conflicts arising during infancy and childhood; the school of Alfred Adler held personality disorders result from excessive attempts to overcome feelings of inferiority. But his studies convinced Frankl of a third cause: that sense of meaninglessness he had seen in his patients, uselessness, trying to survive lives that were "going nowhere." The primary human motivation was not repressed sexuality or the drive for power, but the search for some kind of meaning to validate one's living. By 1937, he was writing in international psychiatric journals about what would later be known as "logotherapy," literally, "healing through meaning."

With the Nazi invasion of Austria in 1938, Frankl, like other Jewish professionals valuable to the state, was allowed to continue his work as chief of neurology at the Rothschild Hospital in Vienna, the only medical facility in Austria still employing Jewish staff, whose patients were also mostly Jews. There, with his gentile mentor, Dr. Otto Poetzl, Frankl began sabotaging the Nazis' euthanasia program, which decreed that "all life unworthy of life" should be systematically eliminated—retarded persons, psychotics, victims of senile dementia or incurable strokes—even at times children with cerebral palsy—Jews and non-Jews alike. The two doctors methodically falsified medical records of brain-damaged or schizophrenic patients, changing the diagnoses to temporary disorders such as feverish delirium and saved hundreds of helpless people.

In December 1941, Viktor Frankl and Tilly Grosser were among the last Jewish couples allowed to wed, but in the summer of 1942, his entire family was rounded up and herded to the railroad station. At first, they went to Theresienstadt, a "model camp" set up by SS to deceive Red Cross inspectors about the nature of Nazi camps. Then, when the Nazi inhumanity could no longer delude even the most naive, they were shipped off to Auschwitz, the Polish death camp.

"There were 80 people in each car. All had to lie on top of their luggage. The carriages were so full that only the top parts of the windows were free to let in the gray of dawn.... The outlines of an immense camp became visible: long stretches of several rows of barbed wire fences; watch towers; search lights; and long columns of ragged human figures, gray in the grayness of dawn, trekking along the straight desolate roads, to what destination we did not know."

They would soon discover. As they were herded off the train and lined up, they moved slowly forward toward "a tall man who looked slim and fit in his spotless uniform." He eyed each newcomer idly, then pointed his right forefinger limply either to the right or the left. They had no idea that a finger to the right meant work, a finger to the left meant death in the gas chambers. Frankl was pointed to the right. He had no idea both his parents had been pointed to the left.

They were stripped, their entire bodies shaved, whipped through showers, presented to young troopers who assigned them green triangles for criminals, red for politicals, double yellow for Jews, pink for homosexuals—to be sewn on striped jackets and trousers. And numbers.

Viktor Frankl would now be #119-104, tattooed on his forearm till death. Whenever that would be.

The men slept in tiered bunks, each tier seven feet square, accommodating nine men sleeping directly on the boards. The nine shared two blankets, all forced to lie on their sides like spoons in a drawer, unable to turn over, sharing their lice but also the heat of their bodies. One night Frankl was tempted to wake up a bed mate suffering from an agonizing dream but stopped, realizing no nightmare could be worse than being awake in such a hell.

Six million Jews died in Hitler's camps. Few know that 11 million Slavs died as well, and for the same reason—Hitler believed them all to be *Untermenschen*, "less than human." Unlike what most also believe, most of the victims did not die in the gas ovens but rather they died of starvation, overwork, fatigue and typhus. At Auschwitz, prisoners worked twelve-hour days on ten ounces of bread and a pint of watery soup. If there was a single prisoner missing at the morning or evening roll call (even if he were dead in a latrine), the whole camp had to stay swaying at attention, no matter what the weather, until he was found. SS commandants rented out the prisoners as slaves to various industries such as Farben, BMW and Messerschmidt for six marks a day. With minor deductions for food and wear on clothing, each prisoner was worth 5.30 marks a day, multiplied by a prisoner's usual life span of 270 days equaling 1,431 marks each. Adding the cost of a profitable disposal of the corpse (first removing gold fillings and clothes, then bones for fertilizer), each human being was worth about 1,600 marks to the Third Reich—times 17 million prisoners.

"Like nearly all the camp inmates, I was suffering from edema. My legs were so swollen and the skin on them so tightly stretched that I could scarcely bend my knees. I had to leave my shoes unlaced in order to make them fit my swollen feet. There would not have been space for socks even if I had had any. So my partly bare feet were always wet and my shoes always full of snow. This, of course, caused frostbite and chilblains. Every single step became real torture."

The prisoner's first response, of course, was utter shock at such pervasive inhumanity. But then, almost inevitably, to preserve sanity they fell into apathy, some even into absolute "absent-presence," what they called "going Moslem"—a depression so deep the sufferers could not move, or wash, or leave the barracks to join a forced march. No entreaties, no blows, no threats would have any effect. They went quickly to the gas chambers. Many prisoners would "surrender" even to the point of committing suicide by throwing themselves on the electrified wires or drinking the Lysol water used to treat those dying of typhus. Frankl was convinced such men had lost all faith in the future and resolved that he would find his purpose in the midst of madness by preventing such total surrender.

He urged his fellow prisoners to joke and sing, to take mental photographs of sunsets, to replay valued thoughts and memories. He himself spent hours, digging ditches or laying railroad track, having conversations in his mind with his wife, Tilly, unsure if she were even still alive. He found a most profound truth—and the foundation of his psychiatric belief—in the words of Friedrich Nietzsche, "He who has a *why* to live for can bear with almost any *how*."

Whenever there was danger of despair, Frankl insisted that they find an *aim* for their lives, a purpose, a meaning. "Think about those you love, one at a time, linger over their faces. Think of what you will do outside. If you believe in God, anchor yourself in him." No matter how their keepers could degrade their bodies, they could never destroy their innermost selves without the prisoner's cooperation. To submit internally to those in power was to cooperate in the rape of their own inner selves and the last vestige of their freedom. There was always that *ultimate* freedom: "to choose one's *attitude* in any given set of circumstances, to choose one's own way."

"Being human always points, and is directed, to something or someone *other* than oneself—be it a purpose to fulfill or another being to encounter. A person can find meaning through work or deed, through the experience of real love or of goodness, beauty, art, or through his or her attitude when faced with tragedy."

After three years, during which Frankl was shunted from the camp at Auschwitz to Dachau to Buchenwald, the war began slowly to grind down. The Russians had broken into Berlin, and the Allies were forging forward in the West. Most of the authorities and SS troopers had deserted the camp, and just as Frankl and a friend were about to slip through the open camp gate, a car painted with large red crosses moved forward into the opening. It was over.

Then began a part of his life no less difficult than the camp—schooling himself to live like a civilized human being again after three years surrounded by "un-men." At first, the world was as shocking in contrast as the first weeks in the camp had been. He found he had lost his mother, father, and brother. His wife had survived the camps but—tragically—had died within days after the liberation. Yet gradually he began to build a new life from the rubble.

From 1947 until his death at 92 in 1997, Frankl served as professor of neurology and psychiatry at the University of Vienna. He was guest lecturer at Harvard, Stanford, Duquesne, and Southern Methodist universities and accepted 29 honorary degrees. He wrote more than 30 books, most eminently *Man's Search for Meaning* in 1946, which he said he dictated in only nine days, having lived it every day for three years. The first segment describes his experience in the camps, the second a brief explanation of logotherapy, and the third "The Case for Tragic Optimism," makes clear how one's attitude can transform any suffering into life. The book has sold over 9 million copies in 24 languages. In a 1991 survey of lifetime readers conducted by the Library of Congress, Frankl's memoir was chosen as one of the ten most influential books in America.

His own terse words sum up his philosophy—and his life: "To give light, you must burn."

Suffering

 n 1831, a young Illinois man failed in business. The following year he ran for the state legislature and was defeated. Another business failed a year later. When he was 25, he was elected to the legislature, but the next year his sweetheart died, and he himself suffered a nervous breakdown in grief. At age 29, he was defeated for speaker of the legislature and at 34, he was defeated for Congress. At 37, he was elected to Congress, but was defeated two years later. At 46, he was defeated for the Senate and the following year defeated for vice president. Defeated for the Senate again at 49, he was elected president of the United States two years afterward. The man's name was Abraham Lincoln.

Aesop's fable about the turtle and the rabbit remains true: "Slow and steady wins the race." There are no biographies in this book which do not bear that out. As Aristotle wrote, as with any other virtue, one learns perseverance by persevering.

Legitimate Suffering

In the broadest sense of the word, "suffering" means giving up something we love or care for or even are just comfortable with. In that sense, getting out of bed in the morning is suffering, leaving behind the warm cocoon of the covers and the peaceful serenity of sleep to face the burdens and mishaps and irritating expectations of the day. The point of all the stories and biographies in this book is that suffering is the only path of growth as a human being, that there is a *purpose* to human suffering—*if* we rise to the challenge.

In that broad sense of "suffering" (a loss in the hope of better) any work is suffering, a forfeiture of freedom for a felt purpose: a paycheck, the well-being of one's family, a sense of being useful. Living together—from a married couple to a family to a community—is suffering: foreswearing independence, curbing resentments, compromising—because we can accomplish more together than we can alone. Wind sprints and weight lifting are painful, but suffered for a purpose, athletic or cosmetic. Learning is suffering, disciplining oneself to persevere with few immediate rewards—which is why so little of it occurs, since those upon whom learning is inflicted often find no purpose in enduring it. Seeing a purpose counteracts the suffering, gives it *meaning*.

Any significant change in one's life is, in its broadest sense, suffering, a loss. Growth itself is suffering, since we have to give up a self we were comfortable with in order to evolve a better self. Such "losses-which-invite-growth" consistently intrude on human life, what Erik Erikson called "natural disequilibriums."

Birth itself is the first suffering. For nine months in the womb we were in paradise—warm, fed, floating—free of all care because we couldn't think. Then through no fault of our own, we were ejected, and our birthday present was a slap on the butt. But without it, we'd die.

Then, just as we got things comfy again, parents started intruding with weaning and potty training, which were unnerving, but without them we'd never have achieved physical independence—which was worth the loss. Then Mommy shoved us out to play with the other snotty kids, even in the cold! But without it, we'd never have learned how to settle disputes without an adult arbitrator—which was worth the loss. Then the terrible betrayal at the kindergarten doorway! Stranding us with all those strangers! But without it, we'd lack skills to survive in the world on our own—which was worth the loss. Then adolescence, when bodies we'd taken for granted for so long began to betray us. But without it, we could never achieve personal identity—which is worth the loss.

Marriage is "suffering," giving up the swinging bachelor life to promise responsibility for another person. But without it you face all challenges alone–which is worth the loss. Having children surrenders the hard-won intimacy and partnership of marriage to allow an intruder in, to whom—sight unseen—you commit yourself to earn and spend one quarter million dollars! But without it, the two of you have nothing but yourselves to spark excitement in your life, none of the uninvited challenges that keep us growing—which is what our humanity invites.

But since we live in an ethos that resists inconvenience—and resists more strongly any effort to make us change our stultifying habits, it is not surprising that our society is composed—in great part—of terminal adolescents. One can pretend to "solve" the question of *legitimate* suffering—loss inflicted on everyone since the Cro-Magnons—either by evading it or by suppressing knowledge of it.

As we saw, Carl Jung insists that *evading* legitimate suffering—ignoring all but our own worlds—always ends in neurosis—anxiety, obsessions, narcissism, blaming our faults on our personalities rather than blaming our personalities for our faults. "I'm lazy" seems self-justifying, as if it were an incurable disease of which I am a victim. But living an illusion, lying to oneself and believing the lies, is very hard work. Thus, what we accept as a substitute for the truth becomes more painful than accepting the truth. What's more, denying the suffering which comes from facing life head-on stunts our growth as a human beings, since growing means leaving the security of the cocoon in order to fly.

Suppressing suffering involved in facing the truth—drowning it in booze or drugs or witless busywork, simply enduring what can be changed—is equally self-destructive. Perhaps the most widespread neurosis is minding one's own business, sticking the thumb in the mouth and letting the rest of the world go by, being stingy with one's attention, affection, time, and money. As Burger said in the film *Ordinary People,* "If you can't feel pain, you're not going to feel anything else, either."

What we saw in the last chapter about responsibility and motivation fits what Viktor Frankl said about the camps, though the working conditions in a high school are hardly as dramatically inhuman. But, as Frankl himself said, pain is like a gas; it fills the container with the same pressure whether the container is huge or tiny.

Sophomore year is often called "the tunnel"—the novelty has worn off, and the next three years stretch darkly ahead with little light—or payback. In that sense, high school itself is one long tunnel between grade school and college, when one is neither child nor adult, often treated like the former too long and yearning to be the latter too soon. Not to diminish the camp victims by the comparison, there nonetheless is a valid comparison; like the camps, schooling is inescapable—except for those who surrender their lives to mediocrity by dropping out, for those without discipline, drive, determination, and a dream. One can get by without a diploma, but not without the "Four D's." But even for those who don't drop out, schooling becomes for many a meaningless endurance, making them hardly more humanly alive than those who do quit entirely.

Since schooling is inescapable, there are only two options: tolerate it mindlessly like a sheep, utterly wasting four whole years of a life that could end tomorrow, or embrace schooling as if one's entire future depends on it—which it does. Nietzsche was right, "Whoever has a *why* to live for can bear with almost any *how*." And Frankl was right: The ultimate freedom is the *attitude* with which we face unpleasant challenges. But it is a freedom. We *can* settle for mere survival.

Unmerited Suffering

So much for "the thousand natural shocks that flesh is heir to," as Shakespeare wrote in *Hamlet*—the predictable, but unpleasant, challenges to keep growing as a human being—challenges faced by every human who ever lived. But there are also unpredictable and unmerited suffer-ings many of us are called on to endure—and through which we must *persevere*—sufferings that we as an individuals carry *no* responsibility for causing: my parents broke up, my brother sells drugs, my doctor says I have cancer, a fire destroyed my whole neighborhood, my best friend betrayed my confidence, someone of another race beat me out for "my" scholarship, my mother's an alcoholic. None of them are my fault, by I have to live with them.

Wisdom is making peace with the unchangeable. We have the freedom to face the unavoidable with dignity, to understand how our *attitude* can transform suffering. Are we responsible for our unmerited suffer-ings? The answer is no—and yes. We are not responsible for the cause of our predicament—whether it be cancer or job loss or the death of a child or spouse. But we are responsible for what we *do* with the effects— what we build from the rubble fate has made of our lives. As sailor and author David Adams recounts, "You can't direct the wind, but you can adjust the sails."

As Frankl asks, "Is (the prisoner) still spiritually responsible for what is happening to him psychically, for what the concentration camp has 'made' of him? Our answer is: he is. For even in this socially limited environment, in spite of this societal restriction upon his personal free-dom, the ultimate freedom remains his: the freedom even in the camp to give some shape to his existence."

The only hand we have to play is the hand fate deals us. We need not be victims of our *biological* fate. Stephen Hawking is a good example of this—he is a brilliant physicist despite being confined to a wheelchair and unable to speak due to Lou Gehrig's disease. Another example— one night the evening news reported a young man receiving his Eagle Scout Award. There is nothing newsworthy in that, except the young man was 22 years old and couldn't give an acceptance speech. Instead, his father spoke it as his son, who had cerebral palsy, pointed to letters on a board atop his wheelchair. For his merit badge in hiking, he had pushed his chair nine miles, then crawled the rest of the way.

We need not be victims of our *psychological* fate. We are, surely, driven by the winds, but a skillful sailor can use the wind, whereas saying "I'm doomed" or "I'm nobody" can become self-fulfilling prophecies. As Frankl starkly and firmly asserts: "A faulty upbringing exonerates nobody."

Those with callous upbringings in shoddy circumstances are in truth victims of others' mistakes, but it is the inescapable burden they were delivered, and they are no more hamstrung by it than the boy with cerebral palsy. Each of our stories is unique, with its own demons and dragons. Accept that and get on with what you have left—*you.*

We need not be victims of our *situational* fate, imprisoned by its "laws," living a makeshift existence, settling for mere "survival." People who went down on the *Titanic* went down singing. People have gotten off third-generation welfare. Women and men survived Dachau, Auschwitz, the Gulag, Teheran, Bosnia. And they came through battered but unbowed, with their own souls clasped firmly in their own hands. If such heroism is possible for so many ordinary people, surely it is possible to say "no" to soulless societies and soulless selves, to the naysayers and nobodies we're surrounded by. Surely it is possible to say "no" to the values preached incessantly by the media.

Here is a meaning to "value" totally unfamiliar in a utilitarian society where "dignity, integrity, altruism" are scarce. But in a view of life where one's character means more than one's bank balance, the fighting alone counts. There is no lost cause if the cause is just. In the going, I'm already there.

Dr. Martin Luther King, Jr., wrote: "The value of unmerited suffering (calls us) either to react with bitterness or seek to transform the suffering into a creative force. If only to save myself from bitterness, I have attempted to see my personal ordeals as an opportunity to transfigure myself and heal the people involved in the tragic situation which now obtains. I have lived these last few years with the conviction that unearned suffering is redemptive."

What suffering—accepted with an attitude of challenge—erases is our misplaced feeling of uselessness, of meaninglessness, of being dismissible as human beings.

There are only two alternatives: rise to the challenge or drown in self-pity.

A Dilemma

"I think I've had it. I'm pretty sure I can't take any more of this crap. The only thing that made any sense this year was when what's-his-name,

Macbeth, gives that speech about tomorrow and tomorrow, and about life being a tale told by an idiot. *That* made sense. I mean day after day dragging my butt from room to room to sit through it. Like do I care about some dumb old pushy salesman whose sons are bums and who talks to guys who aren't even there? It'll make my life better to know the area of a circle is pi-r-squared? I mean does anybody *use* that kinda stuff? The Trojan War, Napoleon, Eisenhower. Who cares? Knowing about them is gonna make going to Bosnia or Iraq or some other godforsaken place and risking my ass for—whatever—any easier?

"You know, I tried. I really did. Last year when that guy came and talked to us about the SATs, and how our wives and kids are gonna end up in tenements unless we've got a college degree? I did it all, made a schedule, got everything done on time, hell, I even did the extra reading. Two whole weeks! Nada. My grades didn't even burp. All I got from it was tired.

"So I did some research. Don't laugh! I did some research in this set of biography books in the library. Bill Gates—the richest man in the universe—did not finish college. Fact. Peter Jennings, now he's a very smart man, did not finish *high* school. Walter Cronkite didn't finish college, neither did Dear Abby and Ann Landers. Two guys, I forget their names, but one of them wrote that *Grapes of Wrath* that we plowed through. The one about the dust. Well, they won the Nobel bloody Prize, and they never finished college.

"So I talked to my Dad last night. He's mad as a hornet about it, but I'm going down tomorrow and sign up for the Marines."

A Conversation About Perseverance

What's your reaction to the following statements?

A = Agree, ? = Uncertain, D = Disagree.

1. The story of Berenice tells us nothing about getting on in the real world. A ? D

2. All neurosis is rooted in unresolved sexual conflicts or feelings of inferiority. A   ?   D

3. When Frankl and his colleague falsified records, it was illegal, therefore immoral. A   ?   D

4. The men and women who ran the Nazi camps were still human beings. A   ?   D

5. Slow and steady wins the race. A   ?   D

6. Learning is suffering, which is why so little occurs. A   ?   D

7. Getting married and having children is a completely logical, rational act. A   ?   D

8. Parents too cautious in shielding their children also shield them from adulthood. A   ?   D

9. You can get away for a long time—perhaps a lifetime—negating the truth. A   ?   D

10. If you refuse to feel pain, you won't really be able to feel anything else either. A   ?   D

Help me understand what you understand by any of these statements.

1. The ultimate freedom is the freedom to choose one's own attitude in the face of suffering.

2. "Whoever has a *why* to live for can bear with almost any *how*."

3. "Being human always points to something or someone *other* than oneself."

4. "To give light, you must burn."

5. In the broadest sense of the word "suffering," all life and growth is suffering.

6. Neurosis always roots itself in evading or suppressing *legitimate* suffering.

7. Though there is a stark contrast between the camps and school, there is also a real similarity.

8. Wisdom is making peace with the unchangeable.

9. We need not be the prisoners our fate—biological, psychological, situational.

10. "Unearned suffering is redemptive."

Questions

❧ Help me understand the people and the challenges you find most difficult, the things that appear as unavoidable "sufferings" to you. As Nietzsche said, "Whoever has a *why* to live for can bear with almost any *how*." Since the problem is unavoidable (the person, the school subject, the job), can the two of us come up with some "why" that justifies dealing with him/her/it, makes it yield at least some *value*—if only the satisfaction that you haven't quit? Think also of what Frankl said, that the one freedom we have—no matter how awful and inescapable the situation—is our freedom to choose our *attitude* to it. How can you, inside yourself, challenge this long-running sense of "defeat" and change it into something you can be proud of?

❧ Some of the shortcomings each of us has are unchangeable: "I'm too short (or too tall!), I'm Black in a White world, I'm a woman in a man's world," and on and on. But Beethoven was deaf, Milton blind, Dostoevsky an epileptic, Christy Nolan at least seemed to be a gibbering idiot, Oprah Winfrey started out on a pig farm. Sit awhile with your eyes closed and ponder, deep down, how a change in attitude would turn your shortcoming into an asset.

❧ OK, time to take the gloves off. In the most honest place inside yourself, what do you think are shortcomings that can be changed? "I'm lazy, I procrastinate, I'm too shy, I'm too pushy" What are the things you do that consistently get (Mom/Dad) and me ticked off? Don't make me rattle them off; you tell me. Do you think the family would be a happier place to be if you could get control of that? Don't give me "Well, I probably could" or "Maybe I might." How about a deep-down resolution? Want to shake on that?

Dignity

No One Degrades You Without Your Cooperation

The only kind of dignity which is genuine is that which
is not diminished by the indifference of others.
—*Dag Hammarskjold*

Astrid

 nce upon a time, long, long ago, when rulers seemed
above the law, there lived a warrior named Jurgen the Jute, who had
never even heard of the law. He had stout ships, treasure from a lifetime's looting, and a band of gold-braided, beefy men who wanted to
be just like him when they grew up. What they lacked in intelligence,
mercy, or decency, they offset in blood lust.

They swooped from longboats to carry off the comeliest women and
children, leaving nothing living behind. On such a raid they had seized
the beautiful, Astrid, daughter of a German chief, then swept her away
to the island of Albion with plenty of summer left for plunder.

When Jurgen and his brutes landed in the heathered north, he first
crushed a new duke, Aldwyn, and Jurgen feasted riotously in Aldwyn's
hall until time to turn their treasure ships home again. But as he gathered

supplies, Jurgen heard Aldwyn was approaching again, this time with the troops of his cousin, Duke Laughlin, who had trained all summer while Jurgen grew fat. Swarms of kilted men hurled themselves down on the invaders till the field was a swamp of blood.

The following day, the two dukes stood amazed at the mountain of booty piled on the seashore, wealth beyond counting. Then as they turned, they saw the final treasure skiff push off from the invaders' ships. In its stern sat a young woman of unsurpassed beauty, her flaxen hair in a single braided rope down to her hips. She sat erect and regal, her chin quivering but set firmly.

"Aldwyn," Laughlin said, mesmerized, "take it all. I have plenty. Those barbarians left your hall a shell, your fields a waste. Leave me Lady Astrid. She is enough. She is everything!"

"Cousin," Aldwyn grinned, "she is comely, but … to put it delicately, 'damaged goods'?"

"What could matter less? She would ennoble even that."

"But you're already pledged to marry Lady Gwendolyn, daughter of Gardred the Great?"

"Who could love that acid little prune? And a forced contract is no contract. Let the gargoyle be hanged. I will have Astrid. His wretched Gwendolyn can wed some fellow snake."

Seeing his cousin's set face, Aldwyn said no more but gathered his spoil, gave Laughlin fine gifts for his help, and marched his men homeward to heal his ravaged duchy.

In the next days, slowly, shyly, Laughlin set himself to gain the Lady Astrid's confidence. He took her riding and told her the English names of everything. She was quick, and they giggled over her mistakes, sharing their hearts. Finally, in the fall, they married with great ceremony.

When word of Laughlin's nuptials reached the hairy ears of Gardred the Great in the wilds of Cornwall, his roar caused cows to miscarry three counties away. "I'll have his arm for a back scratcher!" he boomed. He continued in that rancorous vein, while Gwendolyn sniffed, imagining revenges ever subtler and slower. Gardred ranted till his lungs and imagination were quite exhausted, then set about the serious business of planning a blood bath to restore his pride.

Laughlin heard news Gardred was marching north with an army outnumbering his own five to one, a wasps' nest of Saxons, Vandals, Huns,

Visigoths, and Ostrogoths who had deserted their own tribes, averring they were too softened and sissified.

"Astrid, my love," Laughlin said one evening to his bride, her skin glowing with her pregnancy. "If Jurgen had fled when we outnumbered him, would that have been cowardice?"

"Of course not, my lord. Prudence. To save his men when no victory was possible."

"And could a man live with his conscience if he saved his people at the price of his honor? "

"You mean this barbarian coming from the south? This Gardred? You cannot overcome him with your swords. Therefore—"

"We might all still survive by our wits."

"I see," she said. "As my lord chooses." Her head bowed, guessing not only how much his plan would cost her but what it had already cost her husband.

So Laughlin took his beloved wife, unprotesting, and hid her with her servants in a cottage deep in the forests. And he gave it out, even to his advisors, that Duchess Astrid, in terror at the coming barbarians, had died in premature labor with her child.

When the tidings met Gardred on the way, the news hissed against his fury like water on a firebrand. He sent a message to Laughlin that, if he would honor his pledge to marry Gwendolyn, Gardred would relinquish his oaths to rearrange Laughlin's digestive passages. Laughlin agreed. Gardred arrived with his slavering followers, pushing forward two pagan druids who united the reluctant bridegroom and the sneering bride on the spot.

Little love passed between the ducal couple, for Gwendolyn elicited but grudging tolerance even from her own father, yet the more wretched her husband was, the more her heart—or something—exulted. She longed to kill him but could not deny herself the pleasure of his pain.

Meanwhile, Astrid waited in the forest and delivered a beautiful girl she named Sabrina, and after a while, under pretext of hunting, Laughlin managed to slip away to be with his wife and child. Astrid assured him their sacrifice had saved hundreds. And they waited. Seven years.

Suddenly news came Gardred had fallen ill. And finally he was dead. Immediately, Laughlin renounced his pagan bride and sent her packing back to Cornwall, cursing all the way, and brought his true wife and child home from their exile. And the whole land rejoiced.

Meanwhile in Cornwall, Gwendolyn gave herself over to plans for unbridled revenge. She summoned her troops, who were softening from scarcity of slaughter, and marched north. She would be implacable until Laughlin was dead and his bride and brat in chains, doomed to a lifelong death.

The armies met on a great plateau above the sea-ravaged cliffs. For hours they clashed and hacked one another. But before the sun was locked overhead, Laughlin was hauled from his steed and run through by one of Gwendolyn's mercenaries. The news was cried and the field went suddenly silent, strewn with his dead. And Laughlin's wife and daughter were prisoners.

Astrid and Sabrina stood in chains, pale but undaunted, before the glowering duchess, astride her stamping horse. "Hah!" Gwendolyn scoffed. "The barbarian bitch and her *get*! Well, the cowardly cur that bred you is dead, my girl. Food for crows. No heart in that one."

"No," Astrid said softly. "My husband took his heart and soul with him when he went. He claimed them back at the end. He is safe. And so are we."

"Think you that, trollop? Safe? You will live a lifetime of little deaths." She snapped her fingers at her marshal. "Bring two spades. These two will bury the dead. All of them!"

"But, my lady," the grim old barbarian rasped, "she is a duch—"

"Not any more she isn't. Get the spades or *join* her." He reluctantly obeyed. Gwendolyn bent low over her saddle to the two women, "And that," she rasped, "is only the beginning!"

So for weeks Astrid and Sabrina dug shallow graves and tumbled in the dead, their white hands corroding with blisters and dirt, their noses gradually indifferent to the ghastly smell. But on the second morning, Astrid had risen with her chin set and smiled at her daughter. "Today, Sabrina, while we labor, we will *sing*!" So as the days dragged by in the ghoulish business, the two sang, toiling away from sunrise to sundown until finally the hideous task was done.

When Gwendolyn arrived with her guard, she found the two of them seated beneath an oak, leaning against one another, their skins tawny as peaches, smiling and singly softly.

"What is this!" the Duchess howled, sure she would have found them dead of exhaustion.

Astrid and Sabina rose and bowed, slightly. "As you see, my lady. We have finished."

Gwendolyn scowled, and the hardened men around the duchess seemed oddly shamed by the serenity of the two women. "Well, I am *not*! Send them to the potato harvest!"

So for weeks more, the mother and daughter dug potatoes, but now they were with their own people, and Astrid coaxed the heartsick women and old men to sing. Soon every field began to ring with song But when the harvest ended, Gwendolyn returned, not at all amused.

"Well, now, we will—" she began, but her old marshal touched her elbow lightly.

"My lady," he whispered, "if I might have a word. Alone." So, scowling, Gwendolyn moved aside with him. "My lady," the old man said quietly, "your men are much taken with the courage and spirit of these two women. It has made the men uncomfortable, resistant."

"Resistant? What? I am in power here!"

"My lady, *we* are your power. Without us, you are one frail woman. But these two frail women have a power in them that saps the power from your men. And thus from you. Might I suggest we return to Cornwall? If you do not order us to return, you will face these folk alone."

Gwendolyn took a huge breath and for a moment seemed ready to strike the old marshal. But she looked at all the hot-tempered peasant faces glancing over at her. She took another breath, grinding her teeth. Then she spurred her horse around and began to gallop away toward the south, her hairy mercenaries following.

For a while, all they could hear behind them was joyous singing.

Jackie Robinson

 efore there was Malcolm X, before Medgar Evars and Rosa Parks, before there even was Dr. Martin Luther King, Jr., there was

Jackie Robinson. He gritted his strong white teeth long before any of the other modern greats struggled for more than token freedom for African-Americans. Before any civil rights lawyer or activist or politician even came into the park, Jackie Robinson took a heroic swing against indignity.

Jack Robinson was born in 1919, the last child of five of a sharecropper eking out a living on a plantation near Cairo, Georgia, who almost immediately thereafter deserted his wife and children and headed off for what may have been greener pastures. Jackie's mother, Mallie, felt the family might have a better chance if she moved them to Pasadena, California, and they did, but not without cost. She bought a house in a mostly White neighborhood, and more than a few of her neighbors begged the welfare agency to move them somewhere else. "I remember," Jackie said, "even as a small boy, having a lot of pride in my mother. I thought she must have had some kind of magic to do all the things she did, to work so hard, and never complain, and to make us all feel happy."

While their mother did housework to support them, her children went to school and played sports. Jackie's brother, Mack, became a world-class sprinter, finishing second in the 1936 Berlin Olympics only to the great Jesse Owens, who was also Black and an affront to race-conscious Adolf Hitler. Jackie, meanwhile, was getting into trouble, filching food from groceries, swiping golf balls from posh courses and then selling back to those who had lost them. But luckily he met a mechanic named Carl Anderson who convinced him that if he ran with losers, he'd be a loser. At John Muir Technical High School, he won letters in football, basketball, baseball, and track.

His performance triggered college scholarship offers, and he accepted one to UCLA, where again he was a four-letter man and was named an All-American halfback. When he was a senior, he met Rachel Isum, a freshman, who was to share the rest of his life. But months before he was to graduate, he dropped out, convinced that "no amount of education would help a Black man get a job. It seemed necessary for me to relieve some of my mother's financial burden." During World War II, the army drafted him and, after basic training, he applied for Officers' Training School, but even though he had almost completed college, he was rejected. He was Black. But Joe Louis, the heavyweight champ, who was also at Fort Riley, stood up for him, and he was accepted, and in

1943, he became a first lieutenant. But they wouldn't allow him to play baseball except on "the colored team."

One evening in July, 1944, Jackie was returning on a bus to Fort Hood, Texas, chatting with a fellow officer's wife, who happened to be White. The driver stopped the bus and told him he had to sit in the back with the other Blacks. Jackie refused, knowing that publicity about Black fighters Joe Louis and Ray Robinson refusing to sit in the back of military buses had made the army forbid discrimination on its vehicles. Nonetheless, he was called up for a court martial, and although he was exonerated, he was tagged a troublemaker and removed from consideration for fighting overseas. Six months later, he received an honorable discharge.

From the army, Jackie went to play with Kansas City Monarchs baseball team in one of the Negro Leagues. Today, it seems ludicrous that a country that had just made untold sacrifices fighting a war to confront inhuman racial policies in Europe could still have "colored only" rest rooms, waiting rooms, even drinking fountains back home, as if skin color were somehow contagious. But for a great many—even Blacks—that was simply the way things were. One New York councilman was so incensed by the inequity he published a poster with two pictures and a caption: a dead Black soldier, a Black baseball player, and the words "Good enough to die for his country but not to play baseball." Therefore, because most hotels and restaurants refused Black patrons, players in the Negro Leagues often had to eat and sleep on the team bus.

It was a bleak life, but the money was good, and Jackie thought it was the only way a young Black man like himself could help his mother and make enough money to marry Rachel. But after only a year with the Monarchs, a mentor, an "Obi-Wan Kenobi" appeared in Jackie's life, a White man named Branch Rickey.

When Rickey was a young coach at Ohio Wesleyan in 1904, a Black first baseman named Charlie Thomas was one of his best players. When a hotel refused Charlie a room, Rickey insisted the manager put a cot in his own room, as hotels then did for Black servants of wealthy Whites. That night, Charlie sat on his cot, weeping, rubbing his hands fiercely. "Black skin!" the boy sobbed. "Black skin! If only I could make them White." Rickey said later, "I vowed that I would always do whatever I could to see that other Americans didn't have to face the bitter humiliation that was heaped on Charles Thomas." He kept his word.

When Rickey became president of the Brooklyn Dodgers in 1943, he had already created the farm team system in which major league teams controlled minor league franchises, bringing up young players while at the same time pepping up hometown teams with talented players from all over the United States. Using the farm team concept as a camouflage, Rickey sent scouts around the country to round up talent for a Brown Dodgers team, which would (seemingly) play in Brooklyn when the White team was on the road. But his real reason was to open up all-White major league baseball to Black athletes. But the player he was looking for had to have more than athletic ability. He would have to have the inner courage and unshakable self-esteem to withstand all kinds of degrading abuse. The man he chose was 26-year-old Jackie Robinson.

When Rickey met him, Jackie asked, "Mr. Rickey, do you want a ball-player who's not afraid to fight back?" and Rickey answered, "I want a player with guts enough *not* to fight back."

He began with the Montreal Royals, a Dodger farm team, and things did not bode well. During spring training in Florida, Jackie didn't play well and endured a segregation in which he wasn't allowed to play in many ballparks. But in April 1946, he was the starting second baseman for the opening day game in Jersey City, and a lot of New Yorkers had crossed the river to see not only one of the first ball games after the war, but a new kind of "foreign" invasion.

Jackie's hands were sweating so badly he could hardly grip the bat. In the first inning, he grounded to short and was out at first. In the third inning, there were two on base and no outs, so the Jersey Giants expected a bunt to advance the runners. Instead, Jackie took a full swing and lobbed the ball over the left field fence. He bunted safely in the fifth inning and began to dance off the first base bag in a way that would intimidate pitchers for years. He stole second. Then he broke for third. Then he stole home! In a 14-1 game, Robinson scored four runs, drove in three, and stole two bases.

But it was still going to be an uphill battle. In Baltimore, fans screamed racial epithets at him for a full nine innings; in Indianapolis, the law prohibited him from playing; in Syracuse, an opposing player threw a black cat on the field, hollering, "Here's your cousin!" The International League's Little World Series was held in Louisville, a town that limited the number of Black fans at its games. "I had been booed pretty soundly before, but nothing like this. A torrent of mass hatred burst from the stands with virtually every move I made." But he toughed it out, even if the Royals won only one of the three games. But in Montreal, home fans poured out to support a man they'd taken to their hearts. The Royals won three games and the series. At the end of the final game, they carried Jackie around the field on their shoulders, "probably the only day in history," a sportswriter wrote, "that a Black man ran from a White mob with love instead of lynching on its mind." The coach, a Mississippian, told him, "You're a great ballplayer and a fine gentleman."

In 1947, Branch Rickey shrewdly decided to have spring training for the Dodgers and Royals together, and in Cuba, where there was no racial segregation. He told Jackie to impress the daylights out of the Dodger players and sportswriters, and he played sensationally. It wasn't enough. The players still resented him. When Jackie, the first Black in the major leagues, played his first game, April 15, 1947, he was pretty much a washout for a whole week. In a home game against Philadelphia, a chorus of venomous racial abuse poured out of the Phillies' dugout, led by their manager. Jackie just kept taking deep breaths and clenching his jaw. He was, as one writer said, the only gentleman on the field. And it turned the tide. The other Dodgers rallied to him. When bigots sent letters threatening Jackie's life, the team suggested they all wear his number so no one could tell which one was the Black. *The Sporting News* named him Rookie of the Year.

In 1949, he had a .342 batting average, stole 37 bases, and was named National League MVP. In the '50s, though, the Brooklyn Dodgers were to the World Series what the Buffalo Bills would become to the Super Bowl, always saying "Wait'll next year!" But finally in 1955, with Jackie slowing up at 35 and rumored to be retiring, they finally managed to beat the Yankees and take the Series.

But in 1957, after 65 years of fan support through near miss seasons and two years after their first World Series win, the Dodgers owner, Walter O'Malley, (no relation to this author, *honest!*), decided to sell Ebbets Field and move to Los Angeles. Some Brooklyn fans still compare him to Benedict Arnold. The New York Giants offered Robinson a contract for $60,000—a huge sum in the days when a three-bedroom house sold for less than $20,000. But Jackie said, typically, "It would be unfair to the Giants and their fans to take their money. The Giants are a team that needs youth and rebuilding. The team doesn't need me." So he retired to become an executive with a coffee company. An eloquent speaker, he also served as an effective fund-raiser for the National Association for the Advancement of Colored People (NAACP). In 1964, he raised over $1.5 million to found the Black-owned Freedom National Bank to finance Black businesses in Harlem. And in 1962, he became the first Black ballplayer to enter the Baseball Hall of Fame.

Jackie Robinson often told young audiences, "A life is not important except in the impact it has on others." And throughout his life he believed "the most luxurious possession, the richest treasure anybody has, is his dignity."

Self-Esteem

 t the first act finale of *La Cage aux Folles*, Albine, an aging transvestite is about to reprise *We Are What We Are*, a campy number the chorus has earlier danced. But just as he is going onstage, he hears that his male lover's son—the boy he has raised, cared for, and coddled for 20 years (doing a better job than the boy's absent mother could have)—has refused to allow him to meet his fiancée and her parents. The boy is ashamed of his "mother." With an imperious wave, Albine holds back the chorus and strides onto the stage alone. Jaw set, he begins the song, slowly, ferally: "I ... *am* ... what ... I ... *am*. I am my own *special* creation ... I am what I am, and what I am needs no excuses ... Life's not worth a *damn* till you can shout out loud I *am* what I *am!*"

Albine is not gay in the sense of carefree. On the contrary, at this moment he feels belittled and betrayed, but he is unbowed. He has fought his way through a hell he did not choose and he has made the most of what he has. His is an anthem of unapologetic self-acceptance and self-assertion, which not many can even comprehend, much less take to heart.

The Difference Between Self-Esteem and Self-Absorption

It's of crucial importance to see the stark difference between genuine self-esteem and self-absorption. Self-esteem is based on objective evidence: it's a consistent attempt to strive for one's best and to ride herd on petty meannesses. Self-absorption is really narcissism, and is based on subjective illusion—a series of disguises, lies we tell ourselves, about ourselves—lies we believe. Self-esteem depends on approval from *within*, a conviction that, despite minor failings here and there, I am honestly trying to do my best at everything I attempt or am legitimately requested to do. Its rock foundation is *honesty* about oneself. Self-absorption depends on approval from *without*, from convincing others that "I'm OK!" even when I'm in fact *not* OK, when I consistently slack off, do the minimum, lie and cheat when I'm in a pinch. It has no foundation, since self-absorption consists of denying the objective truth—which is the only place in which to ground *any* belief.

Jesse Jackson rightly encourages young audiences to shout, "I am *some*body!" But that confident battle-cry is legitimate only if one *acts* like a somebody. Humanity invites us to evolve beyond our simian forebears, but we never leave our natural animal inertia behind. It's always inside, trying to drag us back down, tempting us to resist challenge, to weasel our way through. Therefore, anyone who claims to be "on the way" to adulthood (which is what "adolescence" means) ought to have more self-control than someone even a year or two younger. To achieve that, a person of character has to have a chorus of internalized critical voices, which keep him grounded in truth and reality.

A person with authentic self-esteem doesn't run and hide from *legitimate* guilt. Consider the young people who, for no discernible reason, walk into schoolyards and spray bullets around indiscriminately—without the slightest sense of guilt or remorse. They have none of those limiting inner voices. They are what you get without guilt. Just like extermination camp guards, drive-by shooters, terrorists, pimps, pushers.

Unfortunately, as Christopher Lasch points out relentlessly in *The Culture of Narcissism*, almost every area of young people's lives is populated by forces hellbent on keeping them stuck in lifelong childish self-absorption—forces like the media, commercials, athletics, school, sex—there are endless invitations to degrade the self to a narcissism which is really self-distaste rather than self-admiration. For twice as long as youngsters will learn from all their teachers put together, they learn from these cultural forces to mask their inadequate selves, favoring image over substance. As Lasch says, "Nothing succeeds like the appearance of success." For too many, the importance of *personality* far outweighs the importance of *character*.

Most young people validate themselves from the outside: through competition, peer acceptance, grades, appearance. They believe, "I am what others think of me," not "I am what *I* think of me." They certainly don't say "I am what I *am*." There is some truth to "I am what others have done to me," in the sense that we form an idea of self by using others as mirrors, all the way back to Mommy's and Daddy's smiling "*Ah*"s! and disappointed "No-no"s! But to say we are *only* what others have made us is too simplistic. Until we accept and value ourselves—as we are—we will never better ourselves. If we see ourselves only as others see us, we will not treat ourselves with the respect we deserve. Each of us should realize, "I don't *have* a self; I *am* a self."

Get Rid of the "If Only's"

In forging a character, a personally understood and accepted self, the place to start is with the personality—the parts of me that are the result of reacting to other people. The first critical step is to get rid of the "if only"s—"If only I'd had different parents; if only I were rich; if only I weren't so shy"—and even "If only I weren't beautiful." We must be aware of the indelible impact other people's hurtful actions have left on our human spirits, but we must forgive the perpetrators, accept the results, and begin making something of them.

The past is unchangeable, non-negotiable; but the future is both changeable and negotiable, provided we have the courage to take full responsibility for dealing with it. We can't, like Linus, just put the security blanket of "if only"s on the other side of the room or in a drawer someplace. We've got to *throw* them out, burn them up, get rid of them forever.

Ask young people to write down the things they dearly "hate" about themselves; then underline the things that simply *can't* be changed: their DNA, their family, the mistakes they've made because other people (especially parents and siblings) have been too tough, too lenient, too pushy, too meek, too demanding, or too "stand-offish." Whatever the influences, that's the situation *now*. We must face it, accept it, and get on with building a character that capitalizes on the present self's assets and minimizes its liabilities.

Genuine Pride Isn't Arrogance

Self-esteem is genuine pride. But due to a mere semantic difference, most people have no clear idea what genuine pride is. Poor translation of the Greek word *hubris* renders it as "pride," as in "Pride goes before the fall," and "Those whom the gods would smite they first make proud." Wrong. *Hubris* means *arrogance*—narcissism, self-absorption, insulation from others and from the truth.

But that mere slip of a word has made many human beings afraid to proud—when they genuinely deserve to be. When we search for the root cause of a student's shyness or rowdiness or continued failure or pregnancy or brooding or neurosis or psychosis, we often find fear of pride. In 35 years of dealing with young people, I have never encountered a problem that couldn't be reduced to a single cause—the agony of trying to prove the self *without being arrogant*.

No one with a firm grasp on his or her own real goodness and value (despite all their imperfections) would stoop to cheating on a quiz, lying in a tight spot, putting the blame off on someone else. If teachers, instead of becoming more eagle-eyed disciplinarians, worked to find more ways to build young people's self-esteem, we would have a happier, more peaceful school, family, city and world. The amount of litter, crime, and global inhumanity would lessen, if only a fraction at a time. The number of voters, letter writers, public servants, and candidates for Nobel Peace Prizes would increase, if only a fraction at a time. The young are already pitifully enough aware of their faults. If teachers and parents can make them aware of their assets, they might just start making better use of those assets—to their joy and everyone else's.

Between Contentment and Ambition

"Why is fulfillment always in the future?" It's because we fail to understand and accept the difference between contentment and ambition, between a genuine satisfaction with what one has done and the drive to do something better the next time. If there is one burden too many parents lay on children's immature shoulders, it is saying, "You can do better than that," when the child has done his best. If parents could only understand—and if kids could find the words to say, "Yes, I can do better. But that's the best I could do *now*."

Character—which is self-esteem that refuses to demean itself—is made of two contradictory qualities: vulnerability and spine. To be of good character, you must drop your guard against the truth and other people (vulnerability). And you must commit yourself firmly to the truth and be willing to stand up and defend what you believe (spine).

Vulnerability is essential to human growth. To become more human, you must be *humble* before the truth, wherever it leads, and you must be humble before other people, who can open deeper levels of understanding. But to be humble, you must also have confidence in your own self.

Open Mind or Empty Head?

Commitment—spine—is also essential to the formation of character. If you stand for everything, you stand for nothing. Yet, especially nowadays when things change so often and rapidly, most of us balk at commitment, preferring to "keep an open mind"—in case something better comes along—not realizing the *ultimate* open mind is an empty head. Until we take a stand, make a commitment for what we believe, we are mere reflections of other people's choices—we have personality but no character.

Once we reason our way to an opinion (not just mull it over, but gather the evidence, sift it, draw a conclusion), then we have to stand up and defend it—no matter what anyone else says. If they offer substantial and just criticism, then we must go back and rework the opinion and try it out again. Having a personality is inevitable; having character takes work.

When we "give our word" on something, it shows we have a foundation of legitimate pride—a personal integrity. It shows we can accept things—and ourselves—as they are, and then ask, "How can I do better?" Having pride can also mean having a sense of "craft," something that is fast disappearing. A mechanic who takes pride in himself and in his work satisfies not only his customers but *himself*. As Martin Luther King, Jr., said, if your job is to sweep streets, sweep those streets the way Michelangelo would have. The same could be said of any student: if the job at the moment is to write an essay, write it as if you were going to have to deliver it to Congress. If you're getting ready for a test, prepare as if your Dad's next raise depended on it. If you have to clean out the cellar, get it ready for your sweetheart to live there.

Sharks and tigers never suffer doubt. Only humans do. Like genuine guilt, genuine doubt is a healthy hunch things aren't as right as they should be, that ideas you've been sure of so far need rethinking. There is nothing wrong with this kind of doubt as long as you do sit down and figure out a better answer. That shows pride and integrity, it's what we were born for, and it's called evolution.

A Dilemma

Pretend you're a teacher and this is your advisement group. The descriptions after each name are based on your observations and those of other teachers and students. Have ten people role-play these personalities, perhaps discussing one of the other dilemmas in this book. Or, talk to them about character—and let them fight you every step of the way.

Tad:

Thinks of *nothing* but football, not even girls, and surely not grades. Father second-string All-American, convinced son can make the pros. Teachers say he falls asleep in class a lot.

Clarice:

(Called Mary Ellen until she saw *Silence of the Lambs.*) What boys call a "hooker hairdo," hoop earrings, heavy make-up, skirt four inches above the knee. Boys say she's "easy."

Miguel:

A street-smart hustler whose insolence to teachers and students stops short of physical action. He wears a lot of gold chains and reports suggest he's "selling."

Emma:

Thin, pale, perhaps anorexic. Distant, conservative and demanding parents. Girls have reported that, when she gets a B, they can hear her in the girls' bathroom crying quietly.

Kareem:

A very big Black young man with a chip on his shoulder. No one can name a White student to whom he speaks. He believes Black men have no chance against the system.

Justine:

According to the nurse, she has some type of degenerative disease, but she seems to be using it as an excuse not to do any assignments.

Coop:

He wears a black vest with lots of chains; he's into Dungeons & Dragons, he's extremely vocal and intelligent in class discussions, but does no written work unless it interests him.

Courtney:

Students call her "The Queen Bee." She wears designer everything. She has a small coterie of girls whose major activity seems to be shredding other girls' reputations.

Rob:

The best soccer goalie in the county, accepted (at least by word) into a college last November. Hasn't picked up a pen or a book since.

Yvonne:

Dresses very "butch." Female students are very uncomfortable around her. She has made no approaches to anyone, but one very conservative teacher believes she should be expelled.

Now, talk to them about character. If you're in a group, have ten people role-play the personalities. Maybe you can start with one of the other dilemmas in the book.

A Conversation About Dignity

What's your reaction to the following statements?

A = Agree, ? = Uncertain, D = Disagree.

1. The indifference of others ought not to diminish genuine dignity. A ? D

2. Astrid and Sabrina conquered by refusing to be conquered. A ? D

3. No one degrades your inner self without your cooperation. A ? D

4. Albine, the transvestite, had no legitimate grounds on which to claim dignity. A ? D

5. A person of authentic self-esteem doesn't run and hide from legitimate guilt. A ? D

6. It is easier to develop character nowadays than it was even 50 years ago. A ? D

7. I am a result of what others have done to me. A ? D

8. Pride is the same as vanity. A ? D

9. No one with true self-esteem would cheat, lie, lay off the blame. A ? D

10. The most open mind is an empty head. A ? D

Help me understand what you understand by any of these statements.

1. "The richest treasure anybody has is his dignity."

2. "I am somebody" is legitimate only if one *acts* like somebody.

3. Humanity invites us to evolve, but we never leave our animal nature behind.

4. The first critical step toward character is to get rid of all the "if only"s.

5. Vulnerability is essential to growth as a specifically *human* being.

6. Commitment is also essential to growth as a specifically *human* being.

7. One foundation of legitimate pride is having a "word."

8. Another is having a sense of "craft," even in getting an education.

9. Like genuine guilt, genuine doubt is a healthy hunch things need to be set right.

10. Human beings are made to continue evolving *as* human beings.

Questions

⚜ Do you really understand the difference between genuine pride and self-delusive arrogance? In a herd of sheep, anyone with honest self-confidence is going to look arrogant. Are you afraid that, if you honestly affirm your assets as a person, people are going to accuse you of being vain? Think of yourself as a car that's taking you on a journey. If you don't trust the vehicle, how are you ever going to challenge it to take you anywhere?

⚜ When you were a little kid, like all little kids, the world revolved around you and your concerns, your toys, your wants. It was a difficult job trying to make you understand that other people also had concerns and toys and wants. At times we may have gone overboard and made you feel you were the *least* important person in the world. Did you ever feel that? That whatever you did was never quite good enough for us? That if you didn't succeed you wouldn't be loved? If we made you feel that way, be honest with us. If we did, we want to apologize and make sure we change. We have to learn. We have to keep growing, too. That's what life is for.

⚜ (Write this out beforehand, give it to your son and daughter in a sealed envelope before your "session," have them read it—alone, and then sit down and have the conversation. The content of the letter is "These are the ways you make us proud of you." It's almost guaranteed to be a moving conversation.) Well, whatcha think? (This may take some time.) Are there any things we wrote that surprised you, that you didn't realize we were proud of? This is a privileged—maybe even "sacred" time. Can you tell us things you're proud of that we never even realized? Finally, can I have a hug?